FORGING THE SWORD

FORGING THE SWORD
Doctrinal Change in the U.S. Army

Benjamin M. Jensen

Stanford Security Studies
An Imprint of Stanford University Press
Stanford, California

Stanford University Press
Stanford, California

©2016 by the Board of Trustees of the Leland Stanford Junior University. All rights reserved.

No part of this book may be reproduced or transmitted in any form or by any means, electronic or mechanical, including photocopying and recording, or in any information storage or retrieval system without the prior written permission of Stanford University Press.

Printed in the United States of America on acid-free, archival-quality paper

Library of Congress Cataloging-in-Publication Data

Jensen, Benjamin M., author.
  Forging the sword : doctrinal change in the U.S. Army / Benjamin M. Jensen.
    pages cm
  Includes bibliographical references and index.
  ISBN 978-0-8047-9560-9 (cloth : alk. paper) — ISBN 978-0-8047-9737-5 (pbk. : alk. paper)
  1. United States. Army—Reorganization—History—20th century. 2. United States. Army—Reorganization—History—21st century. 3. Military doctrine—United States—History—20th century. 4. Military doctrine—United States—History—21st century. 5. Organizational change—United States—History—20th century. 6. Organizational change—United States—History—21st century. 7. United States—Military policy. I. Title.
  UA25.J525 2016
  355'.033573—dc23
                                                                          2015017618

ISBN 978-0-8047-9738-2 (electronic)

Typeset by Newgen in 10/14 Minion

Contents

	Foreword	vii
	Acknowledgments	xi
1	To Change an Army	1
2	The First Battle of the Next War	25
3	The Central Battle	56
4	The New Warrior Class	87
5	Hearts and Minds Revisited	125
6	Incubators, Advocacy Networks, and Organizational Change	142
	Notes	155
	Index	189

Foreword

One of our most important duties as Army professionals is to think clearly about the problem of future armed conflict. That is because our vision of the future must drive change to ensure that Army forces are prepared to prevent conflict, shape the security environment, and win wars.
—General David G. Perkins, "The U.S. Army Operating Concept: Win in a Complex World"

WAR IS THE FINAL AUDITOR OF MILITARY ORGANIZATIONS. One of the greatest challenges confronting the military professional is how to build a learning organization that implements lessons and anticipates the challenges of future armed conflict. Anticipating the future begins with an analysis of the present and an understanding of history. Consideration of continuities in the nature of war as well as changes in the character of warfare is essential to making wise decisions about future force development. Grounded projections into the future serve as the basis for military innovation and how leaders prepare their soldiers and units for the challenges of future war. As the historian Sir Michael Howard observed, "No matter how clearly one thinks, it is impossible to anticipate precisely the character of future conflict. The key is to not be so far off the mark that it becomes impossible to adjust once that character is revealed."[1] In this book, Benjamin Jensen offers important insights into how militaries learn, adapt, and sustain innovation to ensure that, when called on to fight, they do not find themselves too far off the mark.

Of particular importance is Jensen's emphasis on the need for creative forums in which leaders and soldiers experiment and visualize new forms of warfare. Military leaders need a space to imagine future war and develop new theories of victory to test through experimentation. Innovation begins with leaders cultivating creative space. Jensen's observation that experimentation is necessary to test concepts and challenge assumptions about future war is consistent with the finding of historians MacGregor Knox and Williamson Murray in *The Dynamics of Military Revolution, 1300–2050* that

> the key technique of innovation was open-ended experiment and exercises that tested systems to breakdown rather than aiming at the validation of hopes or theories. Simple honesty and the free flow of ideas between superiors and subordinates—key components of all successful military cultures—were centrally important to the ability to learn from experience. And the overriding purpose of experiments and exercises was to improve the effectiveness of units and of the service as a whole, rather than singling out commanders who had allegedly failed.[2]

Successful military experimentation evaluates ideas, challenges assumptions, and tests new concepts.

The U.S. Army defines innovation as the result of critical and creative thinking and the conversion of new ideas into valued outcomes. Ben Jensen's insights are consistent with the Army's effort to develop and mature concepts, assess those concepts in experimentation and other learning venues, and use what is learned to drive future force development. Critical and creative thinking about future armed conflict requires consideration of threats, enemies, and adversaries; anticipated missions; emerging technologies; and historical observations and lessons learned. Ultimately, innovation requires the development of new tools or methods that permit military forces to anticipate future demands, stay ahead of determined enemies, and accomplish the mission. Invention is not innovation. Innovation often results from the identification of opportunities to use existing capabilities in new ways. And while technology helps shape the character of warfare, military forces gain differential advantage over enemies through the integration of technologies with adaptive leaders and well-trained organizations based on a sound concept of how to fight. As the late historian I. B. Holley Jr. observed, "Unless the armed forces are guided by appropriate doctrines, greater numbers and superior weapons are no guarantee of victory."[3]

The role of doctrine in military innovation is often overlooked. Doctrine, though not prescriptive, is what a military institution teaches in professional education and in the training of operational forces about how those forces accomplish military objectives. Jensen points out the importance of "incubators" (informal subunits outside bureaucratic structures) to develop sound doctrine as well as advocacy networks to implement that doctrine through changes in organization, training, materiel development, leader education, and personnel policies. *Forging the Sword: Doctrinal Change in the U.S. Army* contains important insights into how to foster learning organizations that can anticipate the challenges of future armed conflict and develop the ability to meet those challenges.

Lieutenant General H. R. McMaster
Director, Army Capabilities Integration Center
Deputy Commanding General, Futures,
U.S. Army Training and Doctrine Command

Acknowledgments

As this book shows, no one person owns an idea. Networks of individuals exchange theories and observations, as stories, whose circulation creates a combustible environment conducive to novel insights. While there are many hubs in my network, I thank two people who proved especially helpful to this project in its early stages: Charles Tilly and Christopher Layne. These senior scholars helped a young U.S. Army officer see the world through a different lens. I also thank Dean Jim Goldgeier and the International Affairs Research Institute in the American University School of International Service for creating an academic environment encouraging scholars to bridge the gap and address important policy issues. It funded a book incubator that helped shape the final form of the manuscript. I am similarly grateful to the Smith Richardson Foundation for supporting the research that led to this book. In addition, the book benefited from the generous support provided by Donald L. Bren, the Marine Corps University Foundation, and Marine Corps University. I am also forever indebted to mentors Abdul Aziz Said and John Richardson, as well as my family, for teaching me empathy and patience. Last, this book would not have been possible without the assistance of Stanford University Press, and especially Geoffrey Burns and James Holt.

1 To Change an Army

During the winter encampment at Valley Forge in 1778, Baron von Steuben, a Prussian officer introduced to the American Revolutionary cause by Benjamin Franklin, formed a model company of one hundred hand-selected men. He set out to experiment with drill and tactics for the New World battlefield, documenting his search in a collection of notes that became *Regulations for the Order and Discipline of the Troops of the United States*. On March 29, 1779, John Jay, president of the Continental Congress, signed an order approving the regulations. What started as a soldier's experiment at Valley Forge became the blue book of the U.S. Army, a doctrinal manual outlining how to train and fight an army. Baron von Steuben's work remained the Army's informal doctrinal treatise until 1812.

The process Baron von Steuben initiated at Valley Forge continues in the modern U.S. Army. Despite repeated assertions by pundits and academics alike that the military is a conservative, parochial organization resistant to internal reform, the U.S. Army has a long history of reinventing its war fighting doctrine. This book traces this dynamic process and reflects on the character of military change. Specifically, it analyzes the unique role played by knowledge networks that allowed new ideas to form and diffuse in an otherwise rigid and complex bureaucracy.

The historical cases in this book highlight two institutional processes associated with developing new ways of war in the U.S. Army. Doctrinal change requires *incubators*, informal subunits established outside the hierarchy, and *advocacy networks* championing new concepts that emerge from incubators. Ranging from special study groups to war games, test beds, and field exercises, incubators provide a safe space for experimentation and the construction of new operational concepts. Incubators form sites where officers engage in what scholar-practitioner Thomas Mahnken calls speculation, a search "to identify novel ways to solve existing operational problems."[1] These concepts become the foundation of new doctrine articulating a theory of how to fight and win future conflicts.

Professional soldiers require these safe spaces to visualize new forms of warfare. Outside the formal hierarchy, officers are free from routines and bias that crowd out the space for innovation.[2] Advocacy networks represent crosscutting institutional networks that spread the ideas throughout the broader defense community. These networks connect different constituents in the bureaucracy and infect them with new ideas that officers would otherwise reject. New doctrine requires forums where officers (re)imagine war and networks in which they can tell their story.

Efforts to reform military organizations occur in different sequences, settings, and circumstances as organizations adapt to the changing character of war. Reforms in China by Qin minister Shang Yang in 356 BC broke with the tradition of cohorts of aristocrats in chariots to form a new mode of land warfare dominated by large infantry formations supported by cavalry.[3] The Roman Marius Reforms in 107 BC grew out of a manpower shortage. The method for generating a force that was built around small landowning classes proved unable to fill the legion's ranks to counter threats posed by Germanic Cimbri and Teuton tribes. To address this battlefield shortage, Gaius Marius expanded recruitment to the landless classes and designed a new tactical formation, the cohort, to employ them.[4] Maurice of Nassau, Prince of Orange, resurrected the ancient military tradition of drill and used it alongside new operational concepts like volley fire to increase the power of the Dutch Standing Army in the late sixteenth and early seventeenth centuries. In each case the reforms started with a unique problem and experimentation by military leaders refining their craft.

The emergence of modern military organizations and bureaucracies dedicated to land warfare also illuminates portraits of soldiers grappling with change. In the nineteenth century military leaders across Europe and the Americas copied the Prussian General Staff, created in the wake of the Prussian Army's defeat at Jena in 1806.[5] The emulation involved looking at how to synchronize increasingly complex military functions. Field Marshal Count Helmuth von Moltke wrote *Instructions for Large Unit Commander* in 1869, codifying the practice of moving units separately and then concentrating them before battle.[6] In 1903 while serving as an artillery colonel on the French General Staff (and later as the commandant of the École Militaire), Marshal Ferdinand Foch wrote *Principles of War* in an effort to distill the Napoleonic way of war and how it differed from Helmuth von Moltke and the German school. In it, Foch emphasized the importance of firepower, a central idea in French doctrine since the 1875 official military *Service Regulations*.[7] In 1915, U.S. Navy commodore Dudley W. Knox argued that modern doctrine was a "European intellectual construct designed to help commanding officers teach or train their subordinates so that they would think like their commander or at least understand his intent in war."[8]

This observation presents a conundrum for military leaders. While the structure of bureaucracy provided the controls and procedures necessary to command large armies, it also tended to lock in particular processes and ways of thinking about war. Big structures created deep habits. This standardization suggests modern military bureaucracies should resist change.[9] These organizations—made of bundles of rituals, standard operating procedures, mandates, and bureaucrats focused on turf and budgets—tend to adapt either incrementally or in response to threats to their autonomy.[10] The modern military, like all bureaucracy, is an iron cage prone to crowding out innovation in an effort to promote efficiency and existing processes.

Civilian bureaucrats and military officers are expected to be unwilling or reluctant to escape this iron cage. This organizational resistance to change should be especially pronounced during peacetime, when there are few incentives to challenge existing routines and uncertainty about where or when the next war will be.[11] Change in military organizations should be an anomaly.

Yet anomalous change has become a frequent occurrence in the U.S. Army since the end of the Vietnam War. Since 1975, officers in the U.S. Army have rewritten its flagship doctrinal manual, *Operations*, seven times. These manuals were not just episodes of bureaucratic recycling and updating procedures. Rather, many tended to embody new theories of victory, visions of how to fight and win the next war.[12]

Continual change in an entrenched bureaucracy is the puzzle at the center the book. I seek to show how professional military officers anticipate future wars to develop new military doctrine. The study of doctrine formation helps illuminate the bridge between tactics and strategy. Strategy establishes the ends, the national security objectives that military forces, along with other agencies and instruments of power, seek to achieve. Doctrine is the means, articulating how to fight within a given context.[13]

In this chapter I establish the argument and overarching logic of the book. First, I define doctrine as a formalized theory of victory prescribing how the military professional should execute critical tasks in support of national security objectives. Second, I situate doctrine in relation to the broader study of military innovation. Specifically, I differentiate exogenous and endogenous causal factors to explain change. Third, I define the causal mechanisms at the root of change in U.S. Army doctrine: incubators and advocacy networks. These mechanisms form the analytical framework applied in the historical case studies: the development of the 1976 Active Defense, the 1982 AirLand Battle, the 1993 Full-Dimensional Operations, and the 2006 counterinsurgency (COIN) doctrines. These studies seek to isolate the sequence of change associated with publishing new doctrine and the extent to which these mechanisms were active.

What Is Doctrine?

Military doctrine is a "set of principles the Army uses to guide its actions in support of national objectives."[14] This definition can be linked with J. F. C. Fuller's characterization of doctrine as the "central idea" behind the organization of violence capturing how fighting formations respond to particular historical modes of war.[15] In Clausewitzean terms, doctrine reflects the operative "grammar" of war.[16] As a foundational script, it prescribes how the Army should execute critical tasks.[17] Doctrine is connected to the first attribute James Q. Wilson defines as essential for successful organizational change: identifying critical tasks for dealing with the environment and its challenges.[18]

Doctrine exists in formal and informal forms at multiple levels. Formal doctrine reflects institutionalized knowledge in manuals, training circulars, and pamphlets. Informal doctrine reflects a broader professional discourse captured in articles, field orders, personnel letters, and so on.[19] Most doctrine exists above the level of tactics and deals with synchronizing units conducting a series of battles (e.g., a campaign). In the U.S. context, these units can be service specific (e.g., the Army, Navy, Air Force, Marine Corps), multiservice (e.g., two services), or after 1987, joint. Regardless of whether they are service specific or joint, *doctrine formally prescribes how the military professional should execute critical tasks in support of national security objectives.* The focus of this study is on service-level formal doctrine—specifically, episodes of doctrine formation in the U.S. Army since the end of the Vietnam War.

The U.S. Army has a long history of using both informal and formal doctrine to capture and distill experience. Unofficial treatises such as Henry Bouquet's "Reflections on War with the Savages of North America," William Smith's *An Historical Account of the Expedition Against the Ohio Indians, in the Year 1764*, and James Smith's *A Treatise on the Mode and Manner of Indian War* diffused ideas on fighting frontier wars among officers and elites interested in the military profession.[20] Short of a complete, concept-driven theory of victory, these treatises were more initial reflections and collections of best practices and techniques. The father of Alfred Thayer Mahan, Dennis Hart Mahan, introduced concepts for frontier wars as they related to conflicts against native peoples in the West Point curriculum as early as 1835.[21] At its origins, doctrine, much like Baron von Steuben's reflections on drill, was personalized and informal. Individual thinkers published their reflections, and this knowledge infected officers through the education system and peer recommendations. Doctrine was the distillation of accumulated experience.[22]

Formal doctrine started to emerge after the Spanish-American War and the associated Root Reforms in the form of field service and drill regulation. Drill regulations outlined the organization of military units and duties by sections. For example, the 1905 edition of *Field Service Regulation* discussed how the U.S. Army organized expeditionary forces and issued standardized orders. While the document also dealt with techniques such as establishing bases and maintaining lines of communication, procedures for conducting tactical movements and marches, and the proper employment of cavalry, it did so less in terms of general principles of war and more in line with tactics.[23]

Formal doctrine, as a constitutive framework and general set of principles defining the employment of forces that operate above the level of tactics, did not begin to emerge in the United States until the 1941 edition of *Field Manual 100-5: Field Service Regulations, Operations*, in which it is discussed in relation to "doctrines of combat" for engaging in offensive and defensive actions.[24] The 1962 and 1968 editions of *Field Manual 100-5* make a further shift toward stating general principles of warfare that animate tactics and force employment. The 1962 edition actually began to use the word "doctrine" while linking the employment of land combat to variable contingencies and national security policy.[25] The document moves beyond discussions of force tables and drill techniques to discuss strategy and military force as they related to principles of war and operational concepts.[26] As shown in Table 1.1, as the profession of arms evolved, so did the role and function of doctrine.

As the purpose and meaning of doctrine evolved, the U.S. Army used it to link strategy and force structure.[27] Doctrine became central to planning. According to the Department of the Army posture statement for fiscal year 1992, "[Doctrine] forms the basis for planning and conducting campaigns, major operations, battles, and engagements."[28] Realizing that procurement and organization ultimately reflect congressional intrigue and technological change, services relied on doctrine as a means of maintaining autonomy. Doctrine functioned as a store of accumulated knowledge.[29] It was, and continues to be, a foundational text whose narration intraorganizational elites can directly influence. Furthermore, this store of knowledge is especially important for military professionals, since they must spend long periods not engaged in actual war fighting.[30]

Historically, the U.S. Army used doctrine to initiate organizational reform. In a September 2, 1994, letter to general officers titled "TRADOC Pamphlet 525-5," General Gordon R. Sullivan, chief of staff of the Army from 1991 to 1995, wrote that "no institution can transform itself coherently and successfully without a clear eye on what it wants to become. . . . Physical change invariably has it [sic] underpinnings in imaginative and rigorous thought about the future."[31] In a 1992 article, Sullivan similarly referred to doctrine as a "catalyst" providing "the framework for institutional changes within the Army."[32] Doctrine, as a store of knowledge, is also a template for changing how military professionals solve new problems. It is evolutionary and progressive.

Much of doctrine is built around concepts. Former commanding general of the U.S. Army Training and Doctrine Command (TRADOC) Donn Starry defined concepts as "ideas, thoughts, and general notions about the conduct of military affairs."[33] They broadly depict the conduct of warfare and capture anticipated battlefields and tactical response repertoires. As defined in the 1982 edition of *Field Manual 100-5*, these concepts represent "the core of [Army] doctrine," reflecting "the way the Army fights its battles and campaigns, including tactics, procedures, organizations, support, equipment and training."[34] Therefore, a key task in tracing how military organizations sustain change is to investigate the sequence, setting, and circumstance animating

TABLE 1.1 Doctrinal change in the U.S. Army after World War II (1945–2014)

Year	Doctrinal change	Description
1949	FM 100-5: Field Service Regulations	Focuses on global war with a limited discussion of radioactive battlefield. Introduces the concept of area defense and stresses combined arms, with the tank as the primary land weapon system.
1954	FM 100-5: Field Service Regulations	Formalizes adaptations made during the Korean War.
1956, 1958	FM 100-5: Field Service Regulations	Expands basic concepts in 1954 edition and emphasizes the integration of atomic weapons in developing fire and maneuver schemes (i.e., Pentomic).
1962	FM 100-5: Field Service Regulations	Introduces the Reorganization Objective Army Division as a common force organization that could be adapted and air mobility. Prepares for nuclear and nonnuclear battlefields.
1968	FM 100-5: Operations	Incorporates initial lessons of Vietnam and details the air mobility concept.
1976	FM 100-5: Operations	Shifts the Army to the European battlefield and emphasizes combined arms warfare, including new concepts for employing tactical reserves. Introduces the Active Defense concept.
1982, 1986	FM 100-5: Operations	The 1982 edition shifts from Active Defense to AirLand Battle and deep attack.
1993	FM 100-5: Operations	Introduces the Full-Dimensional Operations concept and military operations other than war.
2001	FM 3-0: Operations	Expresses aspects of the Force XXI, as developed in TRADOC (Training and Doctrine Command) Pamphlet 525-5, and Army After Next concepts. Stresses deployability.
2008	FM 3-0: Operations	Seeks to further institutionalize aspects of counterinsurgency and stability operations derived from *Field Manual 3-24: Counterinsurgency Operations* in 2006 and *Field Manual 3-7: Stability Operations* in 2008 as it relates to the continuum of operations and changes the definition of combat power used to internally organize, shifting from the battlefield operating systems to war fighting functions.
2011	ADP [Army Doctrinal Publication] 3-0: Unified Land Operations	Like the 2008 *FM 3-0* manual, focuses on a wider spectrum of operations in which the Army conducts land warfare to create conditions favorable for resolving conflicts.

SOURCE: Robert A. Doughty, *The Evolution of U.S. Army Tactical Doctrine, 1946–1976* (Fort Leavenworth, KS: Combat Studies Institute, 1979); William O. Odom, *After the Trenches: The Transformation of the U.S. Army, 1918–1939* (College Station: Texas A&M Press, 2008).

NOTE: Major manuals from 1900 to 1945 include field service regulations published in 1905, 1908, 1910, 1913, 1914, 1917, 1923, 1939, 1941, and 1944; thus, the Army publishes an operational manual an average of every five years.

the formation of operational concepts. To this end I uncover and examine the practices associated with the emergence of a new theory of victory that condense to form doctrinal change.

Doctrinal Change

Studies of military reforms in international relations, strategic studies, and history tend to include work on force structure and technology in addition to doctrine. This literature reflects a diverse body of work with little consensus. They share little consistency in a change's source (e.g., major or minor, civilian or military), modality (e.g., innovation, adaptation, or emulation), or causes (e.g., the international system, civil-military relations, bureaucratic politics, cultural norms, or technology).[35]

Many studies differentiate between major and minor change, often paralleling the analytical metaphor of levels of war. Any shift beneath the operational level (for the U.S. Army, the level at which officers plan campaigns and employ large formations) is seen as a minor and potentially isolated battlefield adaptation.[36] With respect to major change, scholars debate the types of actors who have the access, resources, and influence to initiate reforms. For example, Barry Posen argues that civilians intervene to prod reluctant militaries to develop new doctrine and force structure, while Stephen Peter Rosen contends that military elites initiate reform on their own, without civilian interference.[37] A growing body of work resists this top-down perspective in favor of horizontal and bottom-up innovation, in which actors across the military organization adapt to battlefield lessons and experiments to develop new ways of approaching operational problems.[38] That is, minor changes at the tactical level can cascade into major changes in operational art.

There is also a difference with respect to defining the pathway of military change. For Theo Farrell and Terry Terriff, innovation involves "developing new military technologies, tactics, strategies, and structures."[39] Rosen defines military innovation as "a change in one of the primary combat arms of a service in the way it fights or alternatively, as the creation of a new combat arm."[40] In his study of bureaucracy, Wilson defines innovation as "the performance of new tasks or a significant alteration in the way in which existing tasks are performed."[41]

Adaptations, in contrast, exist beneath the level of major changes and tend not to be formally institutionalized by the organization in new doctrine or force structure. Theo Farrell defines adaptation as a "change in tactics, techniques or existing technologies to improve operational performance."[42] It differs from emulation, which "involves importing new tools and ways of war through imitation."[43]

Innovation, as major change, is usually associated with shifts in the "goals, actual strategies and/or structure of a military organization."[44] Classical organizational theory differentiates innovation from routine problem solving.[45] To solve challenges they confront, all organizations contain routines based on the institutionalization of individual memories.[46] Four features define the problem-solving process. First, it involves a standard, routinized sequence. Second, the sequence has a search process that aggregates information. Third, collected data is screened on the basis of preestablished criteria to determine what is relevant. Fourth, a distinguishable program encompasses the three aforementioned steps. However, institutionalized processes and preestablished criteria can bias an organization not to seriously consider new information. The trick therefore is to develop organizational processes that capture new information and enable analysis free of existing processes and their associated bias.

Innovation tends to occur when an existing problem-solving program is incapable of addressing organizational challenges.[47] These challenges can be internal subunits competing for turf, resources, or prestige as well as external threats to a military organization. This insight informs Posen's claim that military organizations innovate only when they risk defeat or losing budget share.[48] In the broader study of military innovation, the challenges take the form of "specific military problems the solution of which offer[] significant advantages to furthering the achievement of national strategy."[49]

Since much of an organization's activity concerns routine programs and problem solving, innovation can be scarce without an immediate threat. Therefore, classical organizational theorists argue, "the creation of a new unit is the only way to secure innovation that is not excessively bound and hampered by tradition and precedent."[50] Anthony Downs makes a similar claim, arguing that organizations need to create new bureaus responsible for new functions as a means of escaping the tendency for internal conflict over roles and missions as well as a preference to uphold the status quo.[51] Distinct practices, as formal and informal rules and rituals, facilitate the emergence and diffusion of new ideas. This dynamic process is the focus of this book.

This book defines doctrinal change as a formal shift in how military professionals articulate the critical tasks required to achieve the ends of national strategy.[52] It is innovation to the extent that it reflects new ways of solving operational problems. These problems generate incentives for the professional to find alternative solutions. In her analysis of U.S. and Soviet military doctrine, Kimberly Marten Zisk similarly defines innovation as a "change in how military planners conceptualize and prepare for future war."[53] This change generates a new idea and corresponding new behaviors not captured in existing routines.[54] Doctrinal innovation reflects intellectual development within the profession of arms. This definition assumes that before a military can redefine its critical tasks, the military professional must first articulate new ways to solve challenges confronting the organization.

Even parochial military organizations can innovate, then, as the process need not change core missions. As long as the new way of war preserves the organization's autonomy, prestige, or resources it need not meet resistance from entrenched elites.[55] To change doctrine is to generate new ideas and assumptions on how to employ forces. Doctrinal change therefore reflects the dynamic process of knowledge creation and diffusion within the profession of arms.

Doctrinal change varies between no shift in problem definition or critical tasks (i.e., status quo prevails) to large-scale redefinitions of both the nature of the threat and ways to respond that indicate an emergent theory of victory. Between these, doctrinal change can be minor, reflecting only partial reform (e.g., a change of degree), or merely the aspect of reform (e.g., old wine in a new bottle). These changes should be observable in doctrinal manuals used for planning, training, and education. The analysis of doctrine here is less concerned with whether change led to improvements in military effectiveness or altered force structure. The multilevel interplay of actors, institutions, interest groups, and states is a complex system unlikely to afford generalizations. Rather, as shown in Figure 1.1, the analysis focuses more on ideas.

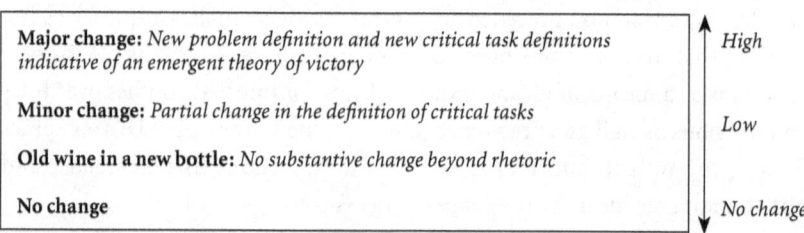

FIGURE 1.1 Threshold of doctrinal change

Sources of Doctrinal Change

By most accounts, doctrinal change should be scarce. Military organizations should have little incentive to challenge a status quo drilled into them. In seeking to explain how military organizations escape their iron cage, scholars tend to posit some form of shock to the system sufficient to create an imperative for change. The first school of thought emphasizes exogenous shocks and competitive bureaucratic pressures. Battlefield defeat or civilian intervention creates catalysts to change an otherwise reluctant bureaucracy.[56] Defeat threatens a military's autonomy and the flow of resources, forcing the leadership to consider large-scale changes. Alternatively, when the balance of power in the international system shifts, civilians intervene to prod reluctant armies, navies, and air forces into altering their doctrine and force structure in a way that aligns military capability with national interests and grand strategy.[57] Similarly, the literature on the revolution in military affairs (RMA) is full of how new technologies produce superior means for waging war and, through this shift in capabilities, fundamentally alter the organization of violence.[58]

Exogenous shocks force otherwise reluctant officers to consider new modes of warfare. Even when external catalysts are present, bureaucracies can repel change. Military organizations tend to resist any innovation that challenges their existing core tasks, missions, and mandates. For Wilson this accounts for the U.S. Army having a Eurocentric focus during the Cold War despite an increasing requirement to be prepared to fight low-intensity conflicts outside Europe.[59] In addition, bureaucracies create standard operating procedures, simplifying complex tasks at the expense of innovation.[60]

Competitive bureaucratic pressures threaten budgets and autonomy as well as increase service rivalry. According to Morton Halperin, "An organization will accept new functions only if it believes that to refuse to do so would be to jeopardize its position with senior officials or if it believes the new function will bring in more funds and give the organization greatest scope to pursue its own activities."[61] Furthermore, bureaus and subunits are competing interest groups in a bureaucracy.[62] Competition over roles and missions between these units, as they search for increased influence over decision making, can result in new and novel ideas. For example, Samuel Huntington argues that service rivalry explains the proliferation of doctrine after World War II.[63] Services used doctrine to compete with rivals to justify the ascendency of their preferred vision of war. Debates on doctrine assumed a "certain

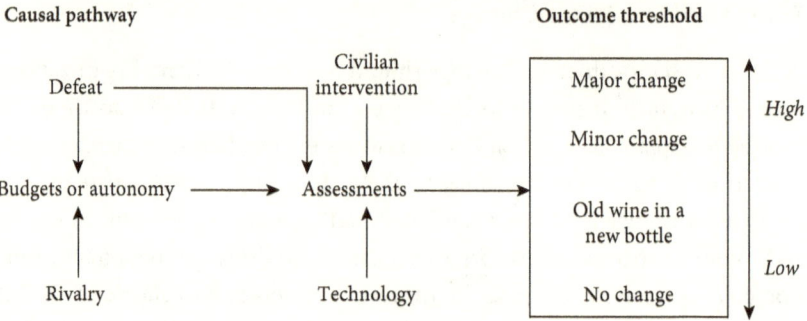

FIGURE 1.2 Doctrinal change by shock and competition

metaphysical quality, in arguments over whether landpower or airpower was the dominant force in modern war and whether guided missiles were aviation or artillery."[64]

Figure 1.2 depicts the pathways connecting these exogenous shocks and competitive interests as they affect the relationship between professional assessments and doctrine. Threats to budget, turf, influence, or autonomy emerge from battlefield defeat or attempts by other services to increase their relative influence. These factors alter how leaders assess the organization. Technology can also push new ways of thinking about war that alter the assessments. Civilians intervene to give existing inputs a higher probability of influencing major change in the organization.

These insights produce the following expected pathways of doctrinal change. First, *threats to the organization's core mission, whether from rivalry or exogenous shock in the form of potential defeat, incentivize reluctant officers to develop new doctrine.* That said, the degree of doctrinal change should be as minimal as possible. Second, *new technology should be associated with the emergence of new doctrine.* Again, the degree of change should moderate because officers try to preserve preexisting organizational interests. Third, *civilian intervention should drive larger-magnitude change in doctrine.* Because of the need to preserve existing organizational interests, external intervention is required to break the gridlock.

Next, strategic and organizational culture shapes the ways military organizations respond to change. Work on strategic culture and constructivism emphasizes the role of norms and social contexts in explaining patterns of military innovation.[65] In her study of interwar doctrine, Elizabeth Kier found that organizational culture influenced how military actors understood themselves and their core missions. For example, the British Army's gentleman's club culture and focus on its colonial mission even beyond World War I made it reluctant to adapt to mechanized warfare.[66] In his work on the military technical revolution, Dima Adamsky demonstrates how cultural factors, in the form of cognitive styles, explain differences in how the United States, Israel, and the Soviet Union responded to precision-strike abilities and advances in command and control systems. D. Michael Shafer, in his study of U.S. counterinsurgency policy, finds an essential role for policy paradigms that form "essential codes" guiding how decision makers frame and solve problems.[67] Russell Weigley argues that since the American Civil War, a distinct attritionist way of war emerged, favoring mass and firepower over maneuver, and dominated how military officers approached conflict.[68] Taken together, these cultural heuristics—whether organizational or strategic—generate logics of appropriateness bounding possible solutions to battlefield challenges.

Figure 1.3 depicts the pathways connecting enduring ideas as micro (e.g., local, organizational) and macro (e.g., larger culture and society) heuristics as they affect the types of assessments military professionals make about future war. These heuristics are the lens through which officers see problems and prescribe solutions. Thus, they shape doctrine. This insight produces the following expected pathway of doctrinal change in the U.S. Army: *any doctrinal change should be weighted toward an enduring American way of war*. It should reflect an attritionist mind-set and favor massing forces and the use of firepower.

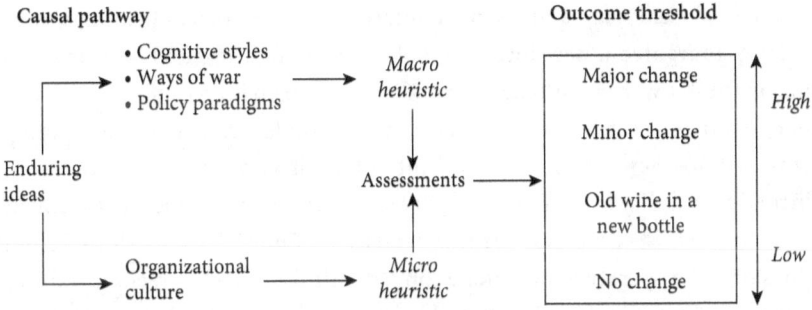

FIGURE 1.3 The cultural antecedents of doctrinal change

While covering a wide spectrum, these accounts do not explain the significant doctrinal and organizational changes in a crucial case, the U.S. Army. Reforms following the Vietnam War and the end of conscription were purely neither the by-product of civilian intervention nor defeat in war. Organizational elites, in the form of professional officers, sought to realign the institution with its primary role of providing a conventional deterrent in Europe while ensuring a higher degree of training and readiness for combat on the basis of their observations of the 1973 Yom Kippur War.[69] Innovation was not dependent on civilian intervention. Rather, it was linked to strategic assessment and definition of new solutions to operational problems. According to their mandate, senior officers scanned the horizon for new threats likely to affect how they fought future wars. This dynamic casts a shadow of doubt on approaches that overemphasize shortsighted military actors who are caught in bureaucratic battles and organizational inertia.

This trend of soldiers catalyzing reform without significant civilian intervention continued through the later stages of the Cold War. AirLand Battle, the doctrine that revolutionized the U.S. Army and shifted it to a more offensive posture in the early 1980s, rested on a series of operational concerns derived from both strategic and technical intelligence about adversary capabilities, specifically the problem of second-echelon forces and Soviet relative advantage in raw numbers. Senior officers studied potential adversaries and extracted information about their disposition and capabilities to initiate organizational change. Professional soldiers changed their organization from the inside out.

After the Cold War, professional soldiers continued to imagine future battlefields and rewrite doctrine. Innovation continued as the security environment shifted from a focus on countering Soviet power to fielding a force able to guarantee a new international order by fighting and winning two major-theater wars simultaneously and respond to an increasing array of military operations other than war. The Army responded in kind, experimenting with not just new RMA-type capabilities but also doctrinal innovations to increase its ability to dominate the full spectrum of engagements that might arise in the post–Cold War security landscape. The U.S. Army shifted from divisions, the operative standalone combat unit since the Napoleonic wars, to an order of battle structured around modular brigades.[70] Soldiers synthesized technology with new understandings of military force and alternative force designs. Military officers reimagined the profession of arms.

The Professional Strikes Back

This book challenges the prevailing wisdom of professional soldiers as unimaginative bureaucrats trapped in an iron cage. Despite over fifty years of intense debate about innovation in military doctrine, existing theories cannot completely explain key changes in the world's dominant land power. They do not decode the logic and sequence of reforms that restructured the very organization of violence in a crucial case, the U.S. Army. There appears to be a significant gap between scholarly models of military innovation and the actual content of change within U.S. Army doctrine since the end of the Vietnam War.

Doctrinal change is not a function of enduring strategic culture or exogenous shock. Rather, it emerges from within as military professionals seek to overcome new operational challenges.[71] Change is a function of anticipation, how soldiers imagine fighting future wars. This process of visualizing new ways of war requires two institutional mechanisms: incubators as sites to think outside the box and advocacy networks to diffuse new concepts.

Two assumptions synthesized from sociology, organizational theory, and policy analysis help situate the argument. First, *the military is a profession*.[72] In the Weberian tradition, the push for rationalization and the need for specialized knowledge drive the formation of a profession. A professional is a person of vocation who rationally organizes a particular domain of activity. As persons of vocation seek to rationalize a particular problem, they require new information and frameworks for synthesizing this information. In the process, they develop education institutions to certify that an agent has the required knowledge. Therefore, the designation and production of expertise are the defining features of a profession. This notion of "profession" combines structure, process, and power; the professional has special knowledge, a fixed doctrine, and identifiable qualifications.[73]

In his study of civil-military relations, Samuel Huntington draws on Max Weber to define the military as a profession with three identifiable features: expertise, responsibility, and corporateness.[74] Expertise is special knowledge. Dedicated institutional actors, steeped in a codified history that is transmitted to new recruits through a formal education system, produce this knowledge. The professional, that person of vocation who is certified by formal institutions of knowledge, has a special responsibility to a larger social system. This responsibility in turn endows the professional with an organic unity and shared consciousness, defined by Huntington as corporateness. Organizational doctrine, as a store of knowledge and network connecting and socializing its members, conditions what officers deem appropriate and rational. It contains a rational and habitual social logic.[75]

For Morris Janowitz, a key attribute of this corporateness is the tendency of senior military leaders to see their careers in terms of fulfilling the organization's national security mission.[76] In this reading, the professional is always scanning the horizon for future threats and seeking out changes necessary to confront them. Military professionals, given their mandate, are always reacting to external threats, albeit from an organizational perspective and in a manner prone to worst-case-scenario bias. While there is a tendency to see such biases as an outgrowth of the search for autonomy and resources, they also reflect a built-in planning parameter. For example, in the U.S. Army, Marines, and joint doctrine, all planning must consider hypothetical most likely and most dangerous scenarios. Key organizational codes mediate how professional officers imagine future wars.

Second, *military professionals engage in problem-directed search* for new ways to respond to their environment. Given the emphasis on knowledge production at the core of a profession, this book treats the military as a special type of epistemic community.[77] Ideas matter in military organizations, especially new concepts outlining how to solve operational challenges that core missions require military leaders to address. For example, stopping the dominant naval power from threatening deepwater ports sparked an intense debate in post–Revolutionary America between Hamiltonians, who emphasized forts and frigates, and Jeffersonians, who emphasized militia-manned sloops swarming British ships.[78] Edward Rhodes's study of the evolution of the U.S. Navy challenges bureaucratic politics models and their emphasis on parochial intraservice communities to show the importance (and durability) of the Mahanian concept of decisive battle and the battle in determining force structure since World War II.[79]

Core missions, environmental pressures, and routine problem solving combine to produce competing ideas inside a military organization.[80] Professional soldiers either reframe an existing challenge to increase their efficiency or respond to new environmental pressures.[81] Doctrinal innovation has internal and external catalysts.

The ideas that emerge from reflecting on operational challenges condense to form a new theory of victory.[82] A theory of victory articulates solutions to a particular operational problem that are based on "frames" and function as a schema of interpretation that organizes how military professionals understand events and interactions.[83] Inherent in any theory of victory are bundles of assumptions about what constitutes a threat, cause-effect relationships related to strategy development, and logics of appropriateness that define procurement and weapons design.[84] The assumptions form a constitutive as opposed to regulative logic shaping how military professionals understand critical tasks in relation to their larger core mission and environment. Thus, the assumptions tend to be focused on technical issues nominally associated with tactics and operational art as opposed to grand strategy, making them the purview of military professionals rather than politicians. New theories therefore emerge from "the presence of specific military problems the solution of which offer[] significant advantages to furthering the achievement of national strategy."[85]

A theory of victory embodies both action repertoires, or implied ways to solve the problem, and standard scenarios, or characterizations of the types of situations in which the organization might be called on to act.[86] Accounts of the failure of the U.S. Army to develop armored warfare doctrine and heavy tanks in the interwar period illustrate how U.S. Army leaders focused on solving a *different* problem than the one confronting them. Military professionals resisted heavy tanks because the standard scenario emphasized speed and off-road mobility, required along the border with Mexico and across the Americas where jungle and mountain terrain presented a different range of operational problems than tank-on-tank engagements on the European plain.[87]

Incubators
These two assumptions, that the military is a profession and military professionals search for a new theory of victory, tell us *why* officers develop new doctrine but not *how*. Earlier treatments building on organizational theory emphasize a range of mechanisms, from reactive innovations as responses to an adapting adversary, to how the personnel system and officer career paths lock in new forms of warfare.[88] Given the difficulty of changing a bureaucracy, explanations of innovation must include how professional military officers escape their iron cage.

This book argues that a key aspect of overcoming organizational inertia is the formation of incubators. Innovation requires new forums or subunits free from the normal push and pull of the bureaucratic hierarchy in which professional military officers are free to visualize new theories of victory. These new spaces contribute to organizational change along two axes. First, incubators enable officers to search for new ways to understand a problem. Articulating new action repertoires and standard scenarios generates rational incentives to innovate. When under time pressure and seeking goal clarity, senior leaders pressure subordinates and link the incubator to core missions and mandates to further catalyze these incentives.[89] The design of organizations affects their capacity for change.

Second, by charting incubators to study different ways of war, military professionals increase organizational complexity. Research from organizational sociology highlights how increases in complexity, in terms of both the division of labor and types of structures present in the organization, increase rates of innovation.[90] In military organizations, generating new theories of victory starts with increasing the diversity of voices and types of studies circulating the corridors of power. This implies that not only the design but the micro-level processes associated with disseminating information determine the capacity of an organization to innovate.

The U.S. Army has a history of using incubators to experiment. Following failures associated with mobilizing the Army for the war with Spain, the secretary of the Army, Eliu Root, initiated a series of reforms leading to the Army War College, a general staff, new doctrine (i.e., field service regulation), and the design of a permanent division.[91] Captain Joseph T. Dickman, a young officer on the General Staff charged with studying organizational design, analyzed European field armies relative to the terrain and infrastructure of the United States. He recommended a smaller force, the division. The Army tested using a smaller force in 1904 in Manassas, Virginia, in large-scale exercises involving both regular and militia units.

After 1914, Army leaders experimented with fielding an expeditionary force capable of fighting on the European battlefield. As part of the effort, they formed the First Expeditionary Division as a core around which deployment of U.S. forces would be organized. General John J. Pershing approved use of divisions in 1917 and personally selected senior leadership, charging them with continuing to experiment and refine new war fighting concepts.[92]

In 1935, General Malin Craig, chief of staff of the Army, ordered new studies on division design. The group recommended a new triangular division that would allow the U.S. Army to streamline division structure and modernize its forces relative to an emerging European threat. After approval of the design in 1937, field exercises and experiments were conducted, including in 1937 tests with the Second Infantry Division and later large-scale tests by Army Ground Forces in 1941 dubbed the Louisiana Maneuvers.[93]

Incubators are an important intervening process that enables endogenous change. If the existence of a professional scanning the horizon is the necessary condition for doctrinal reform, the existence of a forum that enables the professional's search is a sufficient condition. The absence of incubators likely lowers the potential of initiating genuine reform. Responses will tend to be old wine in a new bottle. The presence of an incubator increases the likelihood that direct search will result in new ideas.

Advocacy Networks

Introducing new theories of victory developed in incubators into the broader organization requires advocacy networks to circulate and legitimate emerging ideas. Advocacy networks are loose coalitions of defense and civilian officials championing new reform initiatives.[94] Multiple military innovation studies emphasize the importance of understanding how alliances between senior and midlevel officers influence patterns of adaptation and change.[95] The establishment of Special Operations Command in 1987 provided a collaboration forum for officers and new career paths for them.[96] An alliance between senior officers and midlevel bureaucrats enabled the development of the cruise missile.[97]

Like any other bureaucracy, an army has various internal and external constituents that benefit from a particular mode of operation, or warfare. These networks need not be singularly instrumental and driven by the projected distribution of resources. Advocacy may also emerge from the concatenation of particular threat definitions and implied response repertoires proclaimed by various groups of actors. A professional duty, an operative code of conduct, to maximize the national interest holds these groups together.[98]

Senior leaders act like norm entrepreneurs.[99] They compete with one another to articulate new theories of victory through networks cutting across the organization in order to define the reform agenda. Therefore, regardless of the form, advocacy networks act as positive feedback loops legitimating particular configurations of innovation. They connect intraservice reform agendas with broader national security imperatives and, doing so, circulate and narrate new theories of victory.

Advocacy networks diffuse and legitimate new ideas. By definition, alternative concepts developed in incubators tend to produce conflict within existing units and functions. Bureaucrats view them as threats to their own turf, to resources, and to the overarching paradigm. The call for an incubator assumes existing problem-solving programs, and by proxy, bureaucrats are insufficient.[100] New ideas require a degree of elite protection. In exchange for protecting officers and the thinkers associated with the theory of victory developed through the incubator, senior defense officials gain prestige and influence within the profession.[101]

Advocacy networks that cut across large subsystems in the organization and reach into the broader defense community are more likely to be successful in supporting doctrinal reform than narrow coalitions within any one segment of the bureaucracy.[102] As they connect sites, they enable brokerage. Brokerage represents a relational mechanism that connects "at least two social sites more directly than they were previously connected."[103] Brokerage is closely associated with yoking, by which understanding emerges "from local cultural negotiations."[104] The underlying discussion in this book analyzes brokerage with respect to key policy networks mobilized to legitimate doctrinal innovation initiatives. The connection of critical actors in the defense debate reinforces and legitimates local reform initiatives.

For the broader defense community to adopt a theory of victory that emerges from an incubator, the idea needs to circulate and infect a wide spectrum of officers and civilian officials at multiple levels. New ideas require broad constituencies. Innovators use advocacy networks to broker consent. Whereas most military innovation studies treat constituencies as static and linked to budgets and mandates (services, branches, etc.), this books looks at how the military professional redefines critical tasks and missions to accommodate new visions of warfare.

The U.S. Marine Corps illustrates this pattern of advocacy networks connecting multiple constituencies through professional journals and education institutions. The development of the Small Wars doctrine in the interwar period resulted, in part, from midlevel and junior officer debates in journals and while in resident schools in Quantico, Virginia.[105] Likewise, professional journals and the schoolhouse were used by a coalition of officers and civilian officials to advocate a turn to maneuver warfare in the 1980s.[106] Officers used the *Marine Gazette* and tactical decision games to articulate an alternative to war fighting doctrine based on attrition.

Propositions

Taken together, incubators and advocacy networks reveal the micropolitics of innovation, or how coalitions within defense organizations imagine war and legitimate their vision. Incubators are the institutional sites in which different interpretations coalesce and emerge as new theories of victory, which are legitimated through advocacy networks.[107] These networks reflect two legitimation strategies. In the first, they represent a form of positional legitimation. Knowledge production in defense organizations relies on appeals to authority and the use of position to authorize new ideas. Alternatively, brokerage is legitimation by diffusion. Ideas need to circulate and infect officers throughout the organization, increasing their resonance and broader acceptance. As Figure 1.4 shows, networks of officers and defense officials socialize innovation across the organization.

To illustrate the relationship between incubators and advocacy networks in enabling the emergence of new theories of victory driving doctrinal innovation, this book examines three propositions through a series of historical cases using process tracing and structured focused comparison.[108] The cases cover varying levels of doctrinal change, including the development and publication of the Active Defense, AirLand Battle, Full-Dimensional Operations, and Full-Spectrum Operations doctrines between 1973 and 2008. Each treatment begins by defining the broader strategic context and range of operational challenges identified within the defense establishment as they relate to internal debates within the U.S. Army. While domestic actors like Congress, industrial lobbies, and the broader web of civilian-run national security institutions are critical players to national security strategy and policy, the focus

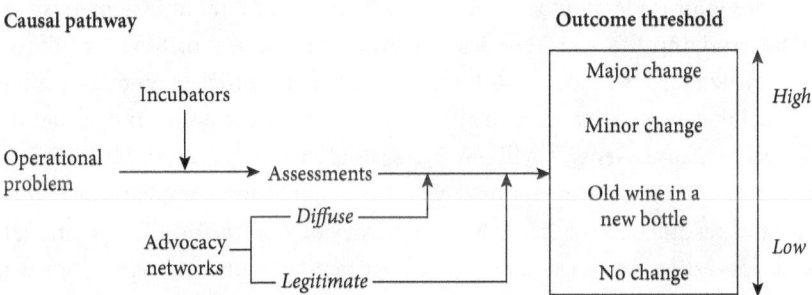

FIGURE 1.4 Doctrinal change and intervening institutional mechanisms

here is more refined and targeted on the operational doctrine within an individual service. The research seeks to analyze how doctrinal innovation occurs at the organizational level, and in the process show how rigid bureaucracies can enable change.

Each case study traces the emergence of new concepts using the historical record, specifically how military professionals understood the security environment and articulated a new theory of victory, to evaluate three propositions. First, *new theories of victory emerge through incubators.* Evidence from historical case studies should indicate the presence of an incubator in periods of successful doctrinal reform. The incubator should serve as a vehicle for senior leaders to bring together a mix of officers and thinkers oriented toward solving a particular operational problem. That is, the incubator should serve as a forum for searching for a new theory of victory.

Second, *advocacy networks diffuse the new theory of victory and infect officers at multiple levels.* The new theory of victory needs to take hold at multiple levels. Debates in the profession socialize officers and orient them to think about war in new terms. This process should be evident in internal debates and professional journals.[109]

Third, *senior leaders in the profession of arms protect new ideas through signaling their concurrence.* New ideas generate new controversies. Successful doctrinal innovation should see senior leaders championing the new theory of victory in speeches and articles. This proposition provides support for Barry Posen's view of senior officials protecting mavericks but, as shown in Table 1.2, does not support the claim that such support must come from outside the military.[110]

The book proceeds by looking in Chapter 2 at a seminal case, the reforms that took the Army out of Vietnam and back to the plains of Europe. The desire of senior leaders to focus on the new lethality of war, an insight gleaned from studying the 1973 Yom Kippur War and analysis of Soviet military modernization, intersected with the focus of senior officials on establishing a credible conventional deterrent in Europe within the political confines of forward defense. General William DePuy used the newly created TRADOC to usher in not only new operational concepts but a renewed emphasis on training and readiness. To develop his new theory of victory and the operational concept—shoot to move, move to concentrate—designed to fight a limited war short of the nuclear threshold, DePuy used multiple forms of incubators. Yet DePuy, focused on realigning the Army with its core mission and

TABLE 1.2 Causal pathways

Core propositions	Expected observation
P1. Incubators increase the likelihood of emergence of new ideas.	The presence of these institutional mechanisms should help professionals scanning the horizon redefine the threat environment and critical tasks required by national strategic objectives.
P2. Advocacy networks diffuse new ideas across the organization.	Networks that cut across large subsystems in the organization and reach into the broader defense community are more likely to be successful in supporting doctrinal reform than narrow coalitions within any one segment of the bureaucracy. The military professional can artificially create buy-in. (This process is a form of outside-in legitimation. While the dynamic is similar to logrolling, it does not rely on bargaining and interest alignment.)
P3. Senior leaders help protect new ideas.	Senior leaders should engage in positional legitimation, or using their place in the hierarchy to signal acceptance of the new theory of victory. This takes the form of articles and speeches reinforcing the new theory of victory and associated doctrinal reforms.

addressing the fallout of Vietnam, did not aggressively pursue crosscutting horizontal advocacy networks. The case is a partial success.

Chapter 3 analyzes the shift from Active Defense to AirLand Battle between 1977 and 1981. General Donn Starry used incubators to test Active Defense and refine new concepts for using general-purpose forces to fight against a Soviet adversary seen as renewing its emphasis on deep operations and first-strike scenarios reliant on achieving a swift conventional surprise attack. In contrast to the Active Defense case, Starry aggressively focused on using multiple forms of advocacy networks to infect the officer corps and broader constituents in the national security community.

Chapter 4 traces how senior leaders used incubators and advocacy networks to change the Army following the end of the Cold War. In this case, multiple, competing visions of the future intersected amid significant budgetary pressures and large cuts to force structure. Army leaders felt themselves caught between embracing new technology and the RMA and organizing to meet the challenges of a broader range of military operations other than war (MOOTW) captured in the 1993 Full-Dimensional Operations doctrine.

Chapter 5 looks at the evolutionary process connecting Full-Dimensional Operations with tactical adaptation to the post–September 11 battlefield and the requirements for stability and counterinsurgency operations. In the case, there was continued expansion of the range of actors involved with developing new concepts for the U.S. Army. The professional was not the sole purveyor of new ideas. The result though was not so much dramatic doctrinal change as it was a return to earlier principles of counterinsurgency. On closer examination, the idea of winning hearts and minds has a deeper intellectual history in the U.S. Army.

The book concludes, in Chapter 6, by reflecting across the cases to consider the major implications for the study of doctrinal innovation. By mapping how military organizations innovate from the inside out, this book makes a contribution to our broader understanding of the ways bureaucracies initiate and sustain major reforms. This issue is especially relevant as military actors, including the United States and most European countries, consider how to reduce their size without significantly affecting their capabilities. The historical observations developed in this work offer important references for policy makers as they consider how to right size defense budgets. Training, exercises, and education are easy targets for officials in times of tight budgets, but these programs nourish incubators.

The book also opens a space to reflect on the profession of arms. The military profession is a vocation organized around specialized education in the art and science of warfare. Like other professions, it has international norms of education and advancement as well as national-level formal and informal regulatory bodies that shape what constitutes legitimate knowledge and practice. Professional military education institutions exchange officers and ideas. Soldiers publish their reflections on their craft in professional journals and at conferences. The book illuminates how new knowledge emerges and is legitimated within the profession.

2   The First Battle of the Next War

IN AUGUST OF 1974, GENERAL WILLIAM E. DEPUY, A DECORATED veteran of World War II and Vietnam, sat down to compose his thoughts on modern warfare. Captured on handwritten notes, much of the language that survives in archival records illustrates a commander grappling with the emergence of a new form of warfare. For DePuy, strategy and tactics were shifting to reflect a "new lethality" as seen in the Arab-Israeli War.[1] The general saw the conflict as a "focusing device."[2] On notebook paper outlining the beginning of a manuscript he never finished, DePuy mused whether an account of a tank battle in the Sinai, part of the larger 1973 Arab-Israeli War, was a window into the future, a means of seeing the coming transformation of ground combat.[3]

DePuy, a senior commander charged with developing doctrine and training, thought about war from the bottom up. He focused on creating professional soldiers. His reflections were not on narratives of sweeping campaigns and abstract leadership traits but on the common soldier and his awakening on the modern battlefield. Thus, the general's unfinished manuscript on modern battle tactics stressed how soldiers employed weapons systems on a battlefield, illustrating a senior leader as a critical institutional node in a larger bureaucratic network that was (re)imaging land warfare following the Arab-Israeli War.

Between 1973 and 1976, DePuy led the U.S. Army Training and Doctrine Command (TRADOC) in developing a new doctrine, Active Defense. This chapter traces the micropolitics of imagining the next war and how DePuy led a small team in developing a new theory of victory and, through it, rewrote the 1976 edition of *Field Manual 100-5: Operations*. What emerges is a portrait of how actors within an entrenched bureaucracy created the possibility of change and an illustration of the ways incubators and advocacy networks enabled doctrinal reform. In this context, the case investigates the internal debates that defined the Army as it reoriented toward the conventional defense of Europe and an anticipated fight, beneath the threshold of nuclear war, against an adversary projected to outnumber NATO forces by as many as six to one in conventional ground forces.[4] While these projections proved to be inflated, worst-case scenarios, they established the context in which military professionals imagined future war.

The remainder of the chapter analyzes doctrinal reforms following the Vietnam War. Specifically, the chapter examines the strategic context in terms of how military planners addressed the Nixon Doctrine and constraints implicit in the all-volunteer force and declining domestic resources. Senior leaders like DePuy used their analysis of the Arab-Israeli War to conceptualize what a future conventional war in Europe might look like. It was the operational problem necessitating new doctrine. From this vantage point, the chapter explores the institutional reform initiatives that gave birth to TRADOC, a principal incubator that provided DePuy and his selected officers the space they needed to rewrite Cold War conventional doctrine.

Rebuilding the Army After Vietnam

In the early 1970s, the U.S. Army was a force in transition in four distinct ways.[5] First, the lingering troubles associated with defeat in Vietnam provided an essential part of the context of reform. The war marked a critical breaking point. Beyond the losses in life and prestige, the conflict left the institution in complete disarray. Drug addiction rates among soldiers were rising, while unit cohesion was withering as racial tension erupted in garrisons across Europe.[6]

Second, in 1973 the armed services shifted from a draft-based system to an all-volunteer force.[7] In addition to this shift in civil-military composition, end strength was reduced by over 50 percent, to 785,000, between 1968 and 1974.[8] In seeking to take advantage of the formal withdrawal from Vietnam and transition to an all-volunteer force, secretaries of defense Melvin

R. Laird and James R. Schlesinger used the reserve force as a way of drawing down the demands on active force components. The decision was not just a budgetary gamble but a strategic initiative designed to maintain a link between the emerging all-volunteer force and the American public. The Army's senior leadership wanted to ensure that the institution would not be turned into an elite system of professionals drawn on to fight wars without involving the public at large. Therefore, they instituted Total Force, in which key combat support and combat service units and round-out brigades, which are nonactive-duty combat arms units designed to bolster active end strength, would be in the reserve component. This shift limited the executive branch's deployment of a volunteer force for sustained amounts of time without drawing in the broader populace. The intent was to "strengthen the Army's ties with the states, the Congress, and the public."[9] This transformation meant a smaller, professional force would have to fight forward before a larger strategic reserve mobilized.

Third, the larger strategic framework shifted toward using general purpose and conventional ground forces. After the mid-1960s, a growing number of NATO members backed détente and a reduction of hostility in Europe. Warsaw Pact feelers on a security and cooperation summit for Europe caused a debate about NATO policy.[10] This shift continued even after the 1968 invasion of Czechoslovakia. A 1969 Central Intelligence Agency memorandum on NATO summarized the dilemma: "Although the British, Germans, and Dutch view the new 'Brezhnev doctrine' of discretionary intervention as a new and permanent danger, they have joined Canada and the Scandinavian members in opposing a resumption of cold-war politics. . . . [T]he central question is not whether to seek to resume detente, but how to achieve it in light of the still-uncertain implications of Czechoslovakia."[11]

Conventional forces were a central part of the answer to this question. Starting in the mid-1960s NATO exercises and high-level meetings increasingly viewed a strong conventional defense as a requirement to support political dialogue and defend against the prospect of limited war. In a December 1967 ministerial meeting, the North Atlantic Council, the political wing of NATO, adopted the "Harmel Report," a statement that followed the Harmel Exercises, proposed by the Belgian foreign minister, Pierre Harmel, to analyze the evolution of NATO and possible ways of strengthening the alliance. The council stated in the official minutes,

> The possibility of a crisis cannot be excluded as long as the central political issues in Europe, first and foremost the German question, remain unsolved. Moreover, the situation of instability and uncertainty still precludes a balanced reduction of military forces. Under these conditions, the Allies will maintain as necessary, a suitable military capability to assure the balance of forces, thereby creating a climate of stability, security and confidence.[12]

Yet U.S. and allied conventional capabilities required to implement flexible response, the official strategic posture since 1961 calling for deterrence at multiple levels (i.e., strategic and conventional), were increasingly called into question. Since at least 1967, high-level war games by the Joint Chiefs of Staff had emphasized a lightning conventional assault on Berlin and Soviet capacity to use a preponderance of conventional forces in a crisis.[13] NATO response to such contingencies required tipping the balance toward conventional forces. According to a February 20, 1969, memorandum to Richard Nixon from Secretary of Defense Laird, many observers believed NATO conventional forces were "not equal to the opposing Warsaw Pact forces," while NATO strategy required a "greater emphasis on conventional forces, since these had been neglected for years in favor of nuclear forces."[14]

The Nixon administration came to see flexible response as largely an unfeasible, suboptimal compromise. NATO defense strategy called for an initial forward defense relying on conventional forces. In estimates prepared for the National Security Council in the late 1960s, the planning assumption was that within "a period of 90 days after an attack on NATO, the requirements for additional conventional defense forces will fall off because (a) diplomatic settlement will be reached, or (b) the Soviets will reach the limit of their conventional capability, or (c) the fighting will escalate to nuclear warfare."[15] Yet according to transition briefs,

> [NATO members have a] general understanding that a Soviet attack on Western Europe would not be countered with an immediate US strategic nuclear attack on the Soviet Union. On the other hand, there is no agreement that a major Soviet attack could be or should be repulsed with conventional forces alone. The most that Europeans are prepared to accept is that NATO strategy should provide for a conventional response to limited aggression.[16]

Fourth, along with the challenges of conventional defense in Europe, the United States was transitioning from the Vietnam War. At a July 25, 1969, press conference in Guam, President Nixon first articulated a policy of disentanglement in Asia that came to be known as the Nixon, or Guam, Doctrine.[17] As a policy, the Nixon Doctrine paved the way for Vietnamization and a broader drawdown of the defense budget as U.S. forces began to shift duties increasingly over to their local national counterparts. Furthermore, the U.S. military posture shifted to a one-and-a-half-war contingency model.[18] That is, whereas the John F. Kennedy and Lyndon B. Johnson administrations used a two-and-a-half-war scenario for planning guidance, or fighting two major regional wars and one lower-level conflict simultaneously, Nixon's team wanted to realign the U.S. security posture toward NATO Europe and the Soviet threat and possible conflicts requiring U.S. intervention in the Middle East, or fighting one major and one lower-level war.[19] This trend continued throughout the early 1970s as the Department of Defense emphasized the strategic importance of Europe and NATO.[20]

Furthermore, this shift in scenario planning drove leading thinkers in the Army to consider the utility of ground troops and their future role given the prevalence of nuclear weapons and deterrence in American military doctrine. In the spring of 1973, the chief of staff of the Army, Creighton Abrams (1972–1974), established the Strategic Assessment Group, under the Office of the Deputy Chief of Staff for Operations and Plans, as an incubator to conceptualize possible conflicts and the future of land combat. Army officers later referred to it as the Astarita group, after Colonel Edward F. Astarita, who was brought in by General Abrams from Pacific Command to lead the initiative.[21] Paralleling the larger concern about conventional defense in Europe, General Abrams tasked the group "to determine if there was a legitimate role for conventional strategy and for the Army in the post-Vietnam world."[22]

After several meetings and internal debate, the group published the "Astarita Report," a classified document that made a case for reinvesting in mechanized forces to support critical alliances and generate military freedom of action short of nuclear war. The report's premise was that the primary thrust of U.S. national security strategy should be directed toward great-powers relationships, especially the U.S.-Europe-Japan and U.S.-USSR-China relationships, given détente. The major concern was the survival of the NATO alliance as a functional conventional deterrent in Europe in the face of divergent security interests created by the German demands for forward defense and debates about the early use of nuclear weapons.[23] As it stood, conventional disparity drove the United States to emphasize responding to a Soviet invasion with nuclear release at either the tactical or the strategic level.

To create the possibility of a credible conventional deterrent and assure key NATO allies like Germany that the United States was capable of defending forward and limiting the thrust of an initial invasion to both spare key population centers and buy time for diplomatic negotiations, the "Astarita Report" called for a renewed emphasis on conventional forces. The authors held that modern mechanized forces were the key to providing assurance to allies and enabling freedom of action in planning short of nuclear release.[24] To disseminate this message, the group leveraged multiple policy networks to provide over one hundred classified briefings in less than a year to audiences ranging from senior Army leaders to the Department of Defense, Department of State, Central Intelligence Agency, and other major national security actors.[25] Such measures clearly point toward advocacy networks used to broker new concepts and sustain particular understandings of warfare that drive innovation.

Thus, the transition out of Vietnam and reorientation toward Europe activated critical debates about the proper use of military power. If read through a strictly bureaucratic lens, the pullback from Vietnam, shift to a one-and-a-half-war standard, and emphasis on alliances threatened the Army's institutional autonomy and share of budgetary resources. In this rendering, initiatives like the "Astarita Report" appear desperate pleas for relevance as opposed to problem-driven attempts to rationalize the strategic environment and its implications for future force development. But that misses the negotiation that took place across the Army. Beyond myopic bureaucratic struggles, the leaders of the Army accepted a shift in the international environment and used it as a means of reconceptualizing the role of land forces at the strategic, operational, and tactical levels. The path that this dialogue took was further defined by institutions and the types of future battles Army officers envisioned.

While the push to innovate correlates on the surface with a military searching for relevance from a traditional bureaucratic view, the next section shows how these domestic interests intersected a new appreciation for the lethality of the modern battlefield. The drive to reorient conventional capabilities did not arise as an isolated response to domestic resource constraints. It was a process etched by speculation about what battles on the periphery foretold about land warfare.

TRADOC

In addition to this broader social and political context, major institutional reforms defined the Army in the early 1970s. In 1973, under Abrams, the Army implemented Operation Steadfast, a massive internal reorganization plan designed to streamline domestic operations and training.[26] Abrams believed that subordinating to Continental Army Command (CONARC) the full range of domestic responsibilities, including support and service, installation management, individual education and training, and force development, was simply unrealistic and stalled innovation.[27] CONARC had become a bureaucratic Gordian knot unable to manage simultaneously the competing requirements of developing future force concepts and managing military installations and personnel.

The origins of Steadfast date back to a series of reviews conducted under chief of staff of the Army William C. Westmoreland (1968–1972). In particular, Winthrop Whipple and John V. Foley's "Pilot Study on the Department of Army Organization" and findings of the follow-up (Charles) Parker Panel outlined the management problems inherent in the U.S. Army in the late 1960s. These studies documented how CONARC had far too many roles and missions to be an effective organization.[28] The Parker Panel turned to private industries, including IBM and Xerox, to see how they dealt with "decision making, systems management (horizontal) vs. functional management (vertical), and the growth and use of ad hoc committees."[29]

DePuy, now vice chief of staff of the Army and its chief planner, wrote the concept paper "Impetus for Change," which outlined many of the key management improvements and functional reorientations that necessitated reorganizing CONARC. The recommendations included reducing staff because of high per capita personnel costs, reorienting the Army away from Vietnam to focus on the broader range of conflicts, increasing unit readiness, and streamlining the process of developing and fielding new weapons, force design, and doctrine.[30] For DePuy, the rationale for reorganization was not limited to the cost and management-efficiency concerns highlighted by the Parker Panel. It arose from a need for a fundamental reorientation of U.S. ground forces. The post–Vietnam Army would be a smaller, professional force operating in a constrained budgetary environment. More forces would be stationed at home, thus requiring high levels of unit readiness to facilitate rapid deployment. Together, these trends put a premium on force readiness, individual tactical and technical proficiency, and future fighting systems and concepts that CONARC would be unable to fulfill.[31] Thus, between 1972 and 1973, in both the "Astarita Report" and the "Impetus for Change" paper, a concept of a new Army, streamlined to field next-generation weapons and respond to conventional challenges, emerged in parallel with the broader Department of Defense reorientation to Europe and NATO. Beyond budgetary battles and the post-Vietnam drawdown, an entirely new conceptualization of the citizen, the state, and military power drove innovation.

Furthermore, DePuy believed that combat development was part of a larger process that integrated training, lessons learned from past combat experience, and new weapons systems. Under the CONARC system, "the crux of the problem was the bureaucratic separation existing between those responsible for combat developments and doctrine on the one hand—the combat development agencies—and the centers of combat developments and doctrinal expertise on the other—the schools."[32] Therefore, to centralize this process, each schoolhouse, which under CONARC had developed its own doctrine, was centralized under a unified command to manage the intricate relationship between operational blueprints for war, soldier readiness, and the emergence of new technology.[33]

The principal idea behind Steadfast was to separate Army Combat Development Command from installation management, which became Forces Command, while elevating its leadership to a four-star-general rank. The reform put combat development back in the hands of functional experts at each respective branch (infantry, armor, etc.). Creation of TRADOC would unify the conceptualization, formation, and implementation of doctrine via its control of education platforms under a four-star command. Combat development, which since the early 1950s had been linked to peacetime research into weapons and new equipment pathways, would be linked to doctrine and training, thus creating a unified site for conceptualizing warfare and the shape of future battles.[34] Imagining war was to be standardized and rationalized by officers beyond technological trends and capabilities. DePuy, the architect of the Steadfast reforms, commanded this new organization designed to manage change and innovation through realigning the Army as a tactical organization in terms of doctrine, training, and development of weapons and equipment to match new requirements.[35]

TRADOC's emergence on July 1, 1973, represented the creation of an institutional space in which senior officers could forge new concepts as blueprints for innovation trajectories. The intent was to use these discursive renderings as constitutive frameworks for altering force structure, training, and future procurement paths. This bureaucratic reorganization was a critical juncture in the history of the U.S. Army. Through transforming the relationship between doctrine and force development, DePuy and the chief of staff of the Army created a path-dependent catalyst for organizational change. They created the institutional space required to enable change in the bureaucracy.

The Pot of Soup

If the emergence of a new volunteer force and the decline in defense budgets provide a domestic context for emergence of conventional doctrine in the post–Vietnam Army, visions of new modalities of warfare provided the systemic impetus. On October 6, 1973, a coalition of Arab states led by Egypt and Syria attacked Israel. The ensuing war came to be known in U.S. Army circles as the Arab-Israeli War. While only three weeks long, the conflict's massive losses to all parties shocked military planners in NATO.

Immediately following the conflict, the U.S. Army dispatched observer teams to derive lessons from it. This process is an age-old military tradition of trying to piece together the substance, logic, and dynamic of particular battles. This lessons-learned cycle is progressive and cumulative. That is, studying war enables adaptation of force design and doctrine. In the case of the Arab-Israeli War, the stakes were high. Israel, as a major purchaser of U.S. military equipment, had just faced top-of-the-line Soviet military equipment in a high-intensity conventional struggle that saw total losses for both the Arab armies and the Israelis of over 3,000 tanks, as high as 3,000 armored personnel carriers, and over 575 artillery tubes.[36] What struck U.S. military observers was that the losses exceeded the total inventory of military equipment the U.S. Army had staged in Europe. According to a TRADOC presentation prepared by DePuy, "Egypt and Syria lost approximately 1,500 to 2,000 tanks. That would equate to all the tanks we have in Europe. Five hundred artillery tubes were lost; almost equal the amount of artillery the American Army has in Europe."[37]

In a January 14, 1974, letter Chief of Staff of the Army Abrams ordered TRADOC to examine the conflict as it related to "tactics, techniques, organization, training, and equipment performance" and work with Army Material Command to determine how the information influenced "weapons systems acquisition."[38] Furthermore, studying the force ratios, weapons performance, and context of major engagements allowed TRADOC analysts to begin to rework standing simulations of conventional engagements in Europe. Specifically, the data brought back to the United States from the Middle East was used by officers to develop new corps-level war games and simulations for proofing new doctrinal concepts, weapons procurement paths, and force design initiatives.[39]

Thus, the chief of staff and commanding general of TRADOC viewed the study of war as elucidating specific paths to follow for weapons development and procurement as well as doctrine and training. The Arab-Israeli War redefined how to view an existing threat in the form of a conventional engagement with the Soviets and their allies in Central Europe. Threat was not merely defined in terms of the balance of power but considered from a functional vantage point that translated assessments of the distribution of capabilities into ideal-typical constructs that integrate future scenarios. This dynamic is described by TRADOC historian John Romjue:

> In November 1974, the TRADOC Chief of Staff, Maj. Gen. Burnside E. Huffman, Jr., outlined the commander's basic approach to the doctrine effort. Tactics had to be based on hard, cold facts, had to be taken out of the abstract. TRADOC had to examine the most recent military experience, and employ the best weapons data—such as that being developed by the Army Material Systems Analysis Agency on hit probabilities of Soviet weapons as a function of range.[40]

As an institution within the national security apparatus of the United States, the Army saw threat in terms of land warfare. The state did not respond as a unitary actor; threat dynamics shaped unique patterns of response for each functional mandate. In many respects, this particular caveat to the logic of the balance of power, as an institutional translation inside the black box of the state, represents a shift from strategic to operational thinking. Doctrine and force development exist at the level of operations. They are specifications. Thus, functionally adapting to threat meant systematically integrating the performance of enemy weapons systems and doctrinal practices as seen in recent conflicts into concept development and analysis. As portrayed in Figure 2.1, innovation thus existed as part of a continuum whereby analysis of threat led to concept development, and this new ideational framework, as a discursive script, shaped force development.

Threat ─────▶ Analysis ─────▶ Concept ─────▶ Doctrine

FIGURE 2.1 Conceptual innovation sequence

Operational concepts nested within a larger strategic shift emphasizing the importance of conventional capabilities and NATO defense strategy. In the case of the emergence of Active Defense, the end operational concept and derivative force development reflected the negotiated understanding of war seen in the analysis of the Arab-Israeli War as an ideal type of conventional war in Europe. This section charts how analysis of the conflict shaped Active Defense.

Officers analyzed the Arab-Israeli War with respect to the major component parts of the combined arms team: air defense and air support, armor, mechanized infantry, and artillery. In a January 4, 1974, letter to the chief of staff of the Army, DePuy outlined TRADOC's lessons learned from the conflict. The first area of interest related to the trade-off between close air support, air superiority, and air defense. In the letter, DePuy discussed how the Israeli Air Force (IAF) shifted from an air superiority campaign, or applying air power to knock out command and control structures, logistics, airfields, and planes in a manner similar to the 1967 conflict, to close air support missions for the Army. As DePuy noted,

> Aircraft losses were high—40 in three and a half days on the Golan front. But more importantly the quality of air support was very low—loft bombing. On the Suez front the IAF was only effective in [close air support] when the Egyptians sallied out from under the SAM envelope.[41]

The "SAM envelope" referred to a new tactic developed by the Soviets and adopted by the Arab armies. Advancing land units would be accompanied by air defense platforms, predominantly surface-to-air missiles (SAMs) and antiaircraft machine gun platforms. The effect was to create an interlocking air defense system that guarded mechanized infantry and tanks as they sought to attack through the front. In the Arab-Israeli War, this tactic limited Israel's use of its air force, compared to 1967, to compensate for its numerical disadvantage on the battlefield.

As a U.S. Army officer analyzing the conflict, DePuy saw both institutional and procurement challenges in applying the SAM envelope. First, he was concerned that the U.S. Army and Air Force would need to reconcile old bureaucratic battles to be successful on the modern battlefield. In the next war, the Army would need to recognize that in order to get quality close air support, an effective air superiority campaign would have to come first. At the same time, the Air Force would need to use the Army's intelligence and weapons platforms to suppress enemy air defense and enable the air superiority campaign.[42]

DePuy further articulated this division of labor and vision of increased integration in drawing an analogy between the infantry and aircraft in a 1974 concept brief given to senior Army leaders and members of the defense community:

> The tank and the aircraft have now joined the infantry in their vulnerability, but this does not mean they cannot be used. It just means they must be used judiciously. The infantryman has been vulnerable to the rifle and the machine gun for many years. He cannot be employed on the battlefield unless the weapons that could kill him are suppressed. We've learned to live with that. The tank cannot now maneuver unless the enemy weapons that can kill the tank are successfully suppressed. So it is with the fighter, the fighter cannot fly through the air over the battlefield unless the enemy weapons that can destroy him have been suppressed.[43]

The division of labor entailed integrating all aspects of combined arms to maximize suppression. This was no bureaucratic battle with the Air Force but a sincere call to reconcile its needs for suppression of air defense with the Army's need for close air support. DePuy was arguing that the lethality of the modern battlefield produced higher loss rates and increased weapon accuracy and range. The Israelis had lost the majority of their aircraft—73 percent—to ground systems, not aircraft.[44] This inhibited close air support in the U.S. Army's estimation of the situation. Therefore, Army systems such as artillery and maneuver forces would be needed to suppress enemy air defense systems to support the Air Force just as the Air Force would be needed to provide close air support to the Army.

The actual statement used in DePuy's letter to Abrams is interesting. The language does much to problematize bureaucratic politics and the notion of constant and enduring interservice rivalries. Writing privately to the chief of staff of the Army in January 1974, DePuy states, "First, the Army must recognize that the air superiority campaign *must* precede and be successful if it is to enjoy effective [close air support]."⁴⁵ If the bureaucratic politics characterizations of military doctrine as being narrow, last-war oriented, and prone to parochial interests are valid, then discussions about how to sideline other services and increase the share of institutional resources pulled into the Army would be expected. Nothing could be further from the historical record. In correspondence with the chief of staff of the Army, DePuy not only acknowledges the importance of the Air Force as a partner but outlines their mutual interests, stating that "Army intelligence, weapons and maneuver can and should play a role in the air superiority campaign."⁴⁶ This sentiment is further echoed in a 1974 concept paper DePuy distributed to the defense community:

> Forward air defense weapons play an increasingly important role in the combat operations of both sides because of their greatly increased lethality and numbers and the practice of moving them with the foremost elements. The Arab/Israeli War of 1973 was the first case in which one side sought completely to deny the airspace over the battlefield to the other side.... Thus is it that air defense suppression in concert and collaboration with the U.S. Air Force is now one of the most important operational problems facing the ground commander.⁴⁷

Another central vein of inquiry was tank performance. The Arab-Israeli War offered a rare view in the performance of frontline Soviet and American tanks in action against one another. The Israelis fielded multiple tank models, including the American-made M60, against Arab armies fielding T-62 tanks. The numbers astounded planners. According to their internal briefing on the implications of the Arab-Israeli War, "Arab forces had some 4,000 tanks.... [T]o put it in perspective, the American Army has approximately 1,700 tanks in Europe."⁴⁸ TRADOC staff projected the pitched tank battles in Golan and Sinai onto the terrain of Central Europe in an attempt to reconcile how a numerically inferior force equipped with comparable equipment could defeat an adversary that outnumbered it by over six to one in many places. While the challenges posed by force ratios and equipment performance created a useful scenario development dimension for the TRADOC analysts, they were further intrigued by the sheer lethality of the modern battlefield. No one had accurately estimated the impact of modern weapons on conventional combat. If the U.S. Army in Europe lost as many tanks as Israel had in the Arab-Israeli War in the opening stages of a conflict with the Warsaw Pact, that would effectively destroy the entire armored capability. World War III, short of nuclear exchange, would be over with a decisive conventional battle before U.S. reinforcements could arrive.[49]

Analysts assessed the lethality of the modern tank battles as a function of evolutionary technological improvements to major weapons systems. In a 1974 Army-wide briefing, DePuy presented charts showing the improvements in hit probability and engagement distances for tanks since World War II. In fact, this use of tables and charts to contextualize lethality quickly became a trademark of early TRADOC publications and the 1976 edition of *Field Manual 100-5: Operations*, which outlines the Active Defense doctrine. Weapons performance in terms of range, accuracy, and destructive capacity were a means of illustrating the devastating firepower that defined the modern battlefield. In the briefing, DePuy traced the evolution of weapons at the tactical level to make the point:

> Back in World War II, a captain commanding a tank company was interested in the terrain his weapons controlled and in the enemy up to as far as he could see. Nonetheless, he was not endangered by very many weapons except those within about 500 meters of him. In those days 500 meters was the distance in which he had a 50-50 chance of getting a first round hit. In Korea that distance had increased to 1,000 meters. Now it has increased to 3,000 meters. . . . You can then see the enormously more difficult problem for the battlefield commander. It's a much more dangerous environment in which to fight. He must worry about a much greater area.[50]

For DePuy, the evolution of technology meant that "what can be seen, can be hit; what can be hit, can be killed."[51] Given the effects of precision-guided munitions, any action on the battlefield, whether offensive or defense, that did not adopt improved tactics and techniques, especially the use of terrain and suppressive fire, would suffer catastrophic losses. In the same passage, DePuy referred to this insight as "the single most important lesson on the Arab-Israeli War."[52] The Army had to be able to shoot first given the higher kill ratios. Yet to shoot, terrain had to be used and key firing points moved to. Movement in turn required suppression of antitank weapons systems. A new theory of victory began to emerge from these special studies of the Arab-Israeli War.

This new lethality would define the next war the United States fought. It was the central operational problem military professionals had to address. The destructive power of modern weapons systems and their integration into effective mechanized units that use all aspects of combined arms would define battlefields in Europe, the Middle East, and North Asia. In the 1974 Army-wide briefing outlining the analysis of the Arab-Israeli War, DePuy summarized this premise:

> The lethality of modern weapons is so much greater than that of the weapons we have used, or against which we have fought in the past, that we are in a new ball game. Our analysis also pointed out that there are more of these lethal weapons on the battlefield than at any other time in history.... [W]e would say that the problem now confronting the U.S. Army is: how to operate on a battlefield which is populated with those very lethal weapons in very large numbers and still get the job done without catastrophic losses; losses for which we are really not prepared.[53]

The observer teams dispatched by TRADOC under the guidance of the chief of staff of the Army came back with a story of twisted metal in the sand. The ammunition burn rates were so high, the sheer numbers of bullets and rockets fired so vast, that the war, though less than three weeks long, stripped two superpowers of a tremendous amount of resources to supply their proxy allies. This forced key players inside TRADOC to come up with a solution to the problem of lethality on the battlefield. Military professionals engaged in a problem-directed search.

In a speech to senior U.S. Army leaders at Fort Benning, Georgia, May 22, 1974, DePuy used the analysis of the Arab-Israeli War to frame the worst-case scenario in a future European conflict. He opened the speech by telling his audience that he was going to talk about what worried him the most about the U.S. Army when he thought about the next war. DePuy referred to the conflict as a "sobering thing" given the high losses relative to the existing combat strength of the Seventh Army in Europe.[54] The focus of his narrative was on lethality and forging America's fighting force. For TRADOC, the traditional American way of war whereby the United States outproduced its enemies was gone. The Soviets had more equipment and, because of the development lag in weapons systems after Vietnam, equal or superior ground combat systems. He told the assembled leaders,

> You are going to be fighting a lot of equipment. In the old days of WWI and WWII, the American way of war was to just provide more of everything than the other guys had. If one Division was not enough we would use two, if two

was not enough we would use four. Our tanks were not as good as the German tanks but we had three times as many. Now it is kind of un-American ... to find out that the other guys have more equipment than we have. Then my next point is that their equipment is just as good.[55]

Therefore, what the nation needed was a new understanding of war itself, a new conceptual framework through which to forge strategy and doctrine. To survive a conventional attack from an invading force that outnumbered them by as much as six to one, U.S. forces in Europe needed to come up with a way to escape a battle of attrition. They would have to rely on mobility to shift forces to the decisive point. They needed a new concept that factored in the increased destructive power unleashed by mechanized forces:

> [The Israeli] performance in battle has helped us to understand the requirements of battle, the concept of operations. While defending on the battlefield or attacking, you must move on the battlefield. . . . In order to move on the battlefield in the face of weapons with high lethality, enemy weapons must be suppressed. You suppress by the combined arms team. . . . To win when fighting outnumbered, it is necessary to concentrate forces at the critical point and at that critical time on the battlefield. . . . We will apply the lessons learned and our concept of operations to the development requirements for specific weapons and material systems.[56]

The concept of suppress, or shoot, to move and move to concentrate centered on the effects of improved firepower. Lethality dictated that units move to survive. To move, they had to suppress enemy weapons systems. Furthermore, movement allowed the outnumbered defenders to concentrate their forces at the critical point to break the attack. Forward defending with a combined arms team was the key ingredient in the rewriting of military doctrine that grew out of the analysis of the Arab-Israeli War. Yet to crystallize the set of operational insights for the defense community, they were linked to the European theater. In his briefing on the analysis of the Arab-Israeli War, DePuy superimposed the derived lessons over the First Armored Division's deployment in Europe to demonstrate how "the outnumbered force has got to see the battlefield better than the enemy and see it in sufficient time, so that he can move his combat elements to the critical place, at the critical time to insure that a suitable force ratio is achieved."[57] In the early 1970s, the First Armored Division was deployed along a sixty-kilometer front with complex terrain. Yet the size of the front meant it was almost impossible for the commander to position his forces in concentrated enough cells to stop a mechanized attack:

> There is no possible way [the] platoons can occupy all positions in sufficient strength to stop an attack. They must know where the attack is coming from and concentrate forces at that point. If the 1st Armored Division commander distributes his force equally, including its anti-tank guided missiles, there is no doubt that it could defeat a small attack. But the enemy will change that equation by concentrating. The enemy will come in great strength and in great depth at one particular point.[58]

Movement and suppression were central themes reiterated throughout the Army-wide briefing on the Arab-Israeli War. According to DePuy, "To win you have got to move. . . . [B]ut if you move in the face of that lethality you will lose unless you suppress."[59] The outnumbered defender must have sufficient forces "at the right place, at the right time, and hope the enemy will have his forces at the wrong place at the right time."[60]

In the suppress-to-move equation, the central idea was to concentrate forces forward and equip them with antitank capabilities to enable the outnumbered defender to see and react faster. It was derived from reading the tea leaves of the Arab-Israeli War to hypothesize what a future struggle in Europe might look like. The defender would use suppressive fire to maneuver their forces to a point where they could engage and delay the enemy until forces assembled for a counterattack. While the idea of suppression is not new, the use of reserve forces forward to fix the enemy is a significant departure from the war fighting doctrine of the day that called for holding one-third of the force in reserve.

From the end of 1973 through the summer of 1974, TRADOC focused its resources on analyzing the Arab-Israeli War through Army-wide briefings, analytical notes sent to key leaders, and conferences. In a letter sent July 23, 1974, to the commanders at each of the Army's schoolhouses, DePuy shifted this analysis to actual doctrine and drew an analogy that is telling in terms of his perspective on doctrine formation:

> In France in the house of a peasant there is always a pot of soup boiling in the fireplace. From time to time someone throws in a potato, leek, some chicken stock or beef gravy, an occasional carrot or whatever. Over time the soup gets

better and better. Everyone can add to it and anyone can partake. I view the attached [concept paper] somewhat the same way.... I want this paper to stay alive and improve, but I want to keep it as an informal TRADOC document which will not see the light of day as a separate official publication. I don't care who sees it or how many copies are made. I just want to keep it like that pot of French soup.[61]

The attached concept paper outlined the critical lessons DePuy took away from the Arab-Israeli War as they related to modern warfare. Two dimensions were at play. Through the TRADOC analysis, DePuy was defining the framework for doctrine formation as an iterative, open process of dialogue and debate that expanded and refined the core concepts until they were ready to push out across the institution. This framework was marked by the United States having to project power and thus fight outnumbered on a mechanized battlefield. In accord with the proposed model of innovation, senior leaders set the reform agenda by outlining operational concepts to define the parameters of doctrinal debate.

For TRADOC, the suppress-to-move, move-to-concentrate concept, as a response repertoire, defined the way the Army should adapt to the configuration of modern warfare as seen in the Arab-Israeli War and its implications for hypothetical pitched battles in Central Europe. How threats are defined cascades into how to conceive of resourcing and employing forces. For example, in the concept papers written for senior leaders in 1974, DePuy discussed how, because of the suppress-to-move, move-to-concentrate concept, "the tank is [now] the central decisive weapon. The infantry and the artillery are used to assist the movement of the tank."[62] A new theory of victory was emerging in the Army.

DePuy was the lead advocate of change, and he created an environment in which debate, disagreement, and competing visions flourished, albeit along lines he could directly influence.[63] DePuy led an organizational debate, letting subordinates at the armor and infantry schoolhouses weigh in on how to defeat the Soviets. He used a synthetic approach to knowledge construction in the profession, linking his experience in Germany and affinity for German tactical concepts with observations drawn from the 1973 conflict, and insights from experiments such as those run by Donn Starry at Fort Knox on the role of the tank in defense in modern war.[64] For example, the Active Defense construct, with its emphasis on covering forces, reflected a fusion of Starry's idea of using multiple, small counterattacks to canalize an advancing enemy and DePuy's notion of using blocking forces to turn an adversary through suppression.

This environment encouraged incubators within incubators, experimentation, and special study groups at various levels within the organization. Starry ran experiments, including the Hunfeld I war game, studying the use of tanks in defensive operations against the Soviets. Starry wrote, "In defensive operations, the closer one can construct the battle to resemble an attack, the greater [the] advantage [that] can be taken of the tank's most sanguine capabilities. That is, the defense should be designed to lure or canalize the enemy onto ground of our choosing."[65] He informally disseminated the results of war games in an article titled "Modern Armor Battle II: The Defense."[66] Starry's arguments were echoed by similar articles highlighting the role of covering forces in suppressing the enemy and enabling maneuver.[67]

Though DePuy fostered dialogue and experimentation with the schoolhouses, he exerted control over writing doctrine, moving creation of *Field Manual 100-5* from the Combined Arms Center at Fort Leavenworth, Kansas, to a small team he assembled at TRADOC. DePuy tasked key generals, like Starry and Paul Gorman, to write specific chapters. In addition to these senior reviewers, he maintained his own group of handpicked field-grade officers known as the "concepts team" and "boathouse gang" because they met at the yacht club at Fort Monroe.[68] The boathouse gang served many purposes: They reviewed and critiqued the larger group's work, and DePuy used them as a "sounding board" for ideas.[69] They wrote and edited the manual, DePuy having them review and critique his work and that of participating general officers.[70] They were connectors, taking draft chapters for review to key constituents in the Army.

Field Manual 100-5: Operations

TRADOC's analysis of the Arab-Israeli War as it related to the modern battlefield became a blueprint for Army operations. This vision was articulated as doctrine in the 1976 publication of *Field Manual 100-5: Operations*. The manual opens by stating its intent to establish "the basic concepts of [the] U.S. Army" and the core "principles for accomplishing the Army's primary mission—winning the land battle."[71] Doctrine, as the conceptual framework defining ground combat, then, was set within a particular context. That context being the Arab-Israeli War, the manual discusses lethality:

We cannot know when or where the US Army will again be ordered into battle, but we must assume the enemy we face will possess weapons generally as effective as our own. And we must calculate that he will have them in greater numbers than we will be able to deploy, at least in the opening stages of the conflict. Because the lethality of modern weapons continues to increase sharply, we can expect very high losses to occur in short periods of time. Entire forces could be destroyed quickly if they are improperly employed. Therefore the first battle of our next war could well be its last battle. . . . The United States could find itself in a short, intense war—the outcome of which may be dictated by the results of initial combat.[72]

Therefore, the manual emphasizes, the U.S. Army must "prepare to win the first battle of the next war."[73] While this battle may take place anywhere, the most dangerous theater for U.S. forces was the "battle in Central Europe against forces of the Warsaw Pact."[74] This battle, as any other the United States would find itself in, would occur "at the end of long, expensive, vulnerable, line of communications," forcing forward-deployed forces to engage "forces with ultra-modern weapons, greater numbers, and nearby supply sources."[75]

The manual defines threat using a formula based on capabilities and scenarios. While a Central European battle was the focus because of the high stakes involved, the manual, as an institutional script, uses the overarching lethality to frame the circumstances of modern ground combat. The losses seen in the Arab-Israeli War were a parameter in determining the types of capabilities enemy forces, whether in Europe, the Middle East, or East Asia, would possess. These capabilities, along with the United States having to project force overseas, formed the building blocks of scenario development. They defined the types of short, intense wars the manual predicted would occur and hence the centrality of preparing units "to fight outnumbered, and win."[76] Thus, lethality, as a concept, framed the invocation of operational response—how the ground forces of a nation would alter their doctrine to ensure continued capacity to secure national security objectives.

To further frame the lethality of the modern battlefield, the manual devotes an entire chapter to a detailed discussion of the evolution of modern weapons in terms of their ranges, accuracy, and destructive capacity. Each main weapons system is reviewed in terms of evolution since World War II, effective engagement range, and hit probabilities and is compared with existing frontline Soviet equipment.[77] The net effect is to both define the new lethality and create a planning tool for positioning equipment on the battlefield on the basis of capabilities.

Furthermore, it was not just the destructive capacity that challenged the U.S. Army but the proliferation of these systems. The manual confronts the reader with this reality in the opening paragraph, stating, "Great numbers of weapons of advanced destructiveness have been provided by major powers to client states; arms purchased by minor but affluent nations have further spread the latest military technology throughout the world."[78]

This emphasis on weapons systems and firepower represented a "deliberate intent to depict a corpus of tactics bound by the concrete. Tactics were tied firmly to the capabilities of weapons employed on the well-studied terrain of most likely deployment, all in the context of actual strategic circumstances believed likely to continue for the foreseeable future."[79] The U.S. Army had to be reformed to meet the challenge of fighting on the battlefield of Central Europe. Doctrine was not just a set of principles and national objectives guiding war but, for DePuy and the other authors of the 1976 edition of *Field Manual 100-5*, an integrated statement of the threat environment and corresponding operational response repertoire. U.S. soldiers needed to know engagement ranges and best practices to survive given the increased lethality and reality of fighting short, intense battles while outnumbered.[80]

After establishing the context of future battlefields, the manual shifts to defining how the U.S. Army would respond in a third chapter, titled "How to Fight."[81] If the key constraint was fighting while outnumbered on an increasingly lethal battlefield, then the Army needed to find a way of obtaining "the maximum combat effectiveness of all forces in the combined arms team."[82] The manual asserts that "to achieve this effectiveness our Army depends on sound doctrine. This doctrine would be derived from an accurate assessment of the dynamics of modern battle, and an understanding of all its implications."[83]

In laying out a doctrinal vision of how to fight on the modern battlefield, the manual established four prerequisites: (1) that weapons and forces should be concentrated at the critical time and place; (2) that command and control should direct the main effort to the decisive point on the battlefield; (3) that cover, concealment, suppression, and the combined arms team had to be employed to enable movement and offset the force ratio imbalances; and (4) that training units should realize the maximum capabilities of their weapons.[84]

In analyzing concentration, the manual emphasizes the role of firepower and movement. Massing firepower is seen as the prerequisite to enabling movement sufficient to concentrate forces at the critical point to stop Soviet breakthrough tactics.[85] Being outnumbered, the United States would need to react quickly and fluidly to an enemy attack. In the defense, to develop a larger covering force, this necessitated altering standing doctrine that called for at least one-third of a commander's forces to be held in reserve.[86] The covering force was to engage an advancing enemy forward of the main battle area in order to determine their disposition and delay the adversary to allow for concentration.

In fact, the manual deals with defensive operations in much more depth than offensive. This was the dimension of the manual that earned the doctrine the name "Active Defense," a system for fighting forward in line with NATO doctrine for the defense of Western Germany. This framework rested on a set of fundamental tasks. First, it required that the commander understand the enemy force and see the battlefield in terms of the effects of enemy doctrine, weapons capabilities, and the effects of terrain. These requirements depended operationally on the covering force. By fighting forward and engaging the enemy, the commanders increased their understanding of where the main attack would be. This was especially critical given the Soviet concept of breakthrough, which massed as many as six divisions on a front ten kilometers wide.[87] This covering force would enable the ground commander sufficient time to concentrate at the critical point and were essential to the conduct of the defense. According to the manual, "units of the covering force should make contact as soon as the enemy advances into the cover force area, and fight there an action in depth which will draw the enemy out from under his forward air defenses and away from his forward artillery. This should be done in such a way that when the enemy strikes into the main battle area, his air defense and artillery support is significantly diminished."[88]

While Army doctrine traditionally favored a strong reserve in the defense, the new doctrine emphasized that failure to position sufficient combat power in the covering force area forward of the main body risked defeat. Officers like DePuy saw this change as the only way to compensate for the new lethality:

> To defend against breakthrough tactics, division commanders must not only concentrate at the right time and place, but they also must take risks on the flanks. A defense which spreads two brigades thinly across a wide area and holds one brigade in reserve for counterattack will be defeated by a breakthrough attack. It will in effect be defeated piecemeal because everywhere it will be too weak and thus overwhelmed.[89]

Yet the covering force, the key to determining where to concentrate, required movement, and the Arab-Israeli War demonstrated to TRADOC analysts that movement required suppression, emphasized as cross-reinforcement in the 1976 edition of *Field Manual 100-5*. For TRADOC staffers, to move into position and fight outnumbered required that the U.S. Army fight as a combined arms team and exploit the advantages of terrain afforded to the defender.[90] The manual conceived of mechanized warfare as the defining feature of the modern battlefield. The tank was central. In fact, the manual asserted, "all great armies of the world rest their land combat power on the tank."[91] This meant the U.S. forces had to cross-reinforce at the brigade and battalion levels to fight as a combined arms team. It was only through integration of all aspects of the combined arms team, the suppressive fire of the mechanized infantry that protected tanks from precision-guided munitions, and the smoke laid down by artillery to obscure movement that the defender was able to fight while outnumbered.[92] In this respect, the idea was to compensate for the lack of manpower through maximizing firepower.[93] Planners invoked an operational concept to frame response repertoires. The studies of the Arab-Israeli War along with DePuy's conceptual paper formed incubators that helped forge this new theory of victory.

Given a conceptual framework that both interpreted modern warfare and advanced a set of premises on how to adapt by suppressing, or shooting, to move and moving to concentrate, TRADOC had to determine how to advance the ideas through the broader security bureaucracy. Advocacy networks needed to link study of external threats and possible response scenarios to the broader institutional array of actors that composed the U.S. Army. What the leadership of TRADOC needed was buy-in from other stakeholders in the defense community. Thus, charting the bureaucratic practices that sought to achieve this helps map critical policy networks.

The initial series of briefings and concept papers came out of the policy networks in which the new mode of warfare circulated. Analyzing the papers' distribution paths makes apparent how TRADOC sought to establish itself as a critical node linking the existing infrastructure of combat development in the Combined Arms Center and the schoolhouses (Infantry, Armor, Aviation, Artillery, etc.) to the office of the chief of staff of the Army. TRADOC acted as a dominant mediator, channeling a vision of warfare to schoolhouses that were supposed to reciprocate with more refined visions and best practices of the future battlefield. These were then to be codified in how-to-fight manuals that prepared individual soldiers for mechanized conflict.

TRADOC represented the interface between the chief of staff, as the senior Army officer, and the articulation of new ways of approaching warfare. The initial policy network of interest was thus the set of institutions created after the Steadfast reforms that enabled TRADOC to assume this role. The institutional design of TRADOC had a path-dependent effect whereby critical debates coalesced around it. The creation of a new organizational layer, as an incubator, generated bureaucratic gravity, pulling debates and dialogue into its halls and offices.

This does not mean that TRADOC resisted seeking broader buy-in from the Army community at large. Rather, the new concept had to be yoked to the need for new doctrine. To this end, TRADOC and Forces Command held a series of workshops that brought together senior leaders from across the Army's constituent communities to demonstrate the new lethality of the battlefield and its implications for combined arms tactics. These conferences, known as Octoberfest, began in October 1974 at Fort Knox, approximately one year after the Arab-Israeli War. In a May 24, 1977, speech, DePuy described the event:

> The subject of that conference was the tactical employment of squads, platoons, and companies. We were concerned about how we planned to employ the combined arms force on the modern battlefield for two reasons. The first was that the Army's attention had not been so focused for many years owing to the war in Vietnam. The second was that the Arab/Israeli War of 1973 had impressed us all with the problems involved in preparing an Army to fight in a modern war. Now that was an interesting meeting. We all got together, talked about it and then rode around in trucks and watched squads and platoons in combat exercises.[94]

The following year, the second Octoberfest conference, Oftcon II, was held at Fort Hood to examine how the realities of mechanized combat and how the Army's shift to mechanized combat would affect the institution's advantages in air mobility. In many respects, this represented the clash of two communities within the Army as a whole. In one corner was the light community, made up of infantry and aviation. In the other corner was the armor community, centered on Fort Knox and the growing mechanized infantry community. The post-Vietnam shift represented a reallocation of resources and emphasis away from the light community and toward the heavy community. This effect of the new concept of warfare drove much of the need to ensure buy-in via conferences and workshops. Advocacy networks in the Army diffused new ideas, legitimating them and co-opting potential opponents.

In fact, this was the express intent. After interviewing DePuy in his later years, Major Paul H. Herbert concluded that

> OFTCON was thus primarily a political conference to placate that community before FM 100-5 went to press. It did not bring about any sweeping changes to the manual but probably force[d] the insertion of several phrases and sections that acknowledge the U.S. Army's continued commitment to world leadership in the use of attack helicopters and air mobility.[95]

There are no black boxes in the study of politics. While the national interest of a state is invoked and acted on as a discursive construct to mobilize resources and legitimate a particular functional view of security, each organization inside the state is itself composed of competing communities. In the case of the U.S. Army, while the path laid out for reform was a function of examining the Arab-Israeli War and its implications for future conflict, this vision still had to integrate multiple constituencies.

Concurrent with these conferences was a form of testing and refinement. This testing was both progressive and discursive. It was progressive in that it represented a vetting of doctrinal concepts and possible refinement. It was discursive in that tested concepts were also being distributed and learned through practice. Describing this effort, DePuy told Army leaders gathered at Fort Knox May 24, 1977, that

> TRADOC schools have been pressing on with company, battalion, brigade and division manuals which are derivative of the doctrine in FM 100-5. During the past 6 months, the III Corps, with 2nd Armored and 1st Cavalry Divisions, has been exercising the tactics set forth in the draft manuals and circulars. They found problems—problems of understanding and problems of execution. In the last week of January, we met with all the involved commanders at Fort Hood (including, for example, all battalion commanders and many company commanders) for two solid days of talks, demonstrations and presentations.[96]

In addition to internal communities, TRADOC actively sought to leverage external policy networks to ensure that its doctrinal vision was translated into further force development via weapons acquisitions. Three communities stand out in the archival documents. First, TRADOC had to lobby the defense policy community to accept its vision of warfare lest civilian analysts influence either the secretary of defense or the Congress to alter future budget priorities and resource flows. Advocacy networks reached beyond the Army to bridge the wider defense community.

For example, in 1975 while completing the initial drafts of *Field Manual 100-5* that would embody the new concept of war, DePuy sent a letter to R. W. Komer of RAND Corporation outlining key differences between the perspective of RAND and TRADOC with respect to the European battlefield. The letter responded to a perceived bias in RAND toward the antitank guided missile (ATGM) that could conceivably influence weapons procurement at the level of the Department of Defense. In response, DePuy tried to show the limits of the ATGM given readily available countermeasures while trying to push analysts at RAND to advocate for the required component parts of mechanized warfare. DePuy yoked his central idea of suppression and movement with the German Army operational concept of *Panzergrenadier* and *Panzer* tactics. Thus, TRADOC sought to caution the defense policy community against overstating the importance of ATGM while reminding them,

> We want to emulate the Germans but in order to do it well, we need a good tank, an infantry fighting vehicle, self-propelled artillery, and effective mobility for the air defense systems. Our greatest defect is the infantry fighting vehicle on which, by the way, we intended to mount an anti-tank missile as well as artillery cannon.[97]

The German concept was strikingly similar to the emerging vision in TRADOC in that it favored mechanized combat and the use of a combined arms team to suppress the enemy as a way to facilitate movement. In many respects, this overlap was by design. DePuy sought to synchronize his operational concept and the new tactical manual with the German military as well as the U.S. Air Force.[98] In 1976 he introduced the term "AirLand battle" to discuss the importance of air-ground integration as part of a new type of theater warfare.[99] The net effect was to make the doctrine appear legitimate.

DePuy and his team leveraged senior stakeholder buy-in as a means of garnering other stakeholders in the larger defense community. For example, they used German acceptance of their concept to get agreement from senior officers in U.S. Army Europe who did not want to be seen going against a key ally.[100] Advocacy was instrumental and targeted at senior stakeholders for maximum effect.

The other dynamic at play in invoking the German Army as a legitimation of the emerging concept was to tie key allies to procurement lines. In the same letter to R. W. Komer, after discussing the doctrinal change at stake in Active Defense and its similarity to *Panzer* and *Panzergrenadier* tactics, DePuy related:

> My chief concern these days is that the German concept depends greatly on the Infantry Fighting Vehicle—the MARDER. We have been pushing for the developing and fielding of the mechanized infantry fighting vehicle which is our MARDER.... [W]e are pushing the adoption of Panzer/Panzergrenadier tactics in the Army even though the M113 armored personnel carrier is a very inadequate infantry fighting vehicle.... In short, we want to emulate the Germans but in order to do it well, we need a good tank, an infantry fighting vehicle, self-propelled artillery, and effective mobility for the air defense systems.[101]

Here, in a discussion with an influential think tank representative, TRADOC was actively trying to circulate a very specific narrative and rationale that linked the adoption of new doctrine to a specific set of equipment requirements. Notice the point that doctrine was changing regardless of existing systems. That is, capabilities may inform, but they do not define, doctrine. Rather, doctrine as a response to a specific threat context and scenario informs equipment and force structure decisions. Furthermore, the letter's audience and the language demonstrate the attempt to circulate this vision through the defense establishment. Shifting procurement requires not just testifying before Congress but working the full range of policy actors, from think tanks to key staffers in the Defense Department. Advocacy networks took the form of personal correspondence and official testimony that reached beyond the institutional Army.

Second, in addition to the defense policy community, TRADOC also was involved with presentations to Congress advocating for the new vision of warfare. In an April 29, 1975, letter to the chief of staff of the Army, Fred Weyland (1974–1976), DePuy recounted being questioned by Senator John Culver (D-IA) over the "differences between the German and U.S. Army as they pertain to tactics and techniques."[102] On May 12, 1975, he responded formally to the senator's concerns with a letter discussing the problem of lethality and TRADOC response:

> As you know, the Army has conducted an intensive analysis of the Mid-East War. This analysis, in fact, is still continuing. Three overriding lessons have

emerged: 1) Modern weapons are vastly more lethal than any weapons we have heretofore encountered on the battlefield. 2) In order to cope with these weapons it is essential that we employ a combined arms team of armor, infantry, artillery and air defense backed by the support required to sustain combat operations. 3) Training of the individual and the team will make the difference between success and failure on the battlefield.[103]

The third critical advocacy network TRADOC leveraged to ensure its concept of warfare was sustained was advocacy of the secretary of defense. What emerges in archival documents is that this distinct path was followed at the level of the chief of staff of the Army. That is, TRADOC in effect lobbied the chief of staff to influence the secretary of defense. In an April 29, 1975, letter to Chief of Staff Weyland, DePuy discusses the secretary of defense's objection to the mechanized infantry fighting vehicle. He explains its importance by placing it within the context of the broader conceptual framework:

> We are involved in moving from a "Dismounted Infantry" oriented doctrine to an "Armored" doctrine, with the Infantry, Artillery, and Air Defense in support of tanks in both the offense and defense. . . . I recite all this because it is the central issue. . . . [I]f the U.S. Army is to fight effectively on the mechanized battlefield against the increased lethality of modern weapons, while also outnumbered, we need to adopt the most advanced tactics and techniques of combat. We think we understand and are moving in that direction.[104]

To the extent that TRADOC did directly lobby the secretary of defense, it was done via trusted intermediaries in the Pentagon. For example, in an April 25, 1975, letter to Major General Gordon Sumner Jr., director of the Near East and South Asia Region, Office of the Assistant Secretary of Defense, DePuy again took up his vision:

> We have not been successful in communicating with the Secretary of Defense. . . . As you know, the German Army believes strongly that the United States Army does not know how to fight on a mechanized battlefield against Russian forces. They believe we are too much organized and oriented toward infantry combat. They also believe that our counterattack plans with large forces sweeping across the front are sheer bunk, or at least simply romantic. They believe, and I agree, that the Panzergrenadier/Panzer tactics are our only hope against superior forces. At TRADOC we have been rewriting the doctrine of the United States Army in general accord with the German concept.[105]

TRADOC was the institutional hub of an Army rebuilding itself to fight conventional warfare. Under the ever-watchful eye of DePuy, teams were dispatched to study modern conflict in the context of the Middle East and the battles of 1973. The resulting insights were adapted to construct worst-case scenarios defining possible engagements against the Soviets in Europe. To reinforce operational concept, TRADOC actively leveraged policy networks. Through working the defense community, select think tank pundits, and members of Congress, the leadership of TRADOC sought to reinforce their operational response and gain advocates.

Conclusion

What emerges from process tracing the emergence of the Active Defense doctrine is a portrait of senior officers articulating a new theory of victory and socializing it throughout the broader defense community. Winning the "first battle of the next war" started with mobilizing senior leaders in the U.S. Army and providing them the institutional space to reimagine warfare.

The new theory of victory at the core of Active Defense, how the new lethality called for cover forces using suppression to enable movement, emerged from several sites outside the normal bureaucratic hierarchy. The case highlights the role of incubators, framing studies, and the TRADOC boathouse gang in forging a new vision. Furthermore, incubators operated at levels throughout the defense community. From the chief of staff of the Army's Astarita group to General Starry's use of concept-driven war games at Fort Knox in the Hunfeld I exercise, incubators generated the conceptual space leaders needed to imagine new strategies, doctrine, and forces.

In the emergence of Active Defense, these incubators took four forms: problem-driven simulation, concept-driven simulation, framing studies, and cohorts. Special study groups engaged in framing studies operated at the strategic (e.g., the Astarita group) and operational levels (e.g., multiple Arab-Israeli War groups). These groups seem to reflect a special class of incubators. Officers need to be separated from their routine duties and given a specific task to enable innovation. Furthermore, the use of exercises and war games seems to indicate that knowledge production and specialization tends to be problem driven, consistent with a theory of victory as a response to the larger strategic environment through an organizational lens.

The ideas that emerged from these incubators relied on multiple advocacy networks. While DePuy and his allies generated new controversies, they were able to use their positions to push through reform. Positional legitimation, the use of position in the bureaucratic hierarchy to signal an issue's importance and legitimacy, was a powerful vehicle. The case highlights multiple instances of leaders using their station and reports produced by special study groups to signal the legitimacy of a new idea. DePuy emerges as a master bureaucratic tactician. When the institutional Army could not support his vision, he simply created new positions, by creating TRADOC, and took command.

The case also highlights how new theories of victory are socialized across the Army. Rather than attempting a mass appeal, DePuy and his coalition seem to have preferred targeting other senior leaders. Diffusing the new concept consisted of distributing targeted letters and concept papers with limited names on the "To" lines. The Army-wide briefings, senior leader conferences, and important conceptual memos like the "pot of soup" paper all targeted leadership. DePuy was an institutional builder interested in not just new doctrine but the reorientation of an entire Army and the grounding of how it fights in how it trains. He concerned himself predominantly with organizational elites, using political conferences to either convince or entrap other constituencies.[106]

Entrapment was a special type of brokerage. Both Octoberfest and Oftcon II, while leveraging positional legitimacy, also used the setting to associate different groups with the new ideas. Participating in these workshops on the new lethality linked participants to the emerging theory of victory. The conferences targeted likely rivals in the light infantry community and entrapped them by associating critics with a new idea and indirectly getting their consent.

The case also highlights two processes of interest: nesting and the role of memory and experience. The findings of the "Harmel Report," senior discussions in the National Security Council, the "Astarita Report," and DePuy's "pot of soup" memo all seem to coalesce around the importance of conventional deterrence in support of the forward defense of Germany. This raises a question: To what extent is legitimacy a function of nesting at multiple levels? That is, does an organizational theory of victory become more resonant if it replicates a higher, more diffuse strategic logic? While nesting would seem vital, the archival record does not contain a large number of explicit references to strategic imperatives. Rather, the focus was on tactical questions inherent in modern war and the European theater in particular.

With respect to memory and experience, the emergence of Active Defense illustrates how soldiers use history, memory, and lessons learned in crafting and disseminating new theories of victory. Leaders like DePuy fused lessons learned from the Arab-Israeli War with their battlefield experiences in World War II. Historical anecdotes and experiences appear to have mixed with a stream of incoming data on weapons, capabilities, and enemy doctrine, which could be legitimacy by proximity. The proximity of a story to a key leader's experience may be more important than truth. Soldiers tell stories about war, and the resonance of those stories with their experiences adds to their weight.

On the alternative causal pathways of innovation, the findings are mixed. There were exogenous shocks, but no real evidence of bureaucratic competition driving doctrinal change came to light. The setbacks in Vietnam factored in to how officers imagined future war only in terms of the larger shift to Europe. From the "Astarita Report" to the after-action reviews of the Arab-Israeli War, the military professional appears to have been engaged in a problem-driven search more than a budget battle or attempt to save face following Vietnam. Given the emphasis on tanks in Active Defense, one might be tempted to see the new doctrine in terms of intraservice rivalry, a coup by armored officers against the traditional light infantry dominance in the Army. Yet DePuy was an infantry officer. The focus again was less on bureaucratic rivals or battlefield defeat and more on imagining future war. There was a progressive attempt to redefine modern land warfare in line with the core mission of the Army.

With respect to technology, the evidence is mixed. Observations of the new lethality contained detailed analysis of the impact of precision weapons. Yet military officers synthesized these observations with an appreciation for combined arms and the cumulative integration of new weapons into battlefield tactics.

Last, there is no significant evidence that Active Defense reflected an enduring, attritionist way of war. On the surface, the doctrine with its emphasis on firepower and suppression appears to continue the larger attrition-based paradigm in the American way of war. Yet closer examination that includes General Starry's experiments with small counterattacks and DePuy's concept of blocking forces, reveals that the central idea behind the defense was to buy time for the larger counterattack. DePuy directly linked this theory of victory to maneuver-based concepts used by the German Army on the defensive in World War II.

3   The Central Battle

IN 1981, GENERAL GLENN K. OTIS, TRADOC COMMANDER FROM 1981 to 1983, opened a speech to a delegation of South American military officers in Brazil with the following statements:

> The military balance has been shifting against us; the uncertainty now about the balance of power portends significant trends. The first is the likelihood of a multipolar world. This is seen in the proliferation of nuclear weapons, modernization of armies, interdependence of nations, breakdown of alliances and international movements, and the creation of new movements. The second trend is continuation of the increase in Soviet power projection capability. The development of the Soviet navy, increased arms sales, recent military actions, and use of proxies support this trend. The third trend, which links directly with the second, is a continuation of the US/Soviet military investment imbalance.[1]

For leading thinkers within the U.S. Army, the 1980s, like the "lost decade" of the 1970s in the United States, was a continuation of a trend toward balance-of-power uncertainty, the central premise of Otis's geopolitical narrative in Brazil. Despite sustained force modernization and doctrinal innovation through the second half of the 1970s, senior officers in the Army entered the 1980s increasingly unsure of their ability to meet threats in the global system.

Officials throughout the Department of Defense perceived a significant gap in U.S. and Soviet military spending and conventional force inventories, as Figures 3.1 and 3.2, from official documents, show. While this gap later

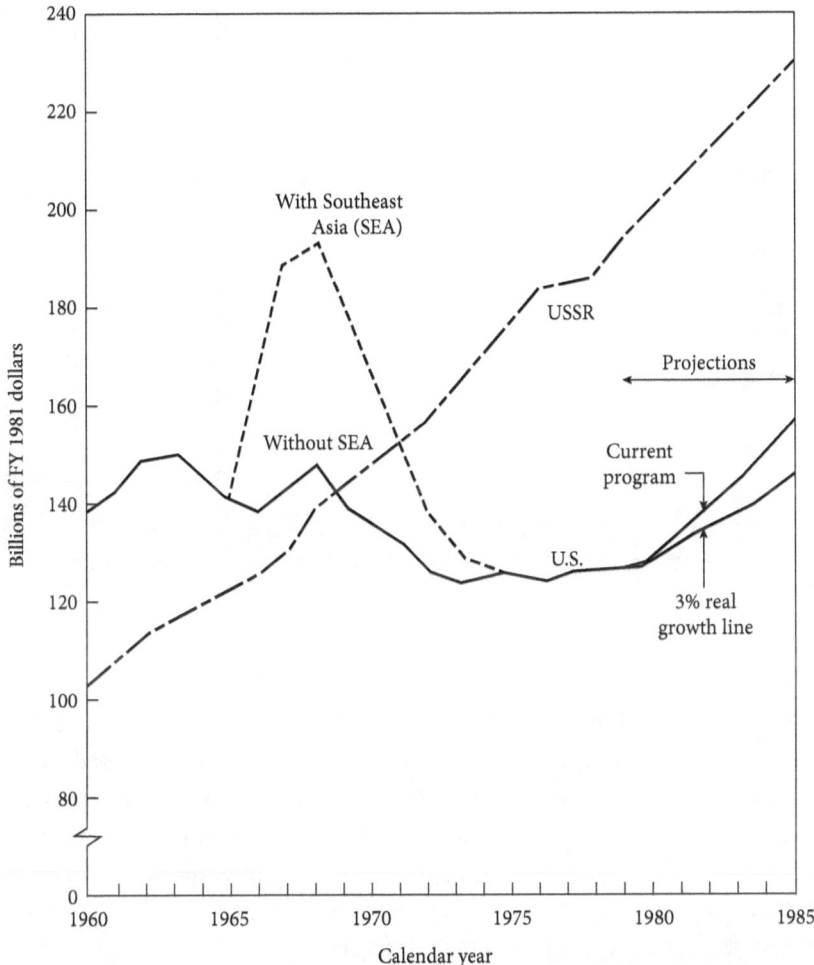

FIGURE 3.1 Comparison of U.S. defense outlays and estimated dollar cost of Soviet defense programs

NOTE: U.S. outlays exclude retirement pay and include Department of Energy and Coast Guard defense outlays. Estimated Soviet costs are based on what it would cost the United States to produce and man the Soviet military force and operate it as the Soviets do. Projections are based on 3 percent annual real growth for the USSR and real growth in outlays as projected by the Future Years Defense Program for the United States.

proved nonexistent, it influenced how military professionals thought about future wars.

Briefings regularly focused not just on the size of the Soviet forces but also on the impact of mass on decision making. In 1977 official assessments

	USSR average	U.S. average	USSR-U.S. ratio
tank	2,770	469	5.9:1
IFV	4,990	1,556	3.2:1
artillery	1,310	162	8:1
aircraft	1,090	573	1.9:1
helicopter	666	733	0.8:1
antitank missile	27,000	27,351	1:1

FIGURE 3.2 Estimated U.S.-USSR relative production rates, 1972–1976
NOTE: Second icon represents mechanized infantry fighting vehicles. Bottom icon represents ground-launched antitank missiles.

assumed the Soviets deployed "27 of its first-line divisions in East Germany, Poland, and Czechoslovakia" with another "4 Soviet divisions . . . in Hungary."[2] In terms of capabilities, U.S. defense officials estimated "ground forces have at their disposal more than 16,000 tanks and hold to a tactical doctrine of rapid armored thrusts that bears a strong family resemblance to what we used to call blitzkrieg."[3] For the Department of Defense, the "atmosphere of détente has arrived because, as the Soviet leadership might put it, the correlation of forces has begun to shift in their favor."[4]

Anxiety further increased after the crises of 1979. The combined impact of the fall of the shah of Iran and the Soviet invasion of Afghanistan pushed fears about surging communist power to new horizons. Defense analysts in both the United States and NATO countries were increasingly concerned about Soviet theater nuclear forces following the deployment of the SS-20, a road-mobile intermediate-range nuclear missile with multiple independently targetable reentry vehicles. At a NATO Defense Planning Committee meeting in Brussels May 15–16, 1979, the official communiqué referred to the SS-20 as adding a "new dimension of threat" constituting a "qualitative change in the Soviet arsenal."[5] To match the SS-20 and Soviet fielding of new Backfire bombers, NATO established a high-level group to review, along with the existing NATO Special Group on Arms Control, NATO's deterrent posture and capability. In December 1979, NATO members agreed on the need to modernize long-range-theater nuclear forces, including "deploying 108 Pershing II missiles on launchers and 464 Ground Launched Cruise Missiles (GLCMs)" by 1983.[6] The U.S. defense planning community had a general perception of a military imbalance in conventional and nuclear forces.

Senior officials in the Army called regional balances into question. In his Brazil speech to the South American military officers, Otis emphasized the trend toward a multipolar world given Soviet advances in high-energy weapons, nuclear proliferation, and a network of client states surrounding areas of strategic importance to the United States in the Middle East, Africa, and Central America.[7] While in retrospect this seems quite overstated, at the time military professionals imagined the future under the shadow of an assertive Soviet foreign policy. The operational problem for the Army was how to provide a credible conventional deterrent to an increasingly capable and assertive Soviet Union and its network of client states.

New Soviet formations in Europe and the threat of worldwide deployments defined the crux of doctrinal development in the early 1980s. In 1982, the Army published a new doctrine, AirLand Battle. The concept called for taking the initiative and making daring assaults across an extended battlefield to destabilize conventionally superior Soviet forces. Though forged in visions of Central European warfare, senior leaders extended the doctrine to non-NATO contingency operations in which planners prepared for the possibility of fighting Soviet-backed armies in areas from the Middle East to the Korean peninsula. A new theory of victory emerged and condensed to form a doctrine that departed from the Active Defense doctrine's covering forces and forward defense.

This theory emerged through a series of special studies and experiments across the Army. Incubators provided a forum for redefining the operational problem just three years after the publication of Active Defense. Advocacy networks then diffused these ideas throughout the Army. Through professional journals, speeches, and conferences, leaders like General Donn Starry made a broad-based appeal to the military profession.

The chapter proceeds by analyzing archival records, official publications, congressional testimony, and secondary sources to reconstruct the emergence of AirLand Battle doctrine. First, the chapter examines the threats that drove national security considerations in the late 1970s and 1980s with an emphasis on the specific concerns voiced by Army leaders. Two stand out: the conventional force balance in Europe and increased planning for non-NATO contingencies in Southwest Asia and the Far East. Second, similar to the previous chapter's discussion of Active Defense in terms of shoot, or suppress, to move and move to concentrate as related to the 1973 Arab-Israeli War, the analysis elucidates the conceptual underpinnings of doctrinal innovation in the development of AirLand Battle. Specifically, the emergence of two concepts, Central Battle and Extended Battlefield, drove doctrinal development in the early 1980s. In both cases, incubators and advocacy networks proved central to helping military professionals define operational problems and spread their new concept across the organization.

The Fulda Gap

Speaking before the Senate Armed Services Committee in 1977, Starry, commanding general of TRADOC (1977–1981), characterized the Army as preparing to fight two types of war: mechanized war, or high-intensity conflict involving heavy forces, in Europe and the Middle East, and "other wars," or contingency conflicts involving power projection by at least one light infantry division.[8] In terms of force strength and institutional orientation, the Army of the 1970s predominantly focused on Europe. Since NATO's adoption of Flexible Response strategy in 1967, conventional forces were a central aspect of alliance planning.[9] In this framework, planners had to be prepared to respond to both conventional and nuclear assaults by the Warsaw Pact. This emphasis on ground forces spawned a lively debate about the utility of conventional deterrence in Europe.[10] While many academics postulated that the Soviets were incapable of conducting a surprise attack, military leaders focused on the worst-case scenario and prepared for situations in which NATO would be left at a significant disadvantage in the opening stages of a Warsaw Pact offensive.[11] Military professionals began to look at this problem through the lens of second-echelon forces and the specifics of how the Soviets might launch a conventional attack.

Much of the debate centered on force ratios. While the U.S. Army planned for combat involving estimated imbalances as high as five to one in Active Defense, civilian analysts put the correlation of forces closer to two to one in the late 1970s. According to John Mearsheimer, the Warsaw Pact had roughly fifty-seven divisions in Central Europe, whereas NATO had twenty-eight.[12]

While many analysts like Mearsheimer also doubted the robustness of this comparison given differences in manning, training, and equipment performance, military planners focused on the prospect of a sudden, violent fight against an adversary that had shorter lines of communication and significant advantages in tanks and artillery tubes.[13]

While the U.S. Army was busy producing training manuals and circulars based on Active Defense, the principal adversary, the Soviet Union, was by no means idle. The Soviets, much like their U.S. Army counterparts, had initiated their own tactical revolution in response to the 1973 Arab-Israeli War. Like their NATO counterparts, Warsaw Pact military leaders held workshops and discussions concerning the impacts of the conflict on the face of battle in Europe. From 1974 to 1975, Soviet leaders engaged in a lengthy and detailed debate on the effects of antitank weaponry.[14] Just as American analysts had responded to the lethality of the Arab-Israeli War, Soviets also studied the impact of precision-guided munitions and antitank weapons on fighting formations in an effort to "rescue Blitzkrieg."[15] This dialogue raised serious doubts about the success of attacking mechanized infantry fighting vehicles like the Soviet BMP, required to support a breakthrough maneuver.[16] In fact, in training exercises Soviet forces were shifting their resources to practice multiprong attacks and meeting engagements that could be exploited by second-echelon forces.[17] Thus, while much of the logic of Active Defense rested on breakthrough-maneuver scenarios—that is, a massed armor attack along a narrow front—by 1976 the Soviets had a new tactical doctrine for fighting and winning a rapid and decisive conventional engagement. The operational problem confronting the Army was in a state of flux.

Alongside these shifts in doctrine, the Soviets began adapting their forces in the mid-1970s to increase their short-warning attack capabilities.[18] In particular, the Soviets' Western Military District saw increases in its absolute numbers and in readiness and logistic support. A new emphasis on command and control procedures necessary to integrate second- and first-echelon forces complemented the Soviets' expansion of offensive capabilities.[19] Collectively, these modernization efforts also called into question whether the United States would be able to meet the conventional deterrent requirements of Flexible Response.[20]

A new appreciation in American military circles for Soviet operational art accompanied changes in Warsaw Pact doctrine and force posture. Senior leaders began to study translated writings detailing a genealogy of Russian warfare dating back to the 1930s. Rediscovered in the 1970s, these texts advocated offensive operations involving deep strikes with continuous attack by mechanized formations.[21] Considering the application of these operations in Central Europe, NATO analysts believed that the Warsaw Pact would seek rapid penetrations of border defenses to fix forward elements for a deep thrust by second-echelon elements into the Allied rear. The principal objective was to put the Soviets' conventional forces in a position to split German lines of communication, disrupt Allied mobilization, and essentially destroy NATO's front-line units. The strategy called for the use of overwhelming combat power in two waves and saw military collapse as a means to decisive political victory short of nuclear war. U.S. military leaders like Starry believed three fundamental principles of war animated the Soviets' offensive planning: mass, momentum, and continuity. In this reading, mass, as the concentration of forces, sustained continuous land-combat operations through the depth of the battlefield to generate sufficient momentum to collapse the opponent's will.[22]

Military leaders in the U.S. Army translated this operational picture into a worst-case scenario in the V Corps sector in NATO's Central Army Group region. Known as the Fulda Gap, the region represented an ideal corridor for large mechanized formations attacking across the German border. According to Starry, the Soviets would specifically attack there because

> [it is] the shortest way to the Rhine. It is the shortest way to the American airfields, which lie down in the southwestern part of Germany. It is the shortest way to the logistic complexes at Kaiserslauten. It is the shortest way to France. It is the shortest way to cut Germany in two.[23]

In their Fulda Gap scenario, Army leaders hypothesized that the Soviets would draw on a modified variant of their breakthrough attack referred to as a "daring thrust" or "preemptive maneuver."[24] In his analysis of conventional deterrence in Central Europe, Mearsheimer called this strategy the "standing start" posture.[25] Like the breakthrough, the preemptive maneuver doctrine reflected evolving Soviet views of warfare. In particular, like those in the U.S. Army, military planners in Moscow were deeply concerned about the impact of antitank guided missiles on the modern battlefield. In Soviet estimates, NATO forces would dig into defensive strong points covered by antitank fighting missiles, making a traditional operational breakthrough based on mass much more costly in terms of troops and equipment losses. Therefore, in the U.S. Army's assessment the most likely Soviet course of action in an offensive would be to "substitute surprise for mass.... [I]nstead of massing the forces, [they] will try to achieve surprise."[26] Military professionals engaged in problem-driven search examined a new challenge: surprise multiprong attacks and meeting engagements followed by second-echelon forces.

Three Days of War

Fighting Soviet proxies worldwide constituted the other-war scenario. From a U.S. perspective, 1979 was a year of twin crises. First, after months of massive street protests the shah fled Iran in January 1979. Along with Saudi Arabia, Iran was part of a "twin pillar" approach to regional security.[27] Under the Nixon Doctrine, the shah's prominence rose because the United States sought to use him as a local ally to offset Soviet influence in the Gulf.[28] Iran acted as a buffer against Soviet units in the Caucasus Mountains and Middle Eastern client states. The collapse of the house of Pahlavi thus upset the regional balance of power. A weak and hostile Iran opened the possibility of Soviet intervention in the Persian Gulf and Indian Ocean.[29]

The Soviet invasion of Afghanistan provided the second crisis. After a buildup of equipment and personnel throughout 1979 to prop up the local communist regime, on December 24 the Soviet Union invaded Afghanistan. Immediately, the military action lent credence to a narrative circulating in Defense corridors of a resurgent, maximalist Soviet foreign policy. In this reading, "the invasion of Afghanistan [was] seen as presaging a move into Pakistan."[30] Many military planners held that the escalation complemented Soviet backing to the People's Democratic Republic of Yemen and efforts to secure strategic bases to threaten U.S. interests in the Gulf, including Saudi Arabia and Oman.[31] The operational problem confronting military professionals in the Army extended beyond mechanized war in the Fulda Gap to include the possibility of short, high-end conflict against Soviet-backed client states.

The economic dimensions of power defined the logic of Soviet aggression to many in the American defense establishment. Planners envisioned the Soviet military using Afghanistan as the pivot in a larger push to the oil-rich areas in Southwest Asia necessary to subvert Western economic interests and further dominate energy markets.[32] In this reading, the Soviets could stop short of seeking access to the Indian Ocean and simply apply military and political pressure through proxies to disrupt flows of oil that were critical to NATO partners.[33] In the late 1970s, Europe received as much as 65 percent of its oil from the Gulf, while the United States received less than 20 percent of its total imports from the region.[34] The situation led many scholars to view Soviet strategy as an effort to disrupt the United States via attacking Europe's Achilles' heel.[35] This prospect of future unrest in the Middle East and an oil-grab scenario set the stage for the Carter Doctrine, which Jimmy Carter proclaimed in his January 23, 1980, State of the Union address: the United States would use force if necessary to protect its interests in the Persian Gulf.[36]

Beyond the troubles in Southwest Asia, military planners also viewed the Soviet Union as playing an instrumental role in emerging conflicts in Africa and Central America. In his 1981 speech in Brazil before South American military officers, Otis noted,

> The Soviets have established direct or indirect presence in Africa, the Middle East, and Southeast Asia. In Africa not only could the Soviets act to deny the west direct access to African sources of raw materials, they also could use footholds on the African littoral to dominate vital sea routes. Over the long term, a combination of Soviet inroads on and around the African continent could give Moscow the potential to manipulate the flow in international trade with disastrous results for the industrial nations of the west. . . . Moscow has not been hesitant to exploit local conditions in the Middle East. Footholds in the People's Democratic Republic of Yemen and Ethiopia afford the Soviet navy important facilities. In addition, large quantities of modern Soviet arms sustain radical Arab states. Soviet-equipped armies in Iraq, Libya, and Syria have the potential to upset regional power balances. . . . Cuban diplomatic and political leverage in Central America, the Caribbean, South America, and with the Nonaligned Nations has increased, primarily as a result of Soviet political and financial support. Cuba will likely continue to back insurgent movements and exploit opportunities for revolutionary change, as evidenced most recently in Nicaragua and El Salvador.[37]

This worst-case scenario characterized Soviet foreign policy for much of the defense establishment in the late 1970s. Concerns over energy security following oil embargos imposed on the West after the 1973 Arab-Israeli War heightened fears. In 1977, President Carter signed Presidential Directive 18 and Presidential Review Memorandum 10 identifying the Persian Gulf as an area vital to U.S. interests and specifying the need for a "rapid reaction mobile force for quick strikes in Third World crises."[38] Concurrently, the secretary of defense issued guidance for the Army to begin planning for a contingency corps composed of light infantry.[39] Furthermore, under the direction of the national security advisor, the Defense Department undertook a series of preliminary staff studies on non-NATO contingencies.[40] These strategic planning exercises paralleled academic studies on general-purpose forces and hypothetical conflicts in the Persian Gulf.[41] There seems to have been parallel planning efforts in the Department of Defense and Army for meeting the objectives of President Carter's new planning directives.

While Carter's directive and memorandum led to the foundation of the Rapid Deployment Joint Task Force, capable of responding to Soviet aggression in the Gulf and beyond, in 1979 newly appointed chief of staff of the Army General Edward C. Meyer began forging his vision of land forces able to balance contingency operations and high-intensity conflict in Central Europe. In June of 1979, he suggested that TRADOC consider revising its doctrine to include third-world contingencies.[42] As outlined in his June 13, 1979, letter to TRADOC commander Starry, Meyer viewed the standing Active Defense doctrine as a high-risk, low-probability threat scenario, whereas he, like many in the upper echelons of the defense establishment, was primarily concerned about the higher probability of the United States being drawn into contingency operations by Soviet involvement at the periphery.[43] Meyer sought to develop a new concept that captured both scenarios and provided the intellectual foundation for doctrinal reform.

Meyer's focus on rapid-deployment-force-type operations circulated in a white paper distributed Army-wide February 25, 1980. The central narrative revolved around Meyer's vision of "three days of war":

> In the most basic sense, the strategic requirement of the 1980s is to prepare for the "Three Days of War": to deter the day before the war, to fight the day of the war; and to terminate the conflict in such a manner that on the day after war, the United States and its allies enjoy an acceptable level of security. The threats to US interests beyond Europe likely to emerge in the decades ahead will be extraordinarily diverse. The increased demand for limited resources worldwide is likely to undergird confrontations. They include not only the USSR, but heavily armed Soviet surrogates and independent, militarily sophisticated Third World nations.[44]

Furthermore, for Meyer these contingencies would span the full spectrum of conflict to include terrorism and insurgency and occur in a variety of environments ranging from urban terrain to deserts, mountainous regions, and rain forest. The Army would have to be sufficiently flexible to "successfully meet threats to vital US interests outside of Europe, without compromising the decisive theater in Central Europe."[45] The new operational problem was how to meet this spectrum of threats without sacrificing the conventional deterrent.

Along these lines, the white paper called for a balancing of force structure and doctrine between the demands of non-NATO contingencies and the conventional fight in Central Europe. It called into question the optimal mix of heavy and light forces. Meyer believed,

> The problems of limited strategic lift and the loss of flexibility which result from expanded prepositioned sets of equipment force us to maximize the utility of light forces both in NATO and in other contingencies. Conversely, where heavy forces are required, both in NATO and elsewhere, we must recognize the need, carefully determine when those forces are required, and make the difficult decisions necessary to make their employment possible.[46]

Thus, while scenarios for supporting the forward defense in NATO called for reinforcements to be moved quickly to heavy weapons already staged around the Fulda Gap, the force packages "for non-NATO contingencies must allow for a continuum or response ranging from counterterrorism through a light show of force to heavy corps-sized force, or even more, the emphasis must be on rapid and successful accomplishments of the task."[47]

In a January 20, 1981, untitled classified memo to the Army chief of staff, Bob Komer of the Office of the Secretary of Defense reiterated his view that the United States required a "10 division D-Day force" to maintain a credible NATO deterrent lest the military "signal the Soviets as well as our allies how we were moving toward reducing the defense of Europe in order to defend [Persian Gulf] oil needed mostly by Europe itself."[48] Furthermore, debate over focusing on mechanized war versus "other wars" also informed force design initiatives. In a March 24, 1981, memorandum to the chief of staff of the Army and TRADOC, "Reorganization of the 101st Airborne Division (Air Assault)," the Forces Command commander states,

> While proceeding with the reorganization effort, I have developed concerns and questions which are sufficient to cause hesitation, specifically, I am concerned

whether the mission statement for the division is appropriate and whether the division is structured too heavy considering the recently assigned [rapid-deployment-force] mission and the attendant strategic lift requirements. . . . [The] focus on NATO Europe and the ability to conduct combined operations or fighting unilateral military actions without full corps support make the division too heavy much less unrealizable given current shortfalls.[49]

Similar concerns plagued many of the intra-Army discussions on rapid deployment forces. In a July 28, 1982, letter to Starry, General Richard Cavazos, commander of U.S. Army Forces, Readiness, made the case that because of strategic mobility shortfalls and equipment issues, the Army was unable to confront non-European contingencies. In these missions, he said,

not only would we suffer from inadequate strategic lift, we simply have not procured equipment in sufficient quantities to enable us to fight in two or more theaters. In addition to our resource shortfalls, we must also dual task units, that is to say, almost all of the force structure is committed to reinforce NATO; any other contingency draws down that force.[50]

While it would be easy to cast Meyer's call to arms as an episode of the isolated Army searching for funds, the role of land forces in non-NATO contingencies and the rapid deployment force were never in doubt. Early on, debate was lively about using air interdiction to delay Soviet forces entering Iran through the Caucasus. Yet air interdiction never transcended standard planning scenarios that called for heavy reliance on ground forces.[51] A requirement to have at least three divisions and a range of special operations forces available as a strategic reserve was part of rapid-deployment-force planning. Rather than resist this mission, military professionals in the Army sought to align their critical tasks and organizational structure to adapt to it. This process required internal debate and critique on the nature of the problem and how best to meet the challenge.

By the early 1980s, planners were shaping force packages for possible deployment. A February 12, 1981, classified Joint Chiefs of Staff memo titled "Planning Guidance" to the Army chief of staff reminded the Army to be prepared to respond given "continuing developments in Southwest Asia" and the "review of military activities in the Persian Gulf/Indian Ocean/Middle East Region within the context of U.S. force requirements."[52] The Army integrated its visions of future war with requirements for major contingency plans.

New Warsaw Pact strategies and capabilities and the prospect of countering Soviet clients in the periphery defined the threat horizon guiding military planning from 1976 to 1982. For the Army, Otis's idea of a "balance of power uncertainty" generated interest in revisiting doctrine and force structure to ensure sufficient combat power to handle multiple crises. To address these operational problems, military professionals in the Army leveraged an array of incubators to create new concepts.

The Central Battle

A conventional defense of Europe had to meet the mass and momentum of Soviet second-echelon forces in a hypothetical attack by armored divisions through the Fulda Gap to destroy logistic points and airfields en route to the Rhine. The problem facing NATO and U.S. Army commanders was how to contain this offensive in a way that both produced sufficient time for reserve forces to marshal and was consistent with NATO's doctrine of forward defense. The challenge confronted Starry in 1976 as the commander of V Corps. Under the Active Defense doctrine, this meant winning the first battle of the next war, pushing covering forces forward at the expense of a tactical reserve to determine the exact breakthrough point so that sufficient combat power could be concentrated to contain the offensive. In a July 1980 TRADOC memorandum titled "Integrated Operations" Starry characterized the V Corps problem as a vehicle for reflecting on the inherent tensions between the tactical and operational levels of war.[53] While a tactical response might be able to hold the initial breakthrough, the second echelons were an operational problem. At the heart was how to structure the initial engagements at the tactical level within a larger operational plan, the Central Battle, to disrupt the momentum of the overall offensive.

To determine how best to achieve these ends, Starry had his staff conduct "150 battle simulations in [the V Corps] sector and a separate array of tank battles [of the] past, together with intensive observation of actual enemy advance maneuvers and intelligence reflecting their locations, routes of movement, and tactics of attack."[54] Starry's team also drew on the extensive array of studies dealing with the 1973 Arab-Israeli War and historical case studies of prior mechanized battles.[55] In Starry's own language, it formed a "battle calculus," a means of inferring the best possible way a defender could use terrain, time, and preestablished defensive points to slow an advance by a numerically superior opponent.

This integration of intelligence estimates, force ratio calculations, and historical studies of command decision and terrain created a conceptual laboratory in which Starry imagined future defensive battles against the Warsaw Pact and in the process determined the optimal mix of targets for the corps to engage. For Starry, a corps commander engaged in either a NATO doctrinal forward defense or the U.S. Army Active Defense had the twin challenges of target servicing and force generation. The division commander would be the principal tactical commander while the corps commander had to position corps-level assets to support the immediate defensive battle. Target servicing was thus selecting the best possible Soviet units, installations, and likely avenues of approach to support the close tactical fight of a division. This quickly added depth to thinking about future battles in Europe.[56] While the near fight would consume tactical units, commanders at the operational or corps level would need to think across the full range of the battlefield to determine the best targets.[57] A new theory of victory was emerging through the V Corps battle calculus incubators.

In the Central Battle, units had to see deep, move fast, strike quickly, and finish rapidly.[58] To see deep, commanders needed to visualize the second-echelon divisions and their reconnaissance elements at ranges of 50 to 150 kilometers, thus putting a premium on intelligence and surveillance capabilities. According to Starry, "To see those targets and bring effective fire on them we have to have the help of assets outside of the control of the corps commander, primarily the U.S. Air Force for surveillance and fires that can bear on those echelons."[59] The brigade commander needed to see the second-echelon regiments of the first-echelon division, just as the division commander would need to see the second-echelon divisions of the first-echelon army and the corps commander the second echelon of the entire army.

Visualizing battlefield depth enabled units on the defensive to maneuver to the critical point of the attack for target servicing. In fact, for Starry there was a distinct decision-making rate associated with each echelon. Battalion commanders would need to be prepared to destroy 200 to 250 targets in a battle that might last ten to fifteen minutes, while a division would engage roughly 2,000 targets over eight hours.[60]

Though Starry had been one of the main architects of Active Defense, he tested the ideas against anticipated future battles. Through battle calculus and other incubators at V Corps, Starry engaged in a problem-driven search indicative of a professional and the premium a profession places on expertise. On assuming command in Europe, he created the space in which his staff could anticipate future battles as a means of redefining critical tasks for Army divisions and corps.

The Extended Battlefield

Parallel to describing the Central Battle, military planners began to develop interdiction strategies. Soviet second-echelon forces in Europe defined a number of Army initiatives during the end of 1979 and the first half of the 1980s. Since 1979, the Field Artillery schoolhouse had worked on developing a deep-strike concept that controlled the tempo of the battle: breaking up the mass slows the momentum. The disruption of second-echelon forces would "shape the central battle."[61] In addition, after assuming the position of NATO's supreme Allied commander in Europe in 1979, U.S. Army general Bernard Rogers tasked his staff to develop a concept using deep conventional strikes to disrupt Soviet follow-on forces. The concept sought to exploit "particularly critical enemy vulnerabilities in the reinforcement process: the rigidity of his planning for an echeloned offense, the density of forces along limited attack routes, and critical transportation facilities."[62] At multiple echelons, senior leaders created a space where their staffs could develop new deep-strike concepts.

At the direction of Starry, Colonel John R. Greenway set up a network of study groups managed from the Combined Arms Center in Fort Leavenworth to study this new concept, Extended Battlefield.[63] Between the fall of 1979 and the winter of 1980, the Combined Arms Center hosted meetings to define how corps Army could interdict Warsaw Pact second-echelon forces. By May, the group had developed an operational concept. Under NATO's forward defense strategy, military planners needed to understand the deep-battle area beyond the forward line of troops (FLOT) in terms of an area of interest, or a zone affected by their weapons systems, and an area of influence, or a zone that could shape the battle in their sector.[64]

In many respects, this characterization was an effort to integrate the target-servicing aspects of the Central Battle with a corps interdiction strategy. As depicted in Table 3.1, at each echelon, commanders needed to see into the deep-battle area and attempt to influence the tempo by attacking follow-on forces given time and distance factors.

TABLE 3.1 Area of influence

Level of command	Time from FLOT (hours)	Distance beyond FLOT (kilometers)
AREA OF INFLUENCE		
Battalion	0–3	5
Brigade	0–12	15
Division	0–24	70
Corps	0–72	150
Echelons above corps	72+	150+
AREA OF INTEREST		
Battalion	0–12	15
Brigade	0–24	70
Division	0–72	150
Corps	0–96	300
Echelons above corps	96+	1,000

SOURCE: John L. Romjue, *From Active Defense to AirLand Battle: The Development of Army Doctrine, 1973–1982* (Fort Monroe, VA: U.S. Army TRADOC, 1984), 90.

The key was to see the full depth of the battlefield and enable deep attacks to delay and disrupt the second echelon. Each level had its role. A battalion commander, guiding the actions of five hundred soldiers in forward defensive positions, had to analyze and plan for Soviet forces that were as far as twelve hours' march or fifteen kilometers from his positions. As his staff worked through options, he had to think about disrupting elements of those advancing forces once they were three hours or five kilometers from his forward troops. Battlefield depth and the ability to influence enemy decision making, based on the position of their forward and rear forces, defined the structure of conflict. As characterized by TRADOC historian John Romjue, the interdiction concept portrayed both offensive and defensive applications:

> [When] defending, the corps conducted operations to destroy assaulting enemy echelons while simultaneously acting to break up the mass, slow the momentum, and disrupt the enemy's ability to conduct operations. When attacking, the corps sought to destroy or bypass enemy forward defenses, to move rapidly into the enemy rear to destroy command and control, logistics, and other soft targets, and reserves.[65]

The Extended Battlefield concept also sought to regain the initiative. Whereas previous doctrine looked to hold the Soviets at bay while diplomats reached a political settlement, the Extended Battlefield concept portrayed a situation in which the only way to avoid defeat was to effectively win the campaign. It was not enough to stop the Soviets at the Fulda Gap. U.S. forces would need to take the initiative and so thoroughly disrupt the numerically superior Warsaw Pact formations that they ceased to function as a fighting force. How military professionals looked at the problem of second-echelon forces drove how they defined critical tasks.

Throughout the course of 1980 and into 1981, planners tested and refined Extended Battlefield. In addition to war games and discussions at the Combined Arms Center, field commanders reviewed the concept. In a May 4, 1981, letter to Starry titled "Extended Battlefield Concept," Lieutenant General James Richardson outlined the response by several corps commanders and their concurrence with "the philosophy that early detection of the enemy's intentions and disrupting his plans or timing will improve our opportunities for success in the close in battle."[66] Furthermore, in the same letter, Richardson tells Starry that Chief of Staff Meyer endorsed the idea and wanted to "stress that this concept is not a fire power/attrition concept but rather a maneuver concept—that by attacking deep we permit openings for counterattacks and friendly maneuver."[67] This concept used multiple incubators, including an extended battle network. Starry's battle calculus circulated among senior leaders, seeking their professional opinion and in the process building momentum for change.

In addition to developing Extended Battlefield, officers at the Field Artillery schoolhouse began to plan for the use of tactical nuclear weapons. Release authority for tactical nuclear strike rested with the national command authority, while the weapons systems existed at the corps level. This produced a significant time lag in the event of a surprise Warsaw Pact invasion as envisioned by the standing start scenario. To address this, the Army began to develop the integrated battlefield concept. That striking the second echelon was the key to success against a numerically superior opponent led commanders to prepare for the use of all assets, including tactical nuclear systems, to this end. There was no such thing as a nonnuclear battlefield. All planning had to be done with respect to the worst-case scenario: the Soviets might use tactical nuclear weapons, and the United States might be delayed in receiving command authority to counter. The Army would include planning for nuclear battlefields as a joint concept within future doctrine and NATO planning.[68]

The importance of conceptualizing all war as nuclear war found further resonance in the Army chief of staff white paper issued in 1980. In it, Meyer noted that "the doctrinal thrust for use of nuclear weapons must increasingly focus on attacking enemy nuclear weapons delivery systems and second echelon forces.... We must continually train to operate in chemical, nuclear, and conventional environments."[69] The Army needed to be prepared for a situation in which the extended battlefield was an integrated battlefield.

That the Army actively pushed to develop war fighting concepts that stressed the integration of air and land forces in a potentially nuclear battlefield shows that worst-case scenario bias shaped how military professionals looked at threats and that service coordination as much as service rivalry can define doctrinal change. Just as the Active Defense doctrine stressed the need to suppress forward air defense elements as a means of enabling the air superiority campaign, the Army's concept of deep attack against Soviet second-echelon forces incorporated close cooperation with the Air Force. While services often do compete over budgetary resources, the historical record demonstrates many points of cooperation in development of operational concepts.

While Army officers were conducting Central Battle studies and studying the Extended Battlefield concept, DARPA (Defense Advanced Research Projects Agency) leveraged incubators to address the problem of second-echelon forces. In 1975 in partnership with the Defense Nuclear Agency, DARPA sponsored a concept development study, the Long Range Research and Development Planning Program, to "broaden the spectrum of strategic alternatives available to the President and the Secretary of Defense against limited Soviet aggression."[70] Panels, boards, and conferences explored potential conflict scenarios and emerging technologies, to determine how NATO forces could respond to a Soviet attack with only limited nuclear use.[71]

DARPA built on the study, combining its findings with other ideas to form the Integrated Target Acquisition and Strike System (ITASS).[72] Like the extended battlefield study and Starry's Central Battle simulations, ITASS would attack "deep in enemy territory using airborne reconnaissance to guide long-range missiles carrying terminally guided submunitions."[73] The Defense

Science Board reviewed the system and recommended a proof-of-concept demonstration, leading to the DARPA Assault Breaker program and tests in 1982 at the White Sands Missile Test Range. The tests caused a cascading ripple effect. Andrew Marshall and his Office of Net Assessment noticed over time that leading Soviet military theorists were panicking about the potential of the system's emerging capabilities, referring to them as a "reconnaissance strike complex." Strategic thinkers began to consider the prospect of non-nuclear weapons achieving strategic effects.[74]

ITASS, Assault Breaker, and the Soviets' perspective of a strike complex were all nested in the emerging idea of an offsetting strategy. Between 1977 and 1981, Secretary of Defense Harold Brown and Undersecretary of Defense William J. Perry started to advocate a new approach to countering Soviet conventional superiority. Perry believed precision technologies were "revolutionizing warfare," giving the United States the ability to match the Soviets without having to "compete tank for tank."[75] He described the strategy years later as "taking advantage of the explosion in information technology which was underway, and applying this technology to a new generation of smart weapons on the theory that this could offset the quantitative superiority of the Soviet forces. And since the United States was the world's leader in that information technology, we reasoned that this would give the United States military what a businessman would call an unfair competitive advantage."[76] Perry used precision technology as part of a broader coalition-building strategy to focus "the attention and support of high-level DoD decision makers, Service Chiefs, and Congress to speed several important technologies from concept to implementation."[77]

Though ITASS emphasizes new technologies, it is hard to make a case for trends in weapons as the defining feature of doctrinal change in the U.S. Army with respect to AirLand Battle. A close examination of the timelines reveals that Starry initiated his battle calculus studies before the ITASS idea circulated through the Department of Defense. Furthermore, the Assault Breaker experiment occurred the same year the Army published the AirLand Battle doctrine, indicating at best parallel development.

AirLand Battle

The AirLand Battle doctrine emerged over the course of 1981 and 1982 as an operational concept integrating Starry's earlier battle calculus studies and the work of the extended battlefield network. In a January 29, 1981, cable from Starry to all TRADOC subordinates titled "The AirLand Battle," Starry instructed officers to use a new term consistently across the Army that embodied these visions of war:

> Now that the integrated battlefield and extended battlefield concepts are being assimilated by the TRADOC community, a need exists to tie these concepts into one overarching descriptive term.... [T]he term "AirLand battle" best describes and ties these two concepts, and all others, together. Henceforth, when we talk about the total battlefield the term "Airland Battle" will be used.[78]

March 25, 1981, marked the formal publication of the AirLand Battle concept. An outline of the new corps structure required to support the doctrine accompanied the document.[79] The document laid out how the U.S. Army would deploy to meet its most pressing challenge, large-scale mechanized conflict in Central Europe, the Middle East, or Korea.[80] To continue functioning as a credible deterrent once limited combat operations started, Army units would assume an aggressive posture, striking deep into the enemy's rear to disrupt their mass and momentum.

To educate Army officers on the nature of the new concept, over the remainder of 1981 and into 1982 individuals connected to the program published a series of articles. Starry penned two pieces that defined Extended Battlefield and demonstrated its application on the modern battlefield.[81] Richardson and his subordinates authored visions of how the new operational concept enabled the Army to fight and win despite the culture of pessimism surrounding the defense of Central Europe.[82] To support these publications, TRADOC affiliates wrote specific articles about how the new way of war affected each battlefield function, from the Infantry to Air Defense Artillery.[83] This approach contrasted with the close-hold, centralized style General DePuy had used to develop Active Defense.

In conjunction with publication of the operational concept and its advocacy campaign, since early 1980 Richardson, TRADOC deputy commander, had led a team of writers consisting of Colonel Clyde J. Tate, Lieutenant Colonel Huba Wass de Czege, Lieutenant Colonel L. D. Holder, and Lieutenant Colonel Richmond B. Henriques in the Department of Tactics at the Command General Staff College in drafting the new edition of *Field Manual 100-5: Operations*.[84] Their job was to translate the new theory of victory into formal doctrine. The writing process was iterative, with each draft chapter submitted directly to Richardson and Starry for review. From 1980 to 1981, they refined aspects of the emerging doctrine, such as defining initiative, addressing the levels of war, and outlining precise applications of offensive and defensive combat on the extended battlefield. For example, with respect to deep attack, the writing team drew a distinction between fires aimed at disrupting and delaying the second echelon and actions that would hit the rear areas to neutralize critical capabilities such as nuclear-capable weapons systems.[85] The team brought the AirLand Battle concept to life as doctrine, taking underlying assumptions and framing them as axioms governing the conduct of war.

Institutionally, TRADOC elements also requested that the Air Force refine the emerging doctrine. Since 1973, TRADOC officers had been working closely with their counterparts in the Air Force Tactical Air Command.[86] In writing AirLand Battle, the Army was preparing to employ operational concepts beyond its current weapons systems. The deep attack called for a corps commander to influence the battlefield up to 150 kilometers forward of his own front line, thus necessitating offensive air support. An agreement on battlefield air interdiction that achieved this goal had been reached in NATO in 1979 as part of their effort to implement Rogers's vision of follow-on forces attack. In September 1980, Air Force Tactical Air Command and TRADOC commanders wrote a memorandum covering offensive air-support coordination outside NATO, making the Army corps commander the primary authority in prioritizing targets for battlefield air interdiction. By 1981, the Air Force had "declared that the agreement was authoritative Air Force doctrine and would be incorporated into relevant Air Force doctrinal manuals."[87] Service coordination, as opposed to rivalry, generated new doctrinal possibilities.

Before publication of *Field Manual 100-5: Operations*, TRADOC leaders also organized a sustained intraservice and defense-community-wide series of briefings to educate principals on the new doctrine. Throughout 1981, the Combined Arms Center sent briefers to field units and across the Beltway. These included presentations to the Republican Congressional Reform Caucus, key appointees within the Department of Defense, the Joint Chiefs of Staff, and Vice President George Bush.[88] By advocating their doctrinal initiatives to policy networks, the Army was seeking to shape opinion in the broader defense establishment.

In August 1982, TRADOC released the new edition of *Field Manual 100-5: Operations*. The document, the residue of three years of dialogue and conceptual experimentation, represented a new vision of warfare against a much broader array of adversaries. The fundamental mission of the U.S. Army remained to "deter war," but the scope of potential battlefields now included an emphasis on the integrated battlefield and contingency operations.[89] In a section titled "Identifying the Challengers" the manual states,

> The U.S. Army must meet a variety of situations and challenges. In the 1980s it can expect to be committed in either of two environments.... It must be ready to fight light, well-equipped forces such as Soviet supported insurgents or sophisticated terrorist groups. It must be prepared to fight highly mechanized forces typical of Warsaw Pact or Soviet surrogates in southwest or northeast Asia. In the areas of greatest strategic concern, it must expect battles of greater scope and intensity than ever fought before. It must anticipate battles fought with nuclear and chemical weapons.[90]

The doctrine thus opens with an explicit statement on the balance of power uncertainty captivating the imaginations of Army planners. To meet these challenges, AirLand Battle outlines its broader intellectual framework in a chapter titled "Combat Fundamentals." The chapter begins with a definition of operational concepts:

> An Army's operational concept is the core of its doctrine. It is the way the Army fights its battles and campaigns, including tactics, procedures, organizations, support, equipment and training. The concept must be broad enough to describe operations in all anticipated circumstances. Yet it must allow sufficient freedom for tactical variations in any situation. It must also be uniformly known and understood.[91]

Indicating a major change in the new theory of victory, the manual formally introduced the idea of an operational level of war. Previously the Army had stressed the strategic and tactical levels of war without outlining how leaders should organize campaigns or corps-level operations. AirLand Battle, in line with the Central Battle concept, focused on the operational level and, in this, the requirement of corps commanders to apply core concepts animating the doctrine on the modern battlefield. Military professionals not only changed critical tasks, such as evaluating the importance of deep strike, but also altered how they defined war itself, integrating the Soviet idea of an operational level.

Four basic tenets defined the idea of AirLand Battle. The first, *initiative*, reflected the "offensive spirit" of all operations.[92] In each encounter, soldiers should seek out opportunities to "seize and retain independence of action" sufficient to keep the enemy disoriented and off balance.[93] This offensive spirit had to exist at each level of command sufficiently for subordinates to "act independently within the context of an overall plan."[94]

Complementing this emphasis on initiative was *depth*, the second tenet, expressed as the "time, distance, and resources" factors that defined momentum and mass on the modern battlefield.[95] Commanders were directed to use the "the entire depth of the battlefield to strike the enemy and to prevent him from concentrating his firepower or maneuvering his forces to a point of his choice."[96] These tenets formed the conceptual blueprint of how military officers should design campaigns at the new operational level of war.

In conjunction with initiative, one sees the rendering of the Extended Battlefield concept, the emphasis on seizing the opportunity to disrupt and delay the second echelon to compensate for fighting outnumbered. V Corps studies drove TRADOC to examine how the United States would deploy to confront other contingencies. When fighting outnumbered in distant lands, the key to success was seizing the initiative and striking deep to disrupt the adversary.

The third and fourth tenets of AirLand Battle related to speed, surprise, and coordination of combat power. The authors stress *agility*, the ability to "act faster than the enemy."[97] Leaders would now need to "know of critical events as they occur and act to avoid enemy strengths and attack enemy vulnerabilities."[98] Organizational flexibility enabled leaders to get in front of enemy planning cycles, thus rendering superior forces unable to coordinate their troops and take advantage of force-ratio imbalances. Agile units would also be able to achieve *synchronization*, the "maximum [concentration] of combat power" before enemy forces could mass.[99] By bringing such power to bear at the right time and place in the defense, commanders enabled operations that achieved "local surprise and shock effect" sufficient to retake the initiative.[100] These ideas were a departure from Active Defense and its emphasis on shoot to move, move to concentrate as a means of facilitating a more deliberate local defense.

The manual also includes a special section of the deep strike. In a section titled "Battle Planning and Coordination," the authors translate the Extended Battlefield concept into military doctrine. A commander's scheme of maneuver would need to focus on "disrupting enemy forces in depth. In either attack or defense, timely and well-executed deep actions against enemy forces not yet in contact are necessary for effective operations."[101] In line with area of interest and area of influence, each level of command from the battalion planned for striking targets in the extended battlefield, but the "corps [was] the focal point for intelligence collection and distribution in the deep battle."[102] Actions in the enemy's rear areas were necessary to "open opportunities for decisive action by reducing the enemy's closure rate and creating periods of friendly superiority in order to gain or to retain the initiative."[103]

In subsequent chapters, these concepts are applied to a wide array of offensive and defensive operations. The manual stresses the need for "speed, surprise, maneuver, and decision action" in the offense to win battles.[104] Commanders were told that the offense was "the decisive form of war, the only means of attaining a positive goal or of completely destroying an enemy force."[105] To illustrate the enduring logic of AirLand Battle's underlying tenets in the offensive, the manual injects a historical anecdote, reconstructing Ulysses S. Grant's siege of Vicksburg as an ideal of the importance of initiative, depth, agility, and synchronization. From this vantage point, the manual details how commanders should conduct offensive operations in a variety of theaters employing the core concepts. Though only six years separated the publication of Active Defense and AirLand Battle, the manuals call for fundamentally different approaches to countering large, mechanized formations.

The same structural logic defines the chapter on defensive operations. Here an effort was made to blur the distinction between offensive and defensive operations in a manner that emphasized the importance of initiative and deep attack in contemporary warfare. Like in the section on offensive operations, the authors construct a historical ideal, this time using the 1914 Battle of Tannenberg, in which heavily outnumbered German forces routed two Russian armies. The ideal defense was a Clausewitzean "shield of blows," offensive action that disrupted the attacking enemy.[106] Once these underlying principles of warfare are demonstrated to have a deep historical resonance, the chapter reviews their usage in contemporary forms of defensive operations. Unlike Active Defense, which stressed blocking forces and localized counterattacks designed to canalize enemy forces, AirLand Battle stretched the battlefield to emphasize fighting the defense in the enemy's rear as opposed to its own front lines.

Furthermore, AirLand Battle placed a new emphasis on contingency operations not seen in the 1976 edition field manual. The chapter on combined operations focuses on not just Europe but the Pacific and the range of contingencies that might require U.S. forces. Meyer's vision of three days of war entered official doctrine, and with it the Army started to emphasize unconventional warfare, including psychological, civil-military, and special operations.[107] The doctrine captured, even if satisficing, interests at senior levels in the profession to prepare for smaller-scale contingencies.

The Concept-Based Revolution

To articulate his vision of Central Battle as a doctrinal statement, Starry engineered a unique institutional array of actors and supporting bureaucratic processes. In October 1979, he established the Office of the Deputy Chief of Staff for Doctrine. Headed initially by Colonel Edwin G. Scribner and later by Brigadier General Donald R. Morelli, the organization had responsibility for operational concepts and doctrinal development.[108] Whereas under DePuy TRADOC had focused on the near-term conventional fight in Europe in terms of weapons systems, tactics, and capabilities, Starry pushed his staff to conceptualize warfare in terms of operational concepts and descriptions "of military combat, combat support, and combat service support systems, organizations, and tactical and training systems necessary to achieve a desired goal."[109] Concepts thus could be differentiated from doctrine, which Starry defined as "what is written, approved, by an appropriate authority and published concerning the conduct of military affairs."[110] Furthermore, according to Starry,

> in its broadest sense a concept describes what is to be done; in its more specific sense it can be used to describe what is done. The Soviet notion that numbers win is an example of the former; the implementing notions of mass, momentum, and continuous land combat are examples of the latter. . . . In the sense that the term is used here, concepts are military in nature, relating to ideas, thoughts, general notions about the conduct of military affairs. . . . [They are] a description of military combat, combat support and combat service support systems, organizations, tactical and training systems necessary to achieve desired a goal.[111]

Thus, concepts were prior to doctrine and reflected multiple dimensions of conflict. They embodied both requirements of a different battlefield as well as the likely tactical considerations that arise from new equipment. They were descriptions of particular visions of warfare that could be tested to forge doctrine. Doctrine was thus a refined series of concepts. This characterization is not at odds with DePuy's methods. For example, through his analysis of the Arab-Israeli War, DePuy pushed his staff to articulate how increased lethality redefined the modern battlefield. As DePuy and his planners worked through this analytical problem, they developed the concept of shoot to move and move to concentrate that was to define Active Defense.

A stark and interesting difference between DePuy and Starry is that Starry emphasized the operational as opposed to the tactical level of war. As seen in his rendering of the Central Battle, his principal concern emerged from target servicing and force generation associated with the corps-level fight, or how to disrupt the second echelon of a Soviet advance. Whereas DePuy had to fashion an entire bureaucratic structure to support his vision of warfare, Starry needed only to reorient TRADOC. Thus, whereas DePuy pushed TRADOC to create a series of publications in support of tactical concepts titled "How to Fight," Starry had his staff produce operational concepts, publishing twenty-one as white papers between June 1980 and December 1982.[112] Starry sought to redefine critical tasks to address a new theory of victory, here an entirely new way of looking at how to array forces on the battlefield given an operational level of war.

On assuming command of TRADOC, Starry outlined his long-term objective for the organization as analytically describing the Central Battle, "the place where all combat systems and combat support systems interact on the battlefield."[113] In August 1977, he tasked Colonel Anthony G. Pokorny, chief of the Combat Development's Analysis Directorate to translate this battle calculus into a major institutional change program that looked eight years out.[114] The "Battlefield Development Plan" used his corps frame of reference to develop a conceptual framework for initiating and managing combat development and force design issues.[115] Starry's team saw the plan as a means of establishing Army-wide priorities for planning, programming, and budgeting.[116] They saw concepts as the foundation of doctrine and doctrine as the intellectual foundation of the profession of arms.

Time and expected technology were key factors in earlier planning frameworks. Under DePuy, TRADOC focused on the near-term fight. Before the Continental Army Command (CONARC) reorganization, the U.S. Army had a twenty-five-year planning horizon. Starry's move can be read as striving for a midpoint between the two. By advocating an eight-year time horizon in the "Battlefield Development Plan," he gave the planners sufficient space to factor in key modernization programs scheduled to become operational in the mid-1980s. Starry sought to reconcile technological push, the rapid development of new systems in the civilian sector, with concept development by military professionals engaged in a problem-driven search.

In this respect, the "Battlefield Development Plan" was essentially a net assessment of relative U.S. and Soviet military capabilities in hypothetical engagements in Europe read in terms of the Central Battle.[117] The document was a scenario-based portrait of future war that could be used to distill planning and programming data. In terms of the underlying scenario, the plan assumed an attack by the Soviets on the basis of a series of meeting engagements followed by rapid exploitation either against rear areas or by second-echelon forces exploiting these initial encounters.[118] From this worst-case scenario, the plan outlined deficiencies that would stop the Army from completing its mission. In November 1978, TRADOC published a first edition containing four chapters: a description of the impact of technological advance on the Army, a net assessment comparing the Army's program to achieve near-term readiness and mid-term modernization with Soviet force capabilities, an analysis of the ability of development programs to meet battlefield demands in the 1980s, and a set of conclusions and recommendations.

Alongside AirLand Battle force design studies and doctrinal development, in the late 1970s TRADOC ran a program headed by Colonel Frederick Franks Jr. and with the help of the Federal Republic of Germany Army staff to study the future of armored forces in the 1990s.[119] Starry pushed Franks to expand the armored concepts and think in terms of an "overarching concept" that would anticipate technological developments over the next decade to arrive at a "concept based material acquisitions strategy."[120] The marriage of concepts and acquisitions was then cemented at the September 1980 TRADOC Commanders Conference. In the words of Major General Donald R. Morelli, the intent was to construct an operational concept that would "drive the labs" and get a handle on material developments by "getting ahead of technology."[121]

In early 1981, the project was renamed AirLand Battle 2000. The institutional mechanism was given further scope by renaming it Concept-Based Requirements System in February 1981, suggesting that not just material acquisitions but doctrine, training, and organization were to emerge from these broader, futuristic narratives of land warfare.[122] In a January 5, 1981, unclassified cable to all major TRADOC subordinate commanders titled "Concept Based Requirement Strategy," Starry stated that under this system AirLand

Battle would be the operational concept that "describes all mission areas." In the same message, Starry outlined the process:

> What we have done is to move from the Battlefield Functional Concepts used in [Battlefield Development Plan] I and II . . . to the emerging mission area breakdown that is more closely aligned to the [Office of the Secretary of Defense] and [Department of the Army] mission areas yet still retain all the critical battlefield tasks that were described by the old [Battlefield Development Plan] functions. What we have then are eight functional mission areas: close combat, fire support, air defense, communications, command and control, intelligence and [electronic warfare], combat service support and combat support, engineer and mine warfare. Aviation and NBC [nuclear, chemical, and biological] are inherent across most all these functional areas and will be integrated as appropriate into the eight concepts.[123]

The Concept-Based Requirements System used operational concepts as responses to threat scenarios to establish the requirements for evaluating doctrine, training, force structure, and procurement. After TRADOC developed concepts in consultation with its subordinate schoolhouses and the Combined Arms Center, they would be subject to analysis and testing by both TRADOC personnel and representatives of key Army constituencies before being submitted to senior leaders for approval. In other words, concepts formed the basis of innovation. To institutionally support this, the Concept Development Directorate was established as part of the Combined Arms Center. Initial concepts were developed as short papers or briefings. The Concept Development Directorate expanded the idea using a wider array of input factors ranging from national threat forecasts to Defense Science Board estimates of future capabilities. These statements were then vetted by analysts in the TRADOC Analysis Center and subject to two additional layers of review: combat performance through war games, assessments by field commanders, and simulations and a general-officer panel review of the concept. How these war fighting concepts, as narratives, were rendered drove doctrinal, training, organizational, and equipment recommendations.

In terms of its vision of future battlefields, the AirLand Battle 2000 umbrella concept altered several underlying concepts of the 1982 doctrine on the basis of assessments of the proliferation of information technology and its effect on war fighting. Given trends in lethality and the prospect of an integrated battlefield, units would need to be self-sufficient and dispersed. War would move from a decisive engagement to a series of small, nonlinear battles, or "islands of conflict," that would seek to destabilize an adversary as opposed to hold terrain.[124]

This vision was further defined by the insertion of the "scan, swarm, strike, scatter" battle sequence in a redrafting of the concept.[125] In this system, commanders would scan the battlefield using all collection assets, including other service components and national platforms, and integrate them into a common operating picture using new computer-based processing applications. With this information dominance, planners would be able to determine the best targets to engage, drawing forces from their dispersed disposition into a concentrated swarm that would then strike key enemy systems and then scatter.[126] Starry attempted to institutionalize problem-driven search by the Army to push constant analysis of change dynamics.

From 1982 to 1986 AirLand Battle 2000 was redrafted and evolved into Army 21.[127] Analysis of future war drove the search for an operational concept that would define long-range combat development. Inside the Army an intense debate emerged among senior officers including the supreme Allied commander in Europe and the chief of staff of the Army regarding the applicability of the concept to all theaters and whether the operational concept was precise enough to develop doctrine.[128]

Concepts also served as a bridge for interservice cooperation. In September 1982, planners from the Army and Air Force integrated AirLand Battle 2000 with Air Force 2000 and called it Focus 21.[129] Concepts were more than marketing mantras designed to increase relative budget allocation. They served as a blueprint for bureaucratic cooperation.

Conclusion

Like Active Defense, the emergence of the AirLand Battle doctrine highlights a special role for problem-driven simulation and experimentation through incubators and the diffusion of ideas through advocacy networks. Starry's initial idea grew out of his central battle experiments while commanding V Corps in Europe. An array of framing studies like the extended battlefield study network and integrated battlefield study further developed the concept. Ideas went through multiple iterations as they passed through a web of incubators before being reintroduced into the bureaucracy by advocacy networks. Starry even went one step further and attempted to institutionalize a process for generating new concepts through the Concept-Based Requirements System and Concept Development Directorate.

Except for the Concept Development Directorate, all incubators were ad hoc groups formed for a specific purpose. Whereas traditional organizational theory recognizes dedicated subunits and new bureaus as sustaining change, the AirLand Battle case illustrates how officers use more temporary bodies to enable organizational change. This contrast presents a paradox. The push to standardize concept generation and place it within the formal bureaucratic hierarchy has the potential to diminish the range of ideas considered. Incubators, by definition, sit outside formal bureaucratic lines. Once formalized, they become subject to pull of procedure and routine. Imagination may not occur according to a schedule.

The emergence of AirLand Battle also illustrates larger defense community studies and experiments on how future technology would enable new operating concepts. Parallel to the emergence of AirLand Battle, DARPA examined how information technology would enable new operating concepts. There appears to have been a concurrent move to develop long-range strike capability between the Army and groups like DARPA in the late 1970s. As Starry recalls the timeline,

> In May 1977 I returned to Israel's battlefields to revisit action at the operational level and then translate that experience to Europe's environment. This led to a concept for extending the battlefield in time (the campaign) and distance (the theater of operations). Most importantly, it resulted in requirements for long-range surveillance and target acquisition systems and long-range weapons systems with which to find and attack Soviet style follow-on echelons.[130]

While complementary theories of victory circulated across multiple agency lines, Starry does not appear to have directly referenced key DARPA studies in developing his vision of the Central Battle.[131] Furthermore, the timeline does not match up. Many of the core underpinnings of AirLand Battle were in place by 1980, but the actual proof-of-concept test for ITASS did not occur until 1982, with the Assault Breaker test at White Sands. This relationship again raises the question of nesting and the extent to which parallel ideas are more resonant.

With respect to advocacy networks the case illustrates a new strategy. Rather than relying disproportionately on positional legitimation and the use of vertical protection rackets, Starry and his team sought broad organizational consensus. They deliberately targeted articles in professional journals to the middle tier of the organization, company and field-grade officers.

The case also highlights how other actors leveraged different types of advocacy networks. The offsetting strategy reflects a form of brokerage by outside-in legitimation. Making it more than just an idea, giving briefings on the concept provided a rationale for new research and development initiatives. The "three days of war" paper, as an Army-wide brief, reflects how senior leaders leveraged their position to legitimate particular views on warfare. It is not enough to be the boss. Senior generals used their position to provide the initial push, socializing their concepts throughout the organization from the top down.

With respect to alternative accounts of change, the AirLand Battle case departs from existing explanations of doctrinal innovation. First, with respect to exogenous shocks and competition, there was no immediate threat to the Army's core mission or autonomy. Budgets were expanding during the time under observation. Furthermore, there was no major military setback sufficient to warrant a fundamental revisiting of the Active Defense doctrine. AirLand Battle appears to be the result of military professionals engaged in problem-driven search. There was no fundamental change in the weapons systems the Army studied for new concepts and doctrine between Active Defense and AirLand Battle at the operational level. At the strategic level the introduction of new nuclear systems altered threat calculations but not in a manner that changed the critical task of providing a credible conventional deterrent.

Furthermore, neither civilian intervention nor strategic culture, in the form of an enduring attritionist way of war, seems to explain the case. In the late 1970s and early 1980s, the Army responded to new estimates of the Soviet threat, which though later proved inaccurate initiated a localized effort to define new operational concepts and doctrine. Civilians do not appear to have initiated these reforms. AirLand Battle is the opposite of an attritionist way of war. It seeks to use deep strike and maneuver to destabilize an adversary as opposed to focusing on firepower and removing units from the battlefield.

4   The New Warrior Class

> As a great democracy we are morally bound to an inherently defensive posture, but as the world's sole superpower in every meaning of the term, we have global interests and responsibilities that require a military force second to none. I have joked occasionally that no, we are not the policeman of the world and we should not claim to be the policeman of the world, but every time somebody gets into trouble, guess who they call to be the cop on the beat—the United States. We have worldwide interests.
> —General Colin L. Powell, Chairman Joint Chiefs of Staff, testimony before the Senate Subcommittee on Appropriations, 102nd Cong. (1991)

THE END OF THE COLD WAR CONFRONTED MILITARY PLANNERS with new threat and budgetary horizons. By 1994, scenarios describing Soviet hordes pouring through the Fulda Gap were a distant, if not cherished, memory to the officer corps. In their place, images of regional strongmen and what TRADOC planners referred to as the new warrior class, bands of nonstate actors challenging the new world order from below, preoccupied Army leadership. A more ambiguous and uncertain security landscape was rewriting the logic of AirLand Battle.

In this new environment, the possibility of defending U.S. interests anywhere meant preparing for war everywhere. As seen in the 1992 and 1995 versions of "National Military Strategy of the United States," the logic of hegemony transcended party lines and two presidential administrations.[1] The U.S. military would meet these challenges by preparing to fight two major wars simultaneously. In the space of five years, the intellectual framework situating land warfare as the basis of exercises and operational planning shifted from AirLand Battle and a forward defense to Full-Dimensional Operations, a power-projection doctrine for enforcing regional security frameworks and guaranteeing primacy.

Furthermore, the new strategy emerged amid declining resources and fundamental questions about the future of warfare. The drawdown from a Cold War footing left military leaders searching for a means of doing more with less. In the constrained budgetary environment of the early 1990s, soldiers relied increasingly on new technology. TRADOC analysts in the Future Battles Directorate and Office of the Chief of Staff of the Army rendered concepts that proposed a shift from mass to information as the organizing principle in which next-generation weapons on a digitized battlefield enabled soldiers to fight outnumbered and win across theaters ranging from city streets to distant jungles. The sword forged was one of integrated circuits and digital command nets that produced a disruptive, leap-ahead capacity. The fog of war, ambiguity about adversary actions and intentions, dissolved into transparent targeting exercises as real-time intelligence allowed engaging the enemy across the entire depth of the battlefield at once. War was no longer a test of wills but a question of the optimal mix of hardware and software.

These two paths, the embrace of technology as a way of waging war and creation of the capacity to fight multiple contingencies, shaped the first post–Cold War doctrine: Full-Dimensional Operations. Officially published in 1993, Army officers refined the underlying operational concept through the remainder of the decade under the Force XXI program. As an episode of doctrinal innovation, the case calls for a more careful approximation of the causal circumstances of organizational change.

The operative strategic paradigm shifted from balancing the Cold War rivalry to maintaining primacy. There was no peace dividend in the mind of military planners who saw the collapse of the stability of the Soviet threat as ushering in an uncertainty. Senior leaders in the Office of the Chief of Staff of the Army and TRADOC scripted concepts that reflected the shift from calculations of conventional threats in Europe to the possibility of fighting outnumbered around the world. In this, declining defense budgets proved a more significant intervening variable than in previous cases as services dealt with the Cold War drawdown. Increased threat scenarios would have to be met with limited resources. The constraints of scarcity led military elite to alter their understanding of technology. Whereas in the previous two episodes new weapons systems increased engagement ranges and destructive power, digitization, as the near-real-time integration of command and control and targeting systems, altered the way officers envisioned operating.

This chapter establishes how senior military officers in TRADOC and the Department of the Army articulated threats following the Cold War. A close reading of actual statements and texts reveals how individuals within the institution perceived shifts in the balance of power, as opposed to an objective historical reconstruction. Against this background, the case examines TRADOC initiatives linked to establishing a new war fighting paradigm that crystallized in the June 1993 publication of *Field Manual 100-5: Operations* and the follow-on 1994 TRADOC Pamphlet 525-5, *Force XXI Operations*.[2] The new *Field Manual 100-5* embodied the broader realignment to a contingency-based force after the end of the Cold War. Force XXI linked this vision of threat everywhere with new concepts governing the optimal mix of information technology.

The chapter seeks to highlight how incubators and advocacy networks helped officers develop and diffuse new ideas about how to array forces at the operational level. The concepts that emerged from incubators evolved into two separate visions of modern warfare: operating across the full spectrum of operations, including military operations other than war (MOOTW), and fielding and fighting a digital force. Similar to the previous chapters, the empirical analysis focuses on primary-source material that enables reconstruction of how the Army internally thought about war and presented the derived concepts to the broader national security community.

The New World Order

Between 1989 and 1991, the Army responded to the collapse of communism and ensuing seismic shift in the international security environment. The end of the Cold War altered the threat and budgetary environment. According to the fiscal year 1992 posture statement,

> In 1990 many aspects of the evolving international environment were hopeful, particularly the rapid unification of Germany, the accelerating relinquishment of Soviet control over the Warsaw Pact, and the less threatening tone of Soviet foreign policy. Mindful of the pressing need to reduce the burgeoning federal deficit, the United States focused more on the opportunities presented by reduced superpower confrontation than on the challenges and risks inherent in the evolving international environment.[3]

By 1994, U.S. ground forces were the smallest they had been since 1939. Between 1989 and 1992, the Army lost two hundred thousand soldiers, equivalent to four corps, fourteen active divisions, and eight National Guard divisions, making it *one corps and six divisions smaller* than the Cold War force.[4] By 1995 total cuts translated into a loss of over four hundred thousand active, reserve component, and civilian personnel, a 20 percent decline.[5] Overall, between 1990 and 1994 the Army budget declined from $92.5 billion to $63 billion, staying at a constant 25–30 percent share of the defense budget.[6] Thus, the reforms of the early 1990s took place in a hostile budget environment that found each service forced to justify its size and expenditures.

Yet while the military was shrinking, perception grew that the future would hold more uncertainty than the Cold War. Already in 1991, senior leaders viewed the threats likely to confront the United States in terms of a wider, diffuse array of challenges that ranged from regional conflicts that threatened economic interests, like the Iraq invasion of Kuwait, to "international drug trafficking, state-sponsored terrorism, insurgency, and subversion of legitimate regimes."[7] Challenges to U.S. interests emerged from "non-state armies and asymmetric threats."[8] A new operational problem emerged, reflecting a line of thinking evolving from General Meyer's three days' war concept.

According to Army planners in the 1992 force posture statement, "the post-Cold War era clearly [had] begun, but with the volatility and unpredictability so characteristic of major transitional periods."[9] In 1992, military planners characterized the growing gap between rich and poor in the global south, the proliferation of weapons of mass destruction, nationalism, corruption, and economic competition as trends likely to increase instability in the international system.[10] This perspective continued in 1993, as Army leaders argued that "international security issues [had] become more complex, with greater political instability caused by the surfacing of traditional sources of friction and discontent and fueled by weapons proliferation."[11] The emerging operational problem indicated trends that could turn otherwise small contingencies on the periphery into significant strategic challenges.

If ideological blocs characterized the Cold War, the new world order was a system of regional balances key to U.S. interests. According to *Fiscal Year 1992 Army Posture Statement*, presented by the chief of staff of the Army to congressional leaders as an indication of Army-wide consensus, the Iraq invasion of Kuwait in 1990 demonstrated "the rapidity with which a regional conflict impacted worldwide military and economic power."[12] Similarly, according to the document, beyond the Middle East were hosts of latent conflicts with the potential to entangle the United States. In Europe, the prospect of "traditional rivalries" demanded the need for a forward-deployed contingency force. The posture statement listed other potential flashpoints, including Yugoslavia, Hungary, Romania, Turkey, and Bulgaria.[13] In Asia, the focal point remained North Korea and the massive arsenal it maintained postured south. In Africa and Latin America, the official Army institutional position was that

> instability in other parts of the world has the potential to nurture threats to U.S. interests. Particularly in developing countries, advances toward democracy and economic prosperity are generally tentative and often not widely distributed. The challenges for these developing countries also are increasingly complex. Radical nationalism and religious and ethnic chauvinism continuously generate friction. Economic and political systems are often unable to meet popular demands for improved standards of living and basic political rights. Adverse climate conditions, population growth, unstable commodity prices, and disease further damage the economic prospects of many developing nations. The situation often leads to the erosion of national unity, political unrest, and violence.[14]

In this reading, two trends further compounded the U.S. concerns about additional destabilization in the developing world. First, the Cold War caused a massive, sustained proliferation of weapons systems. According to Army estimates at the time, "more than a dozen nations [had] 1,000 or more main battle tanks" and several countries persisted in an effort "to acquire chemical, biological, and nuclear warfare capabilities."[15] Second, nonstate actors tied to terrorism and drug trafficking were seen as "major threats" to interests worldwide.[16] In terms of terror networks, the Army closely followed the increase in attacks on U.S. and allied interests following the beginning of Desert Shield, citing a State Department report that seventy incidents were linked to ongoing contingency operations in the Gulf. There was a growing perception among thinkers close to both the chief of staff of the Army and the commanding general of TRADOC that the twenty-first century would be a world defined by a spectrum of war ranging from high-intensity conflict against regional strongmen to nonstate challengers.[17] The emerging operational problem reflected a spectrum of challenges.

Secretary of the Army Michael P. W. Stone echoed this sentiment in March 6, 1991, testimony before the House Committee on Appropriations, stating that the war in the Middle East clearly emphasizes the fact that significant threats remain in many regions of the world where the United States has interests. Regional instability in areas such as Latin America, the proliferation of nuclear, chemical, and missile technology to developing nations, and aggressive, well-armed regional powers such as Iraq pose multiple challenges to United States' interests.[18]

Along the same lines, General Carl Vuono, chief of staff of the Army from 1987 to 1991, briefed senators on the Committee on Appropriations that threats to the United States requiring military power emerged from regional instability brought on by local strongmen and the proliferation of conventional weapons technology. Furthermore, he held that deteriorating economic situations in the developing world fostered narcotrafficking, terrorism, and state failure, each of which would require a military response. General Vuono held out the possibility of a Soviet retrenchment in the future that would necessitate forward-deployed and sustained modernization.[19] While read through a bureaucratic lens these statements could reflect attempts to capture budgets by showing relevance, there appears to have been a significant shift in how senior leaders discussed war in the early 1990s.

According to Vuono, these emergent threats placed "a greater premium on the capability to project power rapidly."[20] In separate testimony before the Senate Committee on Appropriations, Vuono echoed this call for a versatile, rapid deployment, stating that the "United States also will have to maintain the ability to conduct an opposed entry into combat in defense of vital U.S. interests anywhere."[21] The Cold War defensive logic of containment gave way to a framework for U.S. offensive dominance of the international system.

The shift in posture emerged from multiple locations in the Defense Department between 1987 and 1989. The emergence of a new strategic planning paradigm focused on regional, as opposed to global, scenarios coincided with a debate about whether the United States should adjust strategic priorities to the prospect of Soviet decline. On the Joint Staff, the emphasis on regional planning began to emerge in key planning documents like the "Joint Strategic Capabilities Plan" (JSCP) for fiscal year 1988–1990 and later the "National Military Strategy" for fiscal year 1990–1994.[22] Written in 1988, the JSCP for fiscal year 1988–1990 differentiates between the most dangerous threat, a U.S.-Soviet confrontation beginning in Europe, and the most likely, regional conventional conflicts unlikely to involve Soviet forces. This insight was reinforced by work done in response to the March 1989 "National Security Review 12" and analysis by the Joint Staff supporting the "National Military Strategy" for fiscal year 1992–1997, with the latter focusing on both regional scenarios and the prospect of declining budgets to recommend a new concept of forward presence.[23] Furthermore, building on the emergence of integrated planning scenarios used in the late 1970s to examine force sizing and possible non-NATO contingency deployments, the Defense Planning and Resources Board tasked the Joint Staff to develop a new set of regional scenarios likely to drive future threats. The resulting scenarios developed by the Strategic Plans and Policy (J5) directorate strengthened the emerging strategic emphasis on using regional planning to develop force structure.[24]

Starting in 1988, these regional planning scenarios began to address defense commitments given declining budgets. The March 1989 "National Security Review 12" tasked senior officials to "assess how, with limited resources, we can best maintain our strength, preserve our Alliances, and meet our commitments in this changing but still dangerous world."[25] The Program and Budget Analysis Division of the Force Structure, Resources, and Assessment (J8) directorate began to evaluate the potential impact of future cuts to the defense budget on force structure. In the "Quiet Study," members of the J8 analyzed force reduction options with congressional staff members and the Office of Management and Budget.[26]

Analysis of future force-reduction options continued in the October 1989 "Quiet Study II." This study continued the emerging distinction between forward presence and forward defense. According to the 1990 Joint Military Net Assessment the concept of forward presence sought to maintain a conventional deterrent through using fewer permanently forward-based forces but increased periodic deployments alongside increased demands that allies accept greater responsibility for the initial defense.[27]

On being appointed chairman of the Joint Chiefs of Staff, General Colin Powell tasked the J8 and J5 to work together to integrate the Quiet Studies and work on regional defense planning. Powell came to the job with an interest in exploring how changes in the security environment necessitated new strategic thinking and force structure packages. Before being appointed chairman, Powell had discussed the need for deep changes to existing force structure and employment concepts in a May 1989 speech to a symposium of the Association of the United States Army and during his confirmation hearing in September 1989.[28]

In October 1989, Powell tasked a new working group of J5 and J8 members to prepare a brief for the secretary of defense. The team's mission was to help the chairman articulate his vision of the future security environment in 1994 and analyze how it affected force structure decisions. The group met over the course of the month and presented the chairman on November 13 with the finished brief, "View of the 1990s." According to one historical account,

> The "View of the 1990s" study was the important item, since it became the "living" briefing that Powell used repeatedly to convey his strategic vision—first to his staff, then to Secretary Cheney, the Service Chiefs, the CINCs [commanders in chief], and senior officials in [the Office of the Secretary of Defense], then to the President, and, after the budget negotiations of 1990, to the Congress. By March 1990 it had become his text for repeated public statements, both in official testimony and in public fora, stateside and overseas.[29]

The brief called for a shift to regional deterrence through overseas presence as opposed to permanently stationing forces overseas and relying on U.S.-based forces to respond to contingencies. While the shifting strategic rationale called for a smaller force, it also called for one that was lighter, more deployable, and flexible. Powell called the concept Base Force as a means of emphasizing the minimal force needed to maintain U.S. defense commitments. To capture the new regional defense-planning paradigm, Base Force defined conceptual packages that Powell had previously conceived of while at Forces Command.[30] Through a series of special studies diffused through the defense community, a new theory of victory started to emerge around the optimal mix of forces required to meet a range of contingencies. It was less innovative in terms of being a radical break and more adaptive to declining budgets.

In his 1992 State of the Union address, President George H. W. Bush announced that Powell had created a plan to reduce the size of the U.S. military. This included cutting the Army from sixteen Cold War divisions, many of which were forward deployed, to twelve divisions stationed mostly in the United States.[31] More than a reduction strategy, the Base Force model divided military assets into four packages (Strategic, Atlantic, Pacific, and Contingency) designed to ensure deterrence, forward presence, crisis response, and force reconstitution.[32] Powell described it as a series of "conceptual baskets" and "supporting capabilities" that helped planners determine the right mix of units needed for specific situations.[33]

Forces supported "a triad of nuclear forces," a deterrent built around ground-based intercontinental missile systems, submarine-based systems, and the strategic bomber fleet.[34] Atlantic and Pacific forces were linked to regional security frameworks and forward presence required to deter aggression and secure U.S. interests.[35] Contingency forces represented the systemic uncertainty leaders believed embodied the core issues of the security landscape. In testimony before the U.S. Senate, Powell described the different force packages as planning tools for "the next enduring reality—that of the unknown, the uncertainty, the crisis nobody expects, the phone call that comes at 2 in the morning."[36]

The need to shape international events in all regions also gave rise to the war strategy of two major theaters outlined in the classified *1992 Defense Planning Guidance* leaked in a March 8, 1992, *New York Times* article by Patrick Tyler titled "U.S. Strategy Plans for Insuring No Rivals Develop." As described years later by Secretary of Defense Donald Rumsfeld,

> The two MTW [major theater war] approach was an innovation at the end of the Cold War. It was based on the proposition that the U.S. should prepare for the possibility that two regional conflicts could arise at the same time. If the U.S. were engaged in a conflict in one theater, an adversary in a second theater might try to gain his objectives before the U.S. could react. Prudence dictated that the U.S. take this possibility into account. . . . The two MTW approach identified both Southwest Asia and Northeast Asia as areas of high national interest to the U.S. In both regions, regimes hostile to the U.S. and its allies and friends possessed the capability and had exhibited the intent to gain their objectives by the threat or use of force. The approach identified the "force packages" that would be needed for the U.S. to achieve its wartime objectives should two, nearly simultaneous conflicts erupt. These force packages were based on an assessment of the combat capabilities and likely operations of an adversary, on the one hand, and the capabilities and doctrine of U.S. forces—so recently displayed in [Operation] Desert Storm—on the other.[37]

Many aspects of the Base Force concept and emerging regional security paradigm had service-level predecessors. Individual services, sensing a change, had studied how to adapt their forces to a rapidly changing security environment. Predating the Base Force model, the Army began work in November 1988 on adapting current doctrine and force structure to anticipated declines in the Soviet threat and, by proxy, defense budgets. Starting in

1987 Army leaders, especially after the Goldwater-Nichols Act and the removal of many planning authorities, were concerned that the force requirements mandated by the Defense Department were not considering how the future threat environment was likely to evolve or a likely large-scale decline in defense budgets.[38]

Army leaders needed a concept clarifying how requirements for land forces were evolving that they could use in negotiations with the Defense Department and commanders in chief.[39] In 1988, the deputy chief of staff of the Army for Operations and Plans, Lieutenant General John W. Foss, tasked sixteen colonels and representatives from the RAND Corporation to study options for future Army force postures. The study built on earlier conceptual work done at TRADOC for "AirLand Battle Future," a September 1987 study of emerging defense trends and their implications for U.S. Army doctrine, force structure, and training.[40] The new study, named Antaeus after a famous mythic battle between Hercules and a sea giant, similarly envisioned new force packages centered on a contingency force based in the United States. The study also recommended continuing to explore more flexible, "modular" division designs emphasizing increased deployability and flexibility.[41] Officers in both the Joint community and at the service level grappled with how to change Army operating concepts and force structure for the post–Cold War era.

Thus, while Army officers debated the depth of cuts proposed by Base Force, they did not disagree with the need to modify force structure for a new security environment. The emerging regional security paradigm received further clarification in the 1992 "National Military Strategy."[42] For the Army, Base Force emphasized other wars, placing a premium on strategic deterrence, forward presence, crisis response, and reconstitution.[43] Regional security orders defined the new world order. Writing in a January 1992 *Army Times* article, General Gordon R. Sullivan, Army chief of staff from 1991 to 1995, noted that "the world is making a transition to a condition where multiple centers of military, political, and economic power exist. This multipolarity is likely to be less predictable, less stable, and perhaps a bit uncomfortable while we adjust to new rules in the international arena."[44]

For the Army this broader defense debate coincided with an internal series of studies on power-projection and precision-strike capabilities. The lessons of Operations Desert Shield and Desert Storm, the 1990–1991 Gulf War, and Operation Just Cause, the 1989 invasion of Panama, confirmed the need to constitute rapidly and deploy joint task forces for contingencies, a trend that had been increasing since the mid-1970s and the declaration of the Carter Doctrine. Leaders were in awe of their own capabilities. In a January 9, 1992, speech before the Land Warfare Forum titled "The Army in the Postindustrial World," Sullivan outlined how the precision with which the Army simultaneously attacked twenty-seven targets with a mix of light, armored, and Army Special Forces during the 1989 invasion of Panama foretold a new epoch of warfare.[45]

While the U.S. had a clear technological advantage, once its forces were on the ground there were standing concerns about their ability to deploy sufficient combat power for stopping mechanized units and confronting the logistic problems associated with operating in "immature theaters," or areas lacking the infrastructure required to sustain troop buildups. Furthermore, both conflicts demanded worldwide operations, testing the capacity to rapidly move hundreds of thousands of troops and sustain them over great distances. In fact, senior Army leaders were so concerned about U.S. "worldwide mobility" that they lobbied Congress to support the Air Force C-17 program designed to replace the C-141 airlift fleet despite an extremely tight budgetary environment.[46]

The Army began to take a more holistic view of the types of missions it would be tasked with in the coming decade. In studying Desert Storm and Just Cause, planners began to reconsider the importance of security assistance, institution building, and stability operations following major combat operations. In Panama, the Army found itself fighting a limited ground war that quickly transitioned to a "nation-assistance phase."[47] Official posture statements emphasized the possibilities of using land forces as a vehicle for soft power and leveraging Army assets to provide "health, technical, and management assistance to nations to further their development and promote their stability."[48] Planners developed new security assistance programs designed to "promote stability" while building the necessary defense capabilities to have local allies "cope with threats to mutual security interests."[49] Multiple theories of victory seemed to exist in tandem, reflecting a phased approach to war. The Army was evolving beyond conventional deterrence.

In 1992, posture statements began hypothesizing a "continuum of military operations," an "analytical construct [linking] the strategic environment and threats within a theater to appropriate military actions."[50] The continuum spanned three general states: peacetime engagements, hostilities short of war, and war. Peacetime engagements and hostilities short of war consisted of the use of military units alongside other diplomatic measures to deter conflict and build capacity. The U.S. position within a larger regional security order dictated new economy of force missions and shaping strategies ranging from building clinics in client states to peacekeeping missions and training armed forces in developing nations.

Despite the 1992 change in presidential administrations, national security strategy continued to focus on maintaining primacy through preparing to fight regional wars and conducting small-scale contingencies. In 1993, President Bill Clinton's national security advisor, Anthony Lake, framed the operative strategic posture in terms of "democratic engagement." According to Lake, the United States would transcend the Cold War logic of containment to enlarge "the world's free community of market democracies."[51] In this, regional threats were rogue states and nondemocratic regimes that might further limit democracy.[52] In testimony before the Senate Subcommittee on Defense Appropriations, Secretary of Defense Les Aspin noted that while the Clinton administration's view of national security threats expanded to include dangers to democratization and economic dislocation, "regional dangers are what really drive the size of the defense budget. If we look at those other things—nuclear dangers, dangers to democracy, and economic dangers—those are all important. But that is not where the money is. . . . The United States in a national security context, must have the capability to deal with regional bad guys—Saddam Hussein, Libya, North Korea."[53]

For the Army, the logic of engagement furthered the emphasis on rapid deployment and the continuum of military operations. In the 1994 posture statement, senior leaders portrayed the engagement strategy as a proactive strategy

> to strengthen and expand the community of democracies and market economies. An engagement strategy enables the military component of national power to protect the national interest by addressing a threat in its formative stage, rather than dealing only with a full blown crisis.[54]

The blunt hammer of mechanized units engaged in forward defense of Europe was giving way to a light infantry surgical scalpel used in peace and war for deterring threats to international order. Again, the possibility of fighting anywhere translated into being prepared to fight everywhere across the full continuum of operations. A new theory of victory was emerging in this vision of a wider spectrum of operations.

The Clinton national security team translated the strategic priorities associated with primacy into broader defense concepts and force structure requirements, as had the Base Force construct. In 1993, Aspin initiated a bottom-up review to find the optimal mix of military units in a national security strategy of democratic engagement. Rather than emphasize a win-win strategy whereby the United States would simultaneously win a Gulf War–like contest in the Middle East and repulse a full-scale North Korean attack, Aspin sought to leverage advances in technology apparent in the Desert Storm victory to advocate a win-hold framework in which the military would use long-range precision fires to halt one of the attacks, thus buying time for a diplomatic resolution. The Army was thus reduced to ten divisions under the argument that air power and new technologies that increased overall lethality enabled the nation to maintain smaller, more deployable ground forces.[55] Furthermore, the review was used as a budgeting tool. According to Secretary of Defense William J. Perry, just as the Base Force construct specified the types of "force packages" needed for the emerging regional security strategy, bottom-up review specified force structure requirements in the win-hold framework.[56] The chairman of the Joint Chiefs of Staff, John M. Shalikashvili, proposed that military planners determine the force structure required to implement the win-hold framework by identifying long-term threats to U.S. interests, ranging from democratic rollback and state failure to destabilization by rogue regimes like Iran, Iraq, and North Korea.[57]

Yet beyond their subtle differences, both the Bush and Clinton administration approaches to forging U.S. grand strategy revolved around maintaining U.S. position through the use of military force if necessary. From the new world order to democratic engagement, the Army was both a deterrent to aspiring regional hegemonies and a soft-power instrument of statecraft, conducting security assistance and nation-building activities in favored client states. Containment and balancing gave way to an attempt to sustain the centrality of the United States in a broader security order despite the austere budget environment. The demands of the resulting power-projection force shaped the trajectory and character of doctrinal innovation.

A hint of the specter of worst-case-scenario bias rises from the official policy statements and public reflections by senior officers. At the moment of peak power, military leaders obsessed over two particular facets of modern warfare: digitization and asymmetric threats. While the latter can be seen in statements before Congress and internal planning documents, the former requires a more detailed tracing of the specific reform initiatives ushered in under the framework of postindustrial warfare.

Defense officials from the National Security Council and Joint Staff and service-level planners developed visions of the nature of warfare in the post–Cold War environment. This process used multiple incubators, or special studies outside the traditional range of reports produced as part of the day-to-day activities of the defense bureaucracy. The ideas appeared to converge on a central idea, having to increase deployments to meet a wide array of challenges amid declining budgets. For the Army, this represented the operational problem confronting the military professional.

The Postindustrial Army

While the Gulf War demonstrated the problems with power projection, it also seduced the defense establishment with the prospects of a new mode of warfare. In testimony before Congress, Secretary of Defense Richard B. Cheney highlighted the central role played by technology in enabling victory during the Gulf War.[58] U.S. forces possessed qualitative advantages that let them see and shoot first. Between February 25 and 27, 1991, Major General Barry R. McCaffrey's Twenty-Fourth Infantry Division alone moved almost 250 miles, knocking out 360 tanks and armored personnel carriers, 300 artillery tubes, and 1,700 trucks and engineering equipment, and took over five thousand prisoners while *losing only five soldiers*. In a single battle, a brigade in the First Armored Division destroyed as many as 50 tanks and armored personnel carriers in *ten minutes*.[59]

Beginning in 1992, Army leaders began to express concern over maintaining their generational lead in conventional capabilities. It was not just the demands of maintaining a favorable international order with the United States at the center that drove military innovation but the means to maintain what Barry Posen has called a "command of the commons," unrivaled military capability in support of a particular international order favorable to U.S. interests.[60] Despite the resounding Gulf War victory, military leaders began to speculate on the prospect of losing their capabilities edge. According to the fiscal year 1993 force posture statement,

> Many nations are now working to upgrade their own capabilities, contributing to the potential for instability and conflict. The acceleration of technology

transfer worldwide, along with growing intraregional competition, will result in an increasing number of developing states acquiring advanced weapons systems. The proliferation of precision guided munitions and high-technology weapons systems among developing nations with growing mid-intensity combat capabilities will make future Third World battlefields high risk environments. Increasingly lethal weapons, along with the spread of enhanced sensors, sophisticated countermeasures and reduced signature platforms, will provide regional adversaries with capabilities that are disproportionate to overall force size or sophistication. The technological advantages the United States enjoyed in the Gulf War will narrow and could be lost if we do not sustain a robust research and development program.[61]

The integration of threats to regional order and prospects of the proliferation of technologies established a particular understanding of warfare animating doctrinal deliberation. In many ways, estimates of the impact of new weapons systems increasingly established how leaders saw the emerging security environment. As early as 1993, the Army defined the modernization trend as setting a course toward a "capabilities and threat based army."[62] In this, the emphasis was less on any particular threat and more on having sufficient rapid deployment capacity to "demonstrate [U.S.] worldwide commitments, lend credibility to [U.S.] alliances, enhance regional stability, and provide a rapid crisis-response capability while promoting U.S. influence and access."[63] There was no specific, objective threat like the Soviet breakthrough attack guiding combat developments, just a list of capabilities leaders deemed necessary to support U.S. relative power advantages. While attacks by North Korea and Iran were used to model major regional war scenarios, the perception of the need to defend an entire world order was translated through a technological prism into sets of capabilities required to deter attacks against U.S. interests.[64]

Furthermore, efforts to lock in minimal budget shares rationalized the capabilities-based response to sustaining hegemony. By the mid-1990s modernization strategies reported to Congress began to push the argument that "the smaller the Army becomes, the more modern and technologically overmatching it must be."[65] Expecting continued drawdowns, planners anticipated that technology would "create the capability to overmatch any projected threat and attain decisive victory."[66] According to Vuono in testimony before the Senate, while concepts and doctrine would "continue to guide Army's efforts to develop and field combat-ready forces," budgetary constraints pushed the institution to "forgo near-term modernization while continuing with essential long-term modernization."[67] Thus, scenarios began to be stated in terms of the types of operations a technological advantage gave the United States as opposed to objective threats. As force structure was reduced, planners would focus on maintaining basic power-projection capabilities while seeking to develop leap-ahead systems to sustain primacy.[68]

Rather than distill operational concepts from specific threat scenarios, Army planners increasingly focused on the range of operations made possible by new weapons systems. In discussing the 1992 to 1993 fielding of the M1A2 tank and Apache Longbow helicopter, Sullivan claimed the systems marked

> the entry of the United States Army into what Alvin and Heidi Toffler have labeled Third Wave Warfare [in which] the incorporation of information technologies onto existing and future Army systems reflects a fundamental shift in the Army's modernization strategy and portends the development of digitized formations that will be able to capitalize on advanced information technologies to overmatch any potential 21st Century adversary.[69]

The integration of information technology thus represented a paradigm shift for Army leaders, a new logic reified by the austere budget climate and emerging U.S. dominated security order. Just as General Grant led the first American Army campaign of the industrial era, Sullivan saw himself as shepherding in an information age force.[70] In his speech to the Land Warfare Forum in Arlington, Virginia, Sullivan called for sustaining a "technological overmatch" that would ensure U.S. forces could dominate the battlefield in any contingency.[71] Further, the Army was entering a "post-industrial world" where,

> in order to retain this qualitative advantage in the future, we must appreciate the significance of what has been termed the technological revolution. This revolution has affected dramatically many aspects of American society. Industry, business, communications and banking are all much different today due to advanced technology—technology based essentially on the microchip. The same technological revolution today introduces a new era of warfare.[72]

Between 1992 and 1995, Sullivan routinely painted a picture of technological revolution based on the work of the futurist Alvin Toffler. In four influential books between 1980 and 1995, Toffler mapped out a view of the world as passing from an agrarian to industrial and now an information age. The change in epoch was based on the structure of economic activity and technologies that reorder all social interaction, including warfare.[73] Linked to this perspective was the growing sense in defense circles that the U.S. was in the midst of a military revolution. Borrowing from leading Soviet military writers in the 1970s, American military planners began to argue that technological developments related to the flow of information were fundamentally altering warfare and creating a revolution in military affairs (RMA).[74]

Traces of this concept are evident in statements by Army leaders. According to Sullivan, warfare in the information age would be fundamentally different:

> The utility of distributive campaigns that delivered decisive victory during the Industrial Age will fade. In the Information Age, armies will conduct operations resulting in the near-simultaneous paralysis and destruction of enemy forces, war-making capability, and information networks through the depth of a theater. Armies in the Information Age will develop a shared situational awareness resulting from having common, up-to-date, near-complete friendly and enemy information distributed among all elements of a task force.[75]

If the domestic logic of sustained modernization was galvanized by an austere budget environment and the dictates of doing more with less, the ideational factor implicit in such a move was the conceptualization of a whole new way of war. The logic of this paradigm shift was not just instrumental and predicated on building better weapons. For senior military leaders, the United States had to capture a generational lead in combat systems to overmatch future competitors. The twin dictates of digitization and asymmetry galvanized new understandings of warfare.[76] In testimony before the House of Representatives, Sullivan outlined how information age capabilities simultaneously highlighted an affordable means of building a true power-projection Army and illustrated the uncertainty and threat proliferations likely to confront U.S. security interests into the twenty-first century.[77] The world was changing. There was a sense that if the Army institutionally missed the opportunity to transform with it, it would sacrifice a significant historical opportunity.

In separate Senate testimony, Sullivan described this emerging reality as the "post-industrial battlefield" in which the proliferation of modern military capabilities was shifting the structure of war itself:

The U.S. experience in the Persian Gulf revealed the microchip of high technology warfare on the battlefield and the revolution that the microchip has brought to the modern post-industrial battlefield. By post-industrial battlefield I mean the characteristics of warfare that describe the modern environment in which we will fight—increased speed and tempo, and the ability to see the enemy anytime, anywhere, and to take the battle to him.[78]

The paradigm became the rallying point for force modernization in the Army. In an article titled "Doctrine: A Guide to the Future," Sullivan outlined the importance of the "post-industrial period" as establishing the nature and trajectory of doctrinal change in the 1990s.[79] Similarly, in a monograph written for the Strategic Studies Institute at the Army War College, Sullivan claimed that "technological innovations, many of which were dramatically demonstrated in the Gulf War, are giving rise to what is being called a military-technical revolution."[80] Sullivan believed that the United States should leverage inherent "technological advantages in training, development, deploying, and employing forces" to provide the range of land combat capabilities required to secure national interests.[81]

Battlefield Dynamics

An information-age power-projection army had institutional antecedents in efforts to adapt AirLand Battle. In the latter half of the 1980s, TRADOC began to push its doctrine writers to conceptualize future battlefields and imagine how the Army would conduct AirLand Battle in fifteen years. While intelligence estimates and assessments of likely capabilities informed these approximations, the focal point was on a narrative, a conceptual rendering of *how* operations would be conducted "across the continuum of war, conflict, and peacetime competition."[82]

Thus, before larger national security debates underlying Base Force and the two-theater-war models, the Army had sought to extend its doctrinal foundation as a means of developing new modes of warfare. In view of standing arguments related to innovation, this suggests that calculations of external threats driving reform in national security institutions do not require civilian intervention. Rather, they are predicated on assessing the likely thrust and trajectory of change by functional experts. For TRADOC this meant establishing the web of larger concepts animating doctrine and, through it, shaping force structure and future procurement paths. As renderings of war, these narratives offered both responses to external threats and frameworks for lobbying for future funds and resources.

To institutionalize this concept formation process, in the early 1990s TRADOC amended its publication line to include the 525-5 pamphlet series. The idea was to articulate core concepts as bridges to future publications of *Field Manual 100-5: Operations*, the Army's capstone document. The 525-5 series thus provided a space for doctrine writers to establish their operational concepts and encouraged institutional debate and dialogue. In effect, the Army institutionalized a ten-year projection exercise, using worst-case scenarios to track the threats to primacy. Unlike the incubator use highlighted in earlier chapters, the search process and initial development of new concepts would take place inside the bureaucracy.

Along these lines, in 1991, TRADOC published Pamphlet 525-5, *AirLand Operations: A Concept for the Evolution of AirLand Battle for the Strategic Army of the 1990s and Beyond*. Secretary of the Army Stone defined the document as "the basic rationale for leader development, force design, material requirements, and training."[83] The text laid out core concepts to engender institutional dialogue about the future of land warfare. The pamphlet translated standing doctrine into a new four-part engagement cycle based on likely advances in battlefield detection and weapon lethality: detect, shaping fires, decisive maneuver, and reconstitution. Long-range sensors, including Air Force and Army platforms, would detect potential targets. Then, soldiers would use various fire systems to disorient and paralyze the enemy, thus enabling decisive maneuver. After the battle, U.S. forces would then pause to reconstitute, preparing to begin the cycle again. Especially important for the trajectory of innovation in the 1990s, the concept called for application of doctrine across the conflict spectrum, for power projection, and on U.S. technological advantages in iterating the cycle faster than competitors could respond.

In addition to studies on expanding AirLand Battle, lessons learned from the Gulf War provided another catalyst to adapt standing operational concepts. After detailed discussions with Army Chief of Staff Vuono in June 1990, Foss, now TRADOC commander (1989–1991), tasked the Combined Arms Center and School of Advanced Military Studies at Fort Leavenworth to draft a new doctrine that captured both the 1990 white paper and 1991 edition of 525-5. In particular, writers were to fold standing doctrine on low-intensity conflict written in 1986 into the new edition of *Field Manual 100-5*. He further established that the new threat scenario guiding their deliberation should shift from the campaign to reinforce forward-deployed forces to a new case based on Desert Shield that captured the difficulties inherent in deploying to "immature theaters" where logistic infrastructure was lacking.[84]

Senior leaders in TRADOC and the Department of the Army played a significant role in initiating institutional reform agendas. Reform flowed from the top down. Not only did senior leaders like Sullivan set the agenda, framing the particular factors doctrine writers should consider; they also acted as institutional guardians and brokers. While General DePuy was instrumental in providing a safe space for new concepts of mechanized warfare to emerge despite the challenge it posed to the light infantry community, Vuono and Foss, and after them Sullivan and Franks, used TRADOC as the principal vehicle for developing, publishing, and testing new concepts and doctrine. To support this effort, they had senior officers publish articles and initiated new relationships that locked in particular reform agendas. Furthermore, they used the distance of TRADOC headquarters from the Beltway to insulate doctrinal writers from institutional debates that often crippled reform in the Pentagon. One officer close to doctrine development in the early 1990s stated that Sullivan and Franks intentionally moved the formation of concepts away from Fort Leavenworth and the Pentagon to give thinkers space to challenge established practices and stakeholders.[85]

Senior leaders also sought allies across the services. In April 1991, Foss and the Tactical Air Command commander, General John M. Loh, determined that the U.S. Air Force needed to develop parallel tactical air doctrine to support the rewriting of AirLand Battle. Thus, reform is possible in military organizations without external intervention, and it often transcends parochial logic of service rivalry. Yet reform is a fundamentally hierarchical phenomenon initiated and sustained by senior leaders.

After becoming chief of staff of the Army in June 1991, Sullivan directed TRADOC to use doctrine as the principal "engine of change" to forge the post–Cold War army.[86] To oversee this process, he selected the VII Corps commander in the Gulf War, Frederick M. Franks Jr., now a general. While the conflict was seen by many as a vindication of the tenets of AirLand Battle, Franks's experience led him to see significant defects that needed to be revised. The operational emphasis on close, deep, rear fights and interdicting second-echelon forces needed to be adapted to a post-Soviet world where technological advantages gave the United States the distinct ability to simultaneously engage targets across the entire battlefield. The corps commander could now attack the enemy in depth. Furthermore, standing concepts did not deal adequately with moving heavy forces to immature theaters of war or how to tailor forces to new environments.[87]

In addition, TRADOC planners assumed the worst-case scenario as they distilled these lessons into operational concepts. Future adversaries would not give the United States the luxury of a sustained buildup phase, thus putting a premium on forced entry and ensuring infantry forces had sufficient combat power to stop mechanized forces. They imagined an opponent with access to better technology offering them improved air defenses and the capacity to attack U.S. space links vital for sustaining communications. This bias only reinforced the logic of primacy and the broad range of capabilities required to fight anywhere and win everywhere. In this way, the logic of the security dilemma, how threats escalate on the basis of perceptions of adversary capabilities, was not rooted exclusively in intelligence estimates. It had a deeper institutional component, whereby the drive to articulate new forms of warfare was balanced against not current challenges but the whole range of future threats necessitated by planning horizons that spanned ten to fifteen years.

This combination of Gulf War lessons, standing AirLand Battle initiatives, the possibilities gleaned from the application of new technology, and worst-case scenarios led Franks to propose that five battlefield dynamics shaped the future of war. In the summer of 1992, Franks selected Major General Wesley Clark as his deputy chief of staff for Concepts, Doctrine, and Development. The intent was to formulate these arguments as operational concepts that would drive future reform initiatives. Using a Gulf War–like scenario developed by TRADOC Analysis Command, Clark led the Battlefield Dynamics Working Group through a series of seminars and tabletop exercises analyzing combat development that resulted in five concept papers on early entry, depth and simultaneous attack, battle space, command and control, and logistics.[88]

Furthermore, these concepts established ideals for future wars. Early entry embodied the essence of power projection, whereby U.S. forces would fight their way into a theater to gain the necessary lodgment and access to begin a troop buildup. With the inherent U.S. advantages in military technology, depth and simultaneous attack dealt with targeting the enemy across the entire depth of the battlefield. Command and control and battle tempo characterized new distributive formations enabled by the integration of computers and real-time intelligence feeds in tactical units.

To further refine the battlefield dynamics initiative, in April 1992 Franks established six battle laboratories at the TRADOC schools. Rather than invest in developing new capabilities, the battle lab model proposed to adapt existing, off-the-shelf technology to realize the possibilities inherent in digitization.[89] The battle labs were incubators, centers of experimentation isolated from pitched bureaucratic battles, where concepts could be field tested and refined before entering doctrinal discourse. To ensure buy-in across the various constituencies in the Army, six sites were established or planned that matched the Army's branch structure:

> A battle space laboratory for mounted combat at the Armor School at Fort Knox, formed in mid-April, was the pilot effort, with a battle space laboratory for dismounted combat at the Infantry School at Fort Benning, Georgia, and one at the Field Artillery School at Fort Sill, Oklahoma, involving notions of depth and simultaneous attack to follow. Associated with the Fort Sill Battle Lab were the Air Defense Artillery School at Fort Bliss, Texas, and the Intelligence School at Fort Huachuca, Arizona. There would be a command and control and battle tempo (later battle command) laboratory at Fort Leavenworth, supported by the Intelligence School and the Signal School at Fort Gordon, Georgia.[90]

At Fort Monroe, an early entry, lethality, and survivability laboratory worked closely with nearby service headquarters—U.S. Atlantic Fleet, the Air Force Tactical Air Command, and the Marine Corps Combat Development Command. Later planning added the sixth laboratory, for combat service support, at Fort Lee, Virginia. Franks's immediate guidance to the Armor commandant at Fort Knox was to use advanced technology demonstrations and experimentation as well as theory and tinkering.[91] In 1995, the Marine Corps adopted Franks's concept and rolled out the Marine Corps Warfighting Laboratory.

Furthermore, battle labs were the Army's principal mechanism for establishing "needs and solutions for the force projection Army."[92] Situating the initiative historically, Franks linked them to the tradition of using tactical test beds to experiment with fielding new types of fighting organizations, emphasizing the role of the Louisiana Maneuvers in preparing the U.S. Army for World War II in 1941 and the Eleventh Air Assault tests of 1963–1965 that ushered in a new era of air cavalry. In a February 9, 1993, speech to the Association of the United States Army Winter Symposium, Sullivan outlined the battle lab concept to the audience, stressing that the process allowed the Army "to experiment with concepts and equipment across a range of threats by using simulators and simulations to explore hardware and software payoffs."[93] The labs would test concepts and equipment specifications before they were field tested and ultimately sent into production. According to the fiscal year 1994 posture statement,

> The Battle Lab is an institutional means to define the future battlefield requirements; to identify, analyze, create, and evaluate new concepts; to explore alternative solutions; to coordinate with internal and external agencies; and to integrate ideas from external sources. Battle Labs maintain the Army perspective across a wide spectrum of ideas and concepts: conceptualizing, analyzing, simulating, testing, and evaluating command-directed projects at the brigade level and below; aggressively seeking out emerging concepts and technologies worldwide to ensure the Army remains dominant on future battlefields; examining emerging battlefield dynamics; providing feedback to the field; integrating leader development and training; and providing for the current and future needs of Army soldiers. They streamline the Army planning process by providing an organized way to define requirements; allowing industry to develop a focus for developmental work and potential for prototypes; providing industry access to a pool of Army thinkers who can delineate ideas about modernization alternatives and linking combat lessons learned, exercise results, and insights from regional commanders in chief to a formal analytical test bed.[94]

The battle labs thus embodied a move to render operational concepts through studying capabilities as opposed to threats. The post–Cold War ambiguity meant that the Army needed to find an "institutional way to focus on competing ideas and technologies" rather than generating requirements based on an objective threat.[95] In the absence of a clear and present danger like the Fulda Gap scenario, the laboratories' concept pushed planners to situate their work in relation to technological change. Using a vast array of analytical tools ranging from computer simulations to live training exercises, the labs would assess the interaction of capabilities and new modes of violence. Technology became the "focal point for developing the concepts related to the emerging understanding of battlefield dynamics in the post-industrial warfare."[96]

In a parallel effort, in 1991 the chief of staff of the Army established the Louisiana Maneuver (LAM) initiative at Fort Monroe. The project drew on the 1940 plan by Generals George C. Marshall and Leslie J. McNair for assessing key combat formations and tactics. Like the World War II project, the 1990s LAM was an exploratory forum, "a series of related exercises forming a campaign to assess the Army of the 21st Century in areas of policy, doctrine, organization, training, material, leader development, and soldier issues shaping the force."[97] According to the force posture statement, the initiative encompassed "the full range of military operations from force generation through force employment, conflict termination, and force redeployment."[98] It was a "high-technology laboratory for experimenting with conceptual changes in equipment, command, control and communications procedures, intelligence systems, combat tactics, techniques and procedures . . . doctrine and organization."[99] These incubators gave officers spaces to experiment with new ways of incorporating technology outside the traditional bureaucracy.

In a speech to the TRADOC Desert Storm Conference on March 2, 1992, Sullivan outlined his vision for LAM:

> Taking a page from history, my shorthand for this concept is Louisiana Maneuver 94. The original Louisiana Maneuvers were a series of exercises ordered by George Marshall to focus the Army, to train higher commanders, and to study how large field armies operate. Louisiana Maneuvers 94 is not only different, it is more expansive and complex—in many respects reflecting the changing nature of modern warfare. The purpose[s] of the maneuvers are . . . : first it is a focal point for changing the Army. It gives us a common goal as we move toward the future. It brings the institution together and forges cohesion in the reshaped, power projection Army. . . . Second, it will provide an assessment of the progress toward the vision of a trained and ready force, servicing America at home and abroad, capable of decisive victory. It will allow us to test the effects of our doctrine, organization, training, material requirements, and leader development and make necessary changes—mid-course corrections so to speak—before the changes become so institutionalized that we can't discover or undo the changes until after failure or lives lost in combat reveal the weakness.[100]

What made LAM truly unique were its participants. Unlike traditional concept initiatives as seen in DePuy's boathouse gang working at Fort Monroe and Starry's AirLand Battle team at Fort Leavenworth in which the bulk of the participants were professional soldiers, LAM opened up the process. Senior officers associated with the program interviewed science fiction writers, futurists like Alvin and Heidi Toffler, and even movie executives to conceptualize what the future of information technology implied for the conduct of warfare.[101] Furthermore, LAM was intentionally housed at Fort Monroe, outside the gravitational pull of Beltway debates and concerns voiced by the deputy chief of staff for Operations and Intelligence about the radical nature of involving nonmilitary personnel in doctrine development.

Sullivan and Franks wanted a place to think radically about the future of warfare. Thus, while the battle labs gave them a platform to experiment that linked key Army constituencies, LAM gave them the possibility of thinking about the future of warfare divorced from the constraints of near-term threats and probable deployments. The intent was to see over the horizon, fifteen to twenty years into the future, asking what types of capabilities would be available that would fundamentally alter the conduct of warfare. It was assumed that by 2010 the world would be defined by the third wave of warfare, the shift from an industrial to an information epoch.[102] In this, there was an image of a return to a Frederickean Army, a small, highly trained, technologically enabled force that outmatched larger industrial age competitors while maintaining the flexibility to interdict nonstate challenges to U.S. interests.

The Army thus developed a new set of institutional test beds, as incubators, for experimenting for the postindustrial battlefield. In testimony before the House of Representatives, Secretary of the Army Togo D. West stressed how the battle labs and LAM embodied a new "concept-to-production" cycle in acquisition.[103] Planning was quickly becoming divorced from near-term, objective threats and pegged to speculations about the future of technological development. While the regional security framework, with the United States as the center and guarantor, generated the parameters of innovation, the possibility of the third wave of warfare amid austere budgetary environments determined its subsequent trajectory. Just as studies of the 1973 Arab-Israeli War and the Central Battle experiments provided the intellectual framework in which planners imagined warfare, visions of new precision forces cultivated in incubators shaped intellectual development in the profession of arms in the early 1990s. The end of the Cold War, an exogenous shock, set the stage for new theories of victory.

Full-Dimensional Operations

In the early 1990s, there were two forums for translating post–Cold War strategic imperatives and questions about future warfare into doctrine: *Field Manual 100-5* and the 525-5 series. While *Field Manual 100-5* served as a near-term guide for planning, training, and force structure, the 525-5 pamphlets pushed out over the horizon to speculate on decadelong patterns and trends. Related to the discussion above, each took on a very different dimension of the larger national security debate. *Field Manual 100-5* tackled the concerns with force projection and fighting across a full spectrum of future competitors, while 525-5 and the Force XXI initiative sought to transform the Army for the information age.[104]

In a letter to Army general officers on November 22, 1991, Sullivan reiterated to other institutional elites that updating doctrine would serve as the Army's "azimuth as we confront the changes in the international arena, in the *National Military Strategy*, in national budget priorities, and in technology."[105] A similar logic seems to have been contagious during the period because the mid-1990s also saw a surge in service doctrine. The Air Force published *Air Force Manual 1-1: Basic Aerospace Doctrine*, outlining how a technological edge solidified U.S. airpower in the basic missions of power projection, counterspace operations, close air support, and counterair operations.[106] In 1994, the Navy released *Naval Warfare* along the same lines, stressing joint integration to dominate the battle space. There was a sustained push by each branch of service to illustrate how it would harness the power of the ongoing technological revolution to meet security commitments, an institutional move correlated with deeper budgetary cuts and post–Cold War drawdowns.

The Army's response was to unveil its new capstone doctrine, a document over three years in the making. The 1993 edition of *Field Manual 100-5: Operations* was published June 14, the Army's birthday. At a press conference covering the launch, Sullivan referred to the new doctrine as an "intellectual bridge to the future."[107] The manual opens with a definition of doctrine that established its importance as a discursive glue, the collection of conceptions through which reform realizes itself across the organization. Doctrine was said to touch "all aspects of the Army. It facilitates communications between Army personnel no matter where they serve, establishes a shared professional culture and approach to operations, and serves as the basis for curriculum in the Army school system. Doctrine permeates the entire organizational structure of the Army and sets the direction for modernization of the Army and the standard for leadership development and soldier training."[108]

For Sullivan, the new doctrine linked to the "National Military Strategy," establishing the intellectual framework for a "force projection Army that can build and sustain substantial combat power in any region worldwide."[109]

Thus, the manual expanded the focus of AirLand Battle to include five new areas: force projection, joint and combined operations, operations other than war, depth and simultaneous attack, and unit versatility. Furthermore, the 1993 edition added "versatility" to the 1986 edition's tenets of war. For Army planners, versatility addressed "the requirement for Army forces to be able to respond to a wide variety of operations, ranging from war to peace support activities."[110] Versatility was an essential element because it embodied concerns about the myriad nonstate threats likely to confront the nation. In these statements, connection to the three days' war and the Antaeus Study is apparent. The Army expanded its focal point beyond conventional deterrence to factor in new mission sets.

Writing in the 1993 *Army Green Book*, Sullivan declared that the new manual reflected a paradigm shift from a Cold War–deterrent Army to a

> power projection Army with worldwide responsibilities. The Army fights wars and carries on operations other than war (OOTW)—peacekeeping, humanitarian relief, and counter-drug tasks, among others. To engage in operations, we project power from continental America and from overseas forward presence locations.[111]

This shift is embodied in the structure of the language used to describe doctrine. While the two previous cases contained direct references to physical combat with terms like "Active Defense" and "AirLand Battle," the new doctrine was "Full-Spectrum Dimensional Operations," with "operations" referring to the whole continuum of possible tasks the Army might be called on to address. This choice of terms reflected a deeper dialogue in the upper echelons following the Gulf War when senior leaders considered other service terms like the Marines' "small wars" and emerging Army discourse of OOTW. TRADOC doctrine writers strove to find a term that incorporated the essence of OOTW with the need to be simultaneously prepared for high-intensity combat.[112]

The manual echoed this sentiment. In the 1993 edition, the range of challenges that call for the use of land forces reflect the larger emphasis in the "National Security Strategy" and "National Military Strategy" on a broad array of threats ranging from high-intensity conflict to drug trafficking read through a regional security framework.[113] Furthermore, the revision reflected "advances in technology that are continually changing the way warfare is conducted at a pace now greater than ever before."[114] With the twin trends of new

TABLE 4.1 Spectrum of operations

State of the environment	Goal	Military operations	Examples
War	Fight and win	War	• Large-scale combat operations • Attacks • Defense
Conflict	Deter war and resolve conflict	Other than war	• Strikes and raids • Peace enforcement • Support to insurgency • Antiterrorism • Peacekeeping • Noncombatant evacuation operations
Peacetime	Promote peace	Other than war	• Counterdrug operations • Disaster relief • Civil support • Peace building • Nation assistance

NOTE: The states of peacetime, conflict, and war could all exist at once in one strategic environment. The theater commander can respond to requirements with a wide range of military operations. Noncombat operations might occur during war, just as some operations other than war might require combat.

capabilities and worldwide commitments, the Army had to be prepared to operate across a broader continuum of conflict (Table 4.1).

This conceptual shift, the emphasis on the logic of war everywhere across the full range of possible engagements, led to a reexamination of the principles of war.[115] The demands of the force-projection Army called for a new statement of the foundations of all operations. Like the principles of war, each standing tenet from the 1982 and 1986 editions was expressed as it related to power projection and OOTW. For example, the writers discussed initiative as reestablishing centralized, local government control during humanitarian crises and natural disasters, while synchronization was linked to the need for commanders to coordinate early entry forces with follow-on reinforcements in contingency missions.[116] The new tenet, versatility, described "the ability of units to meet diverse mission requirements. Commanders must be able to focus, tailor forces, and move from one role or mission to another rapidly."[117] The Full-Dimensional force would transition from deterrence after early entry to offensive operations, and at the termination of conflict, to operations other than war.

Reflecting the institutional setting and debate from which it emerged, the manual dedicated large sections to discussing "battlefield dynamics" and the lessons of the Gulf War. Along these lines, the manual added new chapters on force projection to help commanders prepare for rapid deployment under varying strategic circumstances. Unable to predict how a future conflict might evolve, commanders were told to prepare to conduct "mobilization and deployment [both] simultaneously and sequentially."[118] Furthermore, the manual discussed force tailoring given the competing demands of rapid deployment and combat power. Light units that could be moved to an area on short notice lacked the sufficient strength to resist mechanized adversaries, while heavy forces took time to build up. The manual also took considerable space to map out how commanders should conduct joint warfare and execute combined operations with multinational allies, both topics of discussion following the Gulf War.[119]

Postindustrial warfare and derivative battlefield dynamics shaped the manual's emphasis on simultaneous attack and operations in depth. Commanders were told to adapt to multiple, connected campaigns, balancing them through a

> unifying strategic concept of operations that synchronizes action taken at each level of war against the enemy, whether the actions occur simultaneously or sequentially. The intent is to destroy or disrupt the enemy's key capabilities and functions and exploit the resulting strategic advantage before the enemy can react. The results should so demoralize the enemy by their combined and simultaneous effects that he perceives he cannot win.[120]

Furthermore, shifting from deep strike against second-echelon forces, the new manual pressed commanders to synchronize deep, close, and rear operations.[121] Fire coordination became a paramount task on an increasingly fluid battlefield. Commanders were expected to leverage inherent advantages in U.S. capabilities and continuously shoot and move.

"Military operations other than war" (MOOTW) entered the Army lexicon. While establishing the historical commonplace of this domain of activity, the manual highlighted how the post–Cold War world was witnessing a proliferation of small-scale force deployments short of major combat operations:

> Today, the Army is often required, in its role as a strategic force, to protect and further the interests of the United States at home and abroad in a variety of ways other than war. Army forces face complex and sensitive situations in a variety of

operations. These range from support to the U.S., state and local governments, disaster relief, nation assistance, and drug interdiction to peacekeeping, support for insurgencies and counterinsurgencies, noncombatant evacuation, and peace enforcement. Operations other than war often are of long duration and undergo a number of shifts in direction during their course. Immediate solutions to difficult problems may not be obvious or may jeopardize long-term objectives. Peacekeeping, for example, demands that the peacekeeping force maintain strict neutrality. . . . Certain military responses to civil disturbance may solve the immediate crisis but subvert the legitimacy of local authorities and cause further civil unrest.[122]

The complexity and nuance of this form of warfare also broadened principles. Beyond mass, offensive, and initiative, leaders were told to consider unity of effort, legitimacy, restraints, perseverance, and security.[123] MOOTW necessitated that commanders apply the minimal amount of force as a means of sustaining the support of the population.

The manual embodied broader trends in the post–Cold War security environment. First, the U.S. position within the international system dictated the emergence of planning for war everywhere across the full spectrum of possible operations. Furthermore, the delineation of operational concepts, as battlefield dynamics, shaped how AirLand Battle evolved in the new doctrine. The vision of a new modality of war found articulation in *Field Manual 100-5* in addition to the larger web of interests implicit in the intersection of external threat, institutional setting, and budgetary constraints. This calculus is best described as an attempt to meld a paradigmatic shift in technology to the requirements of maintaining favorable regional order despite declining domestic resources. The combination of these interests into a reform agenda followed an institutional path that put a premium on elite buy-in through linking dialogue and incubators. The military professional defined, debated, and tested concepts before translating them into doctrine reflecting the varied interests of the institutional Army.

In addition to establishing the doctrinal framework for the post–Cold War Army, the development of *Field Manual 100-5: Operations* also heralded a new model for seeking institutional buy-in across the broader defense establishment. In developing a replacement to AirLand Battle, Franks "chose the vehicle of a precise digest of ideas laying out the reason why a new doctrine was needed and suggesting what lines that doctrine should pursue."[124]

TRADOC conducted a consensus-building campaign to lay the foundation for Army acceptance of the doctrine. Franks and his staff actively generated debate and dialogue in the ranks as a means of shaping the emerging ideas and ensuring that various service constituencies felt included in the discourse. Thus, Army writers not only sought to integrate operational doctrine with the August 1991 "National Security Strategy" but built a broader intellectual community to support their vision.[125] TRADOC historian John Romjue analyzed internal memorandums detailing the campaign and asserts,

> The Plan focused on five groups influential in shaping national security aims and in bringing change to the Army itself. Those groups were the reserve and retired Army leadership; defense industry; other military organizations in the Department of Defense, including the unified and specified commands; other nations bound by treaty or bilateral relationship; and influential entities and individuals including Congress, influential academics, the media, opinion leaders, think tanks such as RAND and the Center for Strategic and International Studies, and other government agencies, particularly those with a stake in operations short of war. TRADOC planners believed that by the time the media had raised an issue, the media's own viewpoint and agenda was set. The Army needed to fully inform media writers and other opinion makers before uninformed opinions formed and were propagated. The proper course of action would be to help set a responsible issue agenda beforehand.[126]

Over the course of the next two years, TRADOC implemented this marketing campaign. TRADOC staffers briefed individual members of Congress and sought to generate a series of articles published in defense-related outlets like *Army, Military Review, Parameters,* and *Defense News*.[127] In summer 1992, Franks began briefing senior leaders on the progress of the doctrinal revision. In a September 1, 1992, memorandum titled "Briefing of FM 100-5, Operations (Preliminary Draft) to CSA [chief of staff of the Army] and ARSTAF [Air Force staff]," he noted how he used a conference methodology, seeking to open up dialogue as a means of generating consensus.[128] In a November 10, 1992, memorandum titled "Notes, FM 100-5 Off Site Conference, Fort Story VA, 5–6 Nov," Franks details how this process had generated sufficient consensus for forging a power-projection Army linked to the new "National Military Strategy" and its emphasis on regional conflict.[129] In the same document, he outlined how the new *Field Manual 100-5* was a "doctrine for a different era" that explored new possibilities afforded by U.S. technological advantages, including the ability to simultaneously attack targets throughout the full depth of the battlefield.

Incubators and advocacy networks laid the foundation for the emergence of Full-Dimensional Operations. The shock of the end of the Cold War left defense officials scrambling to imagine future war. In the Army, this search for new operational problems gravitated toward exploring the difficulties of power projection across multiple contingencies and integrating emerging technology to maintain a significant advantage. Full-Dimensional Operations reflected a solution to these different problems.

Force XXI

Full-Dimensional Operations shifted from forward defense to power projection, and Force XXI represented the follow-up effort to adapt Army force structure for the postindustrial battlefield. In March 1994, Sullivan announced the initiative as a broad-based plan to redesign every Army unit, from the squad to echelons above corps, around new information-based systems. The original plan called for "testing a fully-digitized brigade during 1996–1997, and testing of the experimental division in 1997–1998."[130]

In testimony before the House of Representatives, Sullivan referred to the new doctrine as "the intellectual foundation for growth into the 21st Century."[131] Force XXI would prepare the Army to take advantage of the "ongoing technological revolution."[132] These statements clearly situate the initiative within the larger paradigmatic shift in how senior leaders thought about technology in the early 1990s. In this rendering, technology transformed from a means of building weapons with superior engagement ranges and destructive capacity to an entirely new social logic that altered command relationships and the speed of decision making, illustrating the paths Army leaders could follow to meet increased power-projection commitments amid declining resources.

In a November 10, 1994, letter to general officers titled "Force XXI Campaign Plan: Execution and Synchronization," Sullivan stated the overall strategic objective of Force XXI as transforming "the force from an Industrial Age Army to a knowledge and capabilities based, power projection Army capable of land force dominance across the continuum of 21st century military operations."[133] Describing the "fundamental hypothesis" of Force XXI, he said,

If we know the performance of a currently equipped baseline organization, then we can apply Information Age technologies to that organization, train to standard as we conduct experiments, and gain insights to improved battlefield performance that will cause us to redesign operational concepts and units to enhance our nation's military capabilities.[134]

In 1994, the Army made Force XXI an official operational concept through the publication of TRADOC Pamphlet 525-5, *Force XXI Operations: A Concept for the Evolution of Full-Dimensional Operations for the Strategic Army of the Early Twenty-First Century*. In an opening statement, General William W. Hartzog, Franks's successor at TRADOC, refers to the publication as "a vision for the future," the paradigm for "hypotheses and test[s]" of combat development trends.[135] Force XXI was the gateway to the future. According to Sullivan, it provided "the institutional framework for [Army] experiments and doctrinal debates."[136] As a web of ideas, it helped planners explore "the impact of information systems and other emerging technologies on the operational environment of the future," thus providing "insights into the critical battle dynamics [the Army] should exploit to remain the most powerful and capable Army on earth."[137] Many of the Force XXI authors were drawn from the LAM initiative, including officers from the chief of staff's private think tank and staffers in TRADOC's own guarded think tank in the Future Battles Directorate. Sullivan and Franks each carved out an institutional space to enable radical statements about the future of warfare and handpicked the officers who worked there.[138] They created incubators to render visions of future war.

Force XXI started from the same threat perspective as *Field Manual 100-5*, characterizing the strategic environment in terms of ambiguity and complexity that necessitates a "Full-Dimensions" power-projection force.[139] Major elements of instability threatening U.S. interests included "shifting and unstable power balances at the national and sub national level in the Balkans, Middle East, and throughout Africa and Asia" as well as nationalism and the anticipated "rejection of the west" in the twenty-first century.[140] The world would fracture under the weight of environmental and demographic trends that led to ungovernable states.[141] Conflict entrepreneurs would further have access to a wide array of destructive capabilities as technological innovation accelerated and diffused throughout the international system.

This presented a range of future adversaries beyond nation-states, ranging from "political, racial, religious, cultural, and ethnic conflicts that challenge the defining features and authority of the nation-state from within" to "meta-national threats . . . beyond the nation-state including religious movements, international criminal organizations, and information economic organizations that facilitate weapons proliferation." For professionals developing the new concept, these trends depicted the emergence of a "new warrior class," drawn from the "underclass of society" and "displaced by a conflict."[142] These militants ranged from opportunists and renegade soldiers to ideologically driven "true believers." According to TRADOC analysts in the Future Battles Directorate, this type of enemy

> poses a problem because he does not fight by the rules of conventional warfare: his targets are not force-oriented but are the political will of his opponents; his tactics include terrorism, ambushes, kidnapping, and criminal activities; he does not keep his negotiated word. The nonstate warrior can become a problem during a conflict, but more often prolongs violence after the conflict is formally resolved.[143]

What Force XXI added to this calculus as the critical variable conditioning future war was the concept of a "world in transition."[144] Based on Toffler's view of waves of technological change, the twentieth century was seen as an "industrial age" preceding two "decades of transition" before ending in a new "information age."[145] In this shift,

> information technology [was] expected to make a thousand fold advance over the next 20 years. In fact, the pace of development is so great that it renders our current material management and acquisition system inadequate. Developments in information technology will revolutionize . . . how nations, organizations, and people interact.[146]

The operational concept also continued the institutional narrative that Just Cause and Desert Storm offered "a glimpse of the future" defined by "the revolution in military affairs."[147] In particular, the new mode of warfare in the information age was held to establish five conventional battlefield dynamics. New technology would lead to new communication systems and the "nonhierarchical dissemination of intelligence, targeting, and other data at all levels. Accordingly, units, key nodes, and leaders [would] be more widely dispersed, leading to the continuation of the empty battlefield phenomenon."[148] Furthermore, linked to AirLand Battle's concept of the extended battlefield as it was reinterpreted by Franks as VII Corps commander during the Gulf

War, the concept stated that "recent U.S. operations show that deep battle has advanced beyond the concept of attacking the enemy's follow-on forces in a sequential approach to shape the close battle to one of simultaneous attack to stun, then rapidly defeat the enemy."[149]

The "battlefield dynamics" that reoriented Full-Dimensional Operations received new characterization in the postindustrial battlefield. Battle command now framed not just positioning forces in a linear battlefield, but the effort to synchronize their effects.[150] Continuing the concept of simultaneous attack in depth, Force XXI proposed to "induce massive systemic shock" that broke the enemy's will to resist.[151] The concept also tackled the challenges of early entry operations. Fast strategic lift, lighter forces, prepositioned equipment, and floating stocks were seen as essential for reducing mobilization and deployment times.

Finally, the global scope and breakdown in norms associated with interstate war between formal combatants would dictate shifts in the rules of war, especially in MOOTW environments, and place a premium on "spectrum supremacy."[152] Just as information technology enabled new types of attack, it also left the military increasingly naked before a global audience. According to the new concept,

> military operations, regardless of their importance, dimension, or location, will be conducted on a global stage. Tactical actions and the hardships of soldiers and civilians alike will have an increasing impact on strategic decision making and dramatically alter the concept of time—time from crisis to expected action and time for actual conduct of operations.[153]

Against the backdrop of shrinking budgets and expanding commitments envisioned by each presidential administration following the end of the Cold War, Force XXI and Full-Dimensional Operations embody institutional reform agendas that used doctrine as a means of shepherding larger organizational change. Behind these new logics was the multifaceted relationship between external threat, institutional setting, and budgetary constraints. More than in earlier episodes of change, domestic resources play a significant role in explaining the trajectory of reform. Though many officers close to the initiatives deny they were driven by a pure bureaucratic logic of self-interest and protection of budget share and turf, it is highly likely that this concern over resources at least catalyzed the desire to change the organization. What is similar to previous episodes is the use of conceptual innovation as a means of debating and ultimately developing doctrinal change. This is a process that has a distinct institutional setting, here the role played by incubators and advocacy networks, as senior officers in TRADOC and the Department of the Army set out to establish the parameters of change. Interestingly, the case clearly illustrates the need for senior leaders to carve out protected incubators that allow ideas to be developed and debated before being disseminated across the institution.

Also similar to the two previous cases is the importance of how war is understood by military professionals in terms of new technology. Although, as with Active Defense and AirLand Battle, proposing a direct correlation between new weapons systems and new doctrine would be incorrect. Rather, how technology is understood in terms of its social logic, how it mediates exchanges between individuals, that produces causal incentives within the Army. While Force XXI was a direct response to the perception of postindustrial warfare, it also embodied a response repertoire establishing the ways technology altered human relations as opposed to an exogenous variable defining them.

Conclusion

The Army of the 1990s was an institution and officer corps in flux. Doctrine continued to leverage problem-driven simulation and experimentation. Incubators provided critical institutional mechanisms by which a generation of cold warriors reimagined warfare and their core missions. The Army took the lead. Starting as early as 1987, senior officers began to imagine new forms of warfare through the AirLand Battle Future and Antaeus Studies. Before large-scale budget cuts at the end of the Cold War related to Powell's Base Force concept, the Army used incubators, in the form of concepts and problem-driven studies, to define the character of land warfare in a world where superpower conflict was in decline.

In addition, force experiments and test beds helped a new generation of officers consider how to employ emerging disruptive technologies on the battlefield. From the battle labs to the LAM and Force XXI, officers searched for new theory of victory at the speed of light. In these forums, concepts seemed to follow rather than drive technology and capabilities. The case of Full-Dimensional Operations and the follow-on Force XXI experiments reflect a higher degree of technological pull than the previous cases. Alternatively, in

AirLand Battle, the deep-strike concept emerged before the actual weapons systems that would enable soldiers to employ it on the battlefield. Capabilities followed concepts. In Active Defense, the diffusion of antitank missiles contributed to, but did not exclusively define, the suppress-to-move, move-to-concentrate concept.

With respect to advocacy networks, as with AirLand Battle an attempt was made to rally the base. Leaders in the Army and the wider defense community like Powell used speeches, articles, and traveling briefs to convince the officer corps of the necessity of change. Two forms of advocacy appear as predominant: brokerage and positional legitimation. Through the "View of the 1990s" brief, Powell sought to connect a diffuse network across the defense community to support the Base Force concept. While a Department of Defense–level initiative, the brief opened up a space in which Army officers could advocate their own concepts. In particular, senior leaders used the Antaeus Study to win support from the Joint community for their vision of future war. In the second form of advocacy, senior leaders like Sullivan emerged, as Starry had before him, as masters of positional legitimation, using the authority of their station to circulate new concepts.

Thus, like earlier cases, doctrinal innovation in the early 1990s highlights the importance of incubators where officers can search and experiment and the role of advocacy networks in circulating concepts forged therein among officers. New ideas required protected sites free from the pull of the bureaucracy and champions promoting them across the institution. Arguably these sites were all the more important once defense cuts loomed large on the horizon. Incubators became a vehicle to search for relevance and missions, for how to adapt the Army for a post–Cold War world. This attribute explains the almost constant change in the institution. From AirLand Battle Future to MOOTW and Force XXI, constant conceptual experimentation defined the Army of the 1990s. The rate of organizational change is thus not just a function of the search for a new theory of victory; it is linked to uncertainty about the future. This uncertainty took multiple forms. Like earlier cases it was linked to worst-case bias in the professional ranks. More so than previous cases, it is hard to separate the rate of change from the fear of declining influence. The professional soldier is still part bureaucrat.

With respect to the alternative perspectives on military change, the Full-Dimensional Operations case has mixed results. First, significant cuts to the budget occurred in parallel with efforts to redefine operational concepts.

Furthermore, the end of the Cold War, as an exogenous shock, created a need to revisit ideas about war fighting. Military professionals in the Army found themselves in a situation in which ignoring international and domestic imperatives for change risked organizational autonomy. That said, there was no compelling evidence of civilian intervention. The professional sought to redefine critical tasks in line with the organization's mandate through the use of incubators and advocacy networks.

Second, with respect to the postindustrial Army, it is the first case examined here in which planners emphasized friendly capabilities more than objective threat scenarios (i.e., capability-based concept development more than threat-based). New technologies did appear to exert more causal influence than in previous cases. In fact, the entire enterprise of speculating about future war with respect to emerging capabilities significantly influenced concept development in the 1990s.

Third, with respect to an enduring, attritionist way of war the results are mixed. The idea of optimizing the Army for a wider range of contingencies (e.g., MOOTW) runs counter to this strategic culture. At the same time, the vision of warfare in 525-5 and Force XXI reflected an emphasis on precision firepower indicative of attrition-based warfare.

5 Hearts and Minds Revisited

> Once [a U.S. military unit] settles into the area of operations, its next task is to build trusted networks. This is the true meaning of the phrase "hearts and minds," which comprises two separate components. "Hearts" means persuading people that their best interests are served by COIN success. "Minds" means convincing them that the force can protect them and that resisting it is pointless.... [O]ver time, successful trusted networks grow like roots into the populace. They displace enemy networks, which forces enemies into the open, letting military forces seize the initiative and destroy the insurgents.
>
> —Department of the Army, Field Manual 3-24: Counterinsurgency Operations

DELIBERATING OVER HOW TO COUNTER INSURGENTS IN America, Sir Henry Clinton, the British commander in chief between 1778 and 1782, had a central idea. He called for British forces "to gain the hearts and subdue the minds of America."[1] On assuming the role of higher commissioner during the Malayan Emergency in 1952, British general Gerald Templar worked with his staff to design a campaign that isolated insurgent jungle bases through "coercion and enforcement" while winning the "hearts and minds" of the population.[2] The first task listed in General David Petraeus's "Multi-national Forces–Iraq Commander's Counterinsurgency Guidance" was to "serve and secure the population."[3] Whether framed as gaining hearts, winning minds, or serving the population, there appears to be an enduring question of how to apply military power to subdue restive populations short of salting the earth.

This chapter explores that operational question through examining the development of *Field Manual 3-24: Counterinsurgency Operations* as an episode of doctrinal innovation. While the manual reflects doctrinal change, it is less dramatic than heralded at the time. Incubators and advocacy networks were present and appear to have enabled a group of thinkers around Petraeus, the "coinistas," to shift how the U.S. defense establishment thought about counterinsurgency (COIN). The manual and subsequent surge did change the battle in Iraq, but the core ideas within the manual were neither new nor novel. Rather, they reflected a long tradition in military thinking about how to counter insurgents and guerrillas to wage what was referred to during the American Revolution as *petite guerre* (small war). The doctrine was old wine in a new bottle.

The chapter traces the emergence of the new doctrine between 2004 and 2006. Incubators appear as special study groups and workshops that gave officers a space to reconsider the rise of the insurgency in Iraq. As in the previous case, the advocacy networks that diffused "new" ideas about warfare significantly broadened. From this vantage point, the chapter considers an alternative American way of war and how military professionals deliberate over the conduct of counterinsurgency campaigns. Specifically, the analysis looks at treatments of counterinsurgency in the aftermath of World War II to show a deeper idea also manifest in *Field Manual 3-24*, the balancing of political-military campaigns designed to isolate insurgents and win support among the local populace.

The Rise of the Coinistas

Counterinsurgency doctrine did not begin with Petraeus. The view that no one inside the Department of Defense or broader community of defense analysts cutting across the bureaucracy was interested in counterinsurgency after the successful invasions of Afghanistan (2001) and Iraq (2003) is flawed. Rather, multiple initiatives failed to coalesce. Just months after the invasion in early summer 2003, deputy secretary of defense Paul Wolfowitz called on his deputy assistant secretary, Jim Thomas, and Gary Anderson, a retired Marine Corps colonel, to start exploring ways of managing unrest in post-Saddam Iraq. The two colleagues drafted memos for Wolfowitz and went on site visits in July 2003.[4] Thomas had a background in issues surrounding irregular warfare extending back to the 1990s when he served in the Office of the Under Secretary of Defense for Policy working on asymmetric threats as part of the 1997 *Report of the Quadrennial Defense Review*.[5] Anderson had experience as a marine officer in Somalia and Lebanon and in working through irregular warfare issues while serving in concept development roles, including director of Wargaming and chief of staff of the Warfighting Laboratory at Quantico, Virginia.

The early exploration of irregular threats in post-Saddam Iraq continued throughout 2004. On October 6, 2004, and again on July 6, 2005, Anderson and Thomas, along with marine officer Robert "Rooster" Schmidle, set up conferences on irregular warfare at Quantico.[6] The conferences brought together a diverse network of military officers, analysts, and defense officials. One of the 2004 conference attendees, David Kilcullen, made his way around the Beltway, giving a briefing titled "United States Counterinsurgency: An Australian View."[7]

In 2005, Eliot Cohen, who had attended the 2004 irregular warfare conference, organized a special workshop to discuss counterinsurgency, held June 6–10 at Basin Harbor in Vermont. The closed sessions linked a wide range of defense insiders and thinkers interested in counterinsurgency who would play a significant role in developing Army counterinsurgency doctrine.[8]

These irregular warfare conferences along with briefings and meetings connected a network of defense analysts and officials interested in counterinsurgency. Jim Thomas recruited David Kilcullen and John Nagl, who arrived at the Pentagon following a tour in Iraq, to work on the 2006 *Quadrennial Defense Review Report* irregular warfare section. Over the course of 2005, Kilcullen and Nagl developed a vision of irregular warfare as the future warfare of choice for adversaries of the United States and advocated that the Defense Department develop an irregular warfare road map in an effort to harmonize the wide range of disparate initiatives.[9] While the report further created a space in which irregular warfare and counterinsurgency could be discussed within the Department of Defense, the 2006 *Quadrennial Defense Review Report*, according to John Nagl, "failed to link strategy for the 'Long War' with new development priorities."[10]

Separately, in August 2004 a Defense Science Board task force completed a study, *Transition to and from Hostilities*.[11] Known as the Fields Study after its cochair Craig Fields, the report concluded that the United States would continue to experience significant challenges associated with stabilization and reconstruction after major combat operations, highlighting that the stabilization missions required after conventional operations usually required between five to eight years.[12] Insiders in the defense community not only acknowledged the challenges of counterinsurgency but also predicted as early as 2004 that Iraq could present a challenge for years to come.

On the recommendations of the Fields Study, Secretary of Defense Donald Rumsfeld ordered his staff to draft a new directive on stabilization and reconstruction, assigning Deputy Assistant Secretary for Stability Operations

Jeffrey Nadaner to the task.[13] Nadaner and his staff, which included Janine Davidson who would go on to work in the Office of Assistant Secretary of Defense for Special Operations and Low-Intensity Conflict and found the Consortium for Complex Operations, wrote a ten-page summary of the Fields Study and circulated it throughout the Department of Defense. The summary was so controversial that Rumsfeld had to establish an external commission headed by Martin Hoffman, a former secretary of the Army, to review the findings.[14] The recommendation that stability operations be afforded the same stature as combat operations caused significant controversy on the Joint Staff and in the Department of the Army, where officials claimed it undermined core Army doctrine emphasizing firepower, maneuverability, and mass.[15]

Out of the debate emerged Defense Department "Directive 3000.05."[16] Published November 28, 2004, the document outlined Defense Department guidance on military support for stability, security, transition, and reconstruction. The concept built on earlier work done at the Office of the Coordinator for Reconstruction and Stabilization in the Department of State. Like the 2006 *Quadrennial Defense Review Report* and work that went into it over the course of 2005, the document, while visionary, did not sufficiently mobilize opinion within the Department of Defense.

Like the myriad groups in the Defense Department struggling with how to reconcile irregular warfare with visions of conventional warfare, the institutional Army began exploring a new counterinsurgency doctrine as early as February 2004. The initiative began after General William Scott Wallace and his staff noticed that units training to deploy as part of the Battle Command Training Program were fighting in an overly conventional style for a theater not in major combat operations.[17] Wallace, who had commanded V Corps in Iraq in 2003, came to his new position as commander of the Combined Arms Center intent on using the Battle Command Training Program and Army schoolhouses to connect the institutional Army with lessons learned from currently deployed troops.[18] Having served as division commander of the Fourth Infantry Division during the Force XXI experiments in the early 1990s and later as director of the Joint Warfighting Center, Wallace had a unique appreciation for simulation. During the Iraq invasion, Wallace had successfully employed many of the techniques he experimented with at the Battle Command Training Program in the lead-up to the war.[19] Wallace also previously established informal conferences on Phase IV stability operations following the planning for the Iraq invasion, Victory Scrimmage, held in Germany in January 2003.[20]

Seeing the disconnect between deploying Army officers prepared to fight and the actual missions being conducted, Wallace ordered the Doctrine Directorate to expedite the production of a new counterinsurgency manual.[21] The task fell to Colonel Clinton Ancker III and Lieutenant Colonel Jan Horvath. While the doctrine development process usually took at a minimum two years, Wallace gave them less than a year. The result was *Field Manual–Interim 3-07.22: Counterinsurgency Operations*, published in October 2004, one month before the new Defense Department "Directive 3000.05" on stabilization and transition.[22] Ancker sent a copy to Kalev Sepp, a retired Army Special Forces officer and instructor at the Naval Postgraduate School, whose students offered pointed critiques of the manual.[23] Concept development, at least at the Army level, did not begin in an incubator but within the standing bureaucracy, with officers reaching out to a network of experts to validate their concepts.

In Iraq, senior officials were similarly struggling to determine how to deal with unrest. In the summer of 2005, General George Casey organized a group around his head of Strategy, Plans, and Assessments, Colonel William Hix, to study counterinsurgency and develop a new campaign plan. The group, which included contractors from RAND and Kalev Sepp, debated how to frame the problem. Sepp, who had reviewed the interim field manual on counterinsurgency the previous year, wrote a paper outlining their deliberations, "Successful and Unsuccessful Counterinsurgency Practices."[24]

Casey approved the paper as the concept for the new campaign and concurred with Hix's recommendation to publish it immediately for the ranks of the Army in *Military Review*. Casey also approved Hix's second recommendation, for forming a new training academy.[25] Sepp and Hix had conducted a survey in August 2005 that found that roughly 80 percent of units were either struggling or outright failing to implement effective counterinsurgency practices.[26] In November 2005, Casey opened the COIN Academy at Camp Taji, Iraq.[27]

In addition, the academy captured emerging tactical lessons, especially the experience of the 101st Airborne Division in Mosul during the summer of 2003 and the initial successes of the 3rd Armored Cavalry Regiment in Tal Afar after May 2005. In Tal Afar, Colonel H. R. McMaster received vague orders to "clear and hold" the area.[28] Rather than focusing initially on high-value kill and capture missions, McMaster's units took time to understand the environment, building situational awareness and establishing strong links with local

Iraqi forces. The unit also focused on reestablishing essential services. By engaging with the population, McMaster's troops found it easier to collect information required to identify key insurgent leaders and attack the network.

By May 2006, Casey's staff prepared *Counterinsurgency Handbook*, a collection of lessons learned and best practices distributed at the COIN Academy.[29] The handbook "emphasized [the need for] critical skills in training and operating with Iraqi forces, intelligence, information operations, Iraqi culture, cross cultural communication, and contemporary insurgent tactics,"[30] shortcomings noted by the Sepp-Hix survey. Conceptually, the manual built on Kilcullen's twenty-eight articles, using a short form of the earlier brief.[31] The first commandant of the academy, Colonel Edward Short, emphasized the importance of low-level leaders applying the lessons at the squad, platoon, and company levels.[32] In the foreword, Casey charged each American serviceman and servicewoman to "understand and apply these concepts during every operation."[33]

Petraeus took over from Wallace at the Combined Arms Center in October 2005, inheriting in the process the work Wallace had set in motion on the counterinsurgency manual. Horvath was already engaged in rewriting the interim manual.[34] Yet Petraeus did not place much credence in the existing effort, referring to the eventual rewrite he would push through as "an attempt to fill a doctrinal void."[35] The general had a tentative theory of victory that he had formed both in Iraq and as part of his dialogue with the emerging network of defense analysts, officers, defense officials, and academics on irregular warfare.

Petraeus spent the fall and winter of 2005 touring think tanks and the Department of Defense, delivering a brief titled "Thirteen Observations from Soldiering in Iraq."[36] Like General DePuy with his "pot of soup" memo, Petraeus used his initial counterinsurgency concept as the basis for a larger doctrinal vision. To refine his theory of victory, Petraeus formed an incubator, reaching outside Fort Leavenworth and the Combined Arms Center to establish a small group of thinkers to flesh out his theory of victory.

Petraeus gathered these thinkers, his "coinistas," from his contacts in the faculty at West Point and from workshops. Hosted by Harvard University's Carr Center for Human Rights, headed by Sarah Sewall, and supported by the Carnegie Corporation of New York, the workshops started in 2004 and looked at the emerging conflict in Iraq and its implications for national security.[37] The Carr Center partnered with the U.S. Army War College's Strategic

Studies Institute to hold a groundbreaking workshop, "Counterinsurgency in Iraq: Implications of Irregular Warfare for the USG [U.S. government]," in Washington, D.C., November 7–8, 2005. Petraeus attended, giving a keynote speech based on his "Thirteen Observations" brief. The workshop connected the communities exploring irregular warfare and counterinsurgency in the Department of Defense, institutional Army, and broader defense community.[38] At the conference, Petraeus recruited John Nagl and Conrad Crane—a retired Army officer and historian who had helped Sewall organize the conference—to lead his incubator in rewriting counterinsurgency doctrine.[39]

At the same time, Petraeus set out to wage a war of ideas inside the Army, publishing his brief "Learning Counterinsurgency: Observations from Soldiering in Iraq" in the January–February 2006 edition of *Military Review*.[40] The article crystallized his emerging concept, articulating ten observations as maxims guiding the conduct of counterinsurgency. Combined, the briefing and the speech were used to mobilize opinion in the Army behind a new mental model for fighting and winning counterinsurgencies. As the translation of Petraeus's vision into doctrine commenced, additional articles by the core members of the incubator and the broader community of interest augmented it. In the March–April 2006 edition of *Military Review*, Eliot Cohen, who had organized the earlier Basin Harbor workshop, teamed up with Horvath, Crane, and Nagl to publish "Principles, Imperatives, and Paradoxes of Counterinsurgency."[41]

The process continued, relying on forums to vet and refine the emerging concept. From February 23 to 24, 2006, General Petraeus, working with Marine Corps Lieutenant General James Mattis, put together a conference in counterinsurgency at Fort Leavenworth.[42] The purpose of the conference was twofold. First, it aimed to outline and vet the emerging COIN concept developed by Nagl, Crane, and other members of Petraeus's writing team. According to Nagl, the counterinsurgency concept "was built around two big ideas: first, that protecting the population was the key to success in any counterinsurgency campaign, and second, that to succeed in counterinsurgency, an army has to be able to learn and adapt more rapidly than its enemies."[43] The writing team had arrived at these insights after an exploration of the "lessons of previous successful and unsuccessful counterinsurgency campaigns, confident that, just as there are principles of conventional war that have endured for hundreds of years, there are lasting principles of 'small wars' and insurgencies that are also relevant."[44] The conference in effect vetted these concepts, introducing the ideas to a wide range of experts, human rights advocates, and veterans of earlier COIN campaigns in El Salvador and Vietnam.

Second, the conference diffused and socialized the still-forming doctrine. The conference had approximately a hundred attendees from across the Army, defense and intelligence communities, State Department, and academia. The group of attendees was much broader and eclectic than typical Army workshops. Petraeus built on the advice of his mentor, General John Galvin, and waged a "war of information" in the ranks of the Army.[45] According to Petraeus, "Producing something as important as COIN doctrine, where so many seem to hold a view, needs engagement with a much wider group than standard doctrine has traditionally needed. You have to get as many as possible inside the tent."[46]

As the writing team continued to refine the doctrine, the publication blitz continued. In October 2006, *Military Review* published a special issue reprinting many of the key pieces since 2004 dealing with counterinsurgency and irregular warfare. In the preface, Petraeus stated that the purpose of the special issue was to "complement[] the new Army/Marine Corps field manual on counterinsurgency operations" and referred to the new doctrine as the "graduate level" of war.[47]

In December 2006, the Army revealed its new counterinsurgency doctrine, *Field Manual 3-24*.[48] The doctrine elevated stability tasks as a focus of military forces to the level of offensive and defensive operations. *Field Manual 3-24* was population-centric, a variant of "hearts and minds." The focus was on governance and legitimation. According to the manual, "Political power is the central issue. . . . [E]ach side aims to get the people to accept its . . . authority as legitimate."[49] Central to winning this struggle for legitimacy was the struggle to secure the population. According to the manual, "The cornerstone of any COIN effort is establishing security for the civilian population."[50]

The manual was not without controversy. The Army Intelligence Center filed a protest against it, concerned over how the manual treated intelligence and that it had been developed outside the routine doctrinal process.[51] Defense insider and retired Army officer Ralph Peters read a draft copy that was circulating and attacked the manual as "politically correct war."[52] Despite the criticism, the manual was an instant success and became the first Army field manual published as a book, by the University of Chicago in 2007.[53]

The process in the published manual reveals the importance of incubators and advocacy networks in helping otherwise rigid organizations innovate.

True to the image of the military as a profession, knowledge networks and the codification and circulation of expertise determined the capacity for innovation. In this respect, a professional journal circulating ideas and bridging different informal networks within the Army played a significant role in paving the way for adoption. *Parameters*, a publication of the Army War College, went from publishing three pieces on counterinsurgency in 2004 to publishing eleven in 2005. In the same period *Military Review* went from publishing one piece to twenty-nine. In particular, *Military Review*, under editor Bill Darley, made its page a focal point for the emerging counterinsurgency concept.

To resonate, ideas need to diffuse across a loose network of actors in and around the profession. Bridging networks and workshops played key roles in connecting a wide variety of actors from across the defense community. The curious case of COIN illustrates the strength of weak ties, the phenomenon whereby connecting otherwise isolated actors increases the exchange of information and capacity for innovation. Forums, from the irregular warfare conferences to Eliot Cohen's Basin Harbor workshop and the workshops hosted by the Carr Center, connected a wide range of thinkers, increasing the available information and generating a space in which ideas moved between otherwise disconnected corridors of the defense community. The net result was to create an environment conducive to innovation. Before Petraeus, ideas were circulating. They just needed a senior leader to form a focal point.

Contrast *Field Manual 3-24* with *Field Manual–Interim 3-07.22: Counterinsurgency Operations* with respect to the role of incubators and advocacy networks. First, the interim manual did not use incubators. Rather, Wallace sought to develop the doctrine within the normal institutional channels. Second, Wallace and his team did not use advocacy networks to diffuse their initial ideas or concepts. This failure can be contrasted with Petraeus's championing ideas through briefs, keynote speeches, and articles in military professional journals. No incubator or advocacy network, no significant doctrinal innovation.

Yet the enduring success of the field manual is not certain. After Petraeus's tenure as commanding general at the International Security Assistance Force and then removal from his post as CIA director, criticism of his revolution emerged. The most damning critique sees COIN as an expensive fantasy and comes from a West Point faculty member, a historian, who refers to the counterinsurgency revolution as a "deadly embrace."[54] The adoption of the Army's counterinsurgency doctrine in the surge campaign planning for Afghanistan also drew criticism from Vice President Joe Biden and a wide range of veteran military officers who viewed it as "armed nation building" outside their core mandate.[55]

The New Old Idea

But was population-centric counterinsurgency new? Did the theory of victory offered by *Field Manual 3-24* offer a new vision of warfare that radically departed from existing doctrine in *Field Manual 90-8: Counterguerrilla Operations*, issued in 1986, or *Field Manual 100-20: Military Operations in Low Intensity Conflict*, issued in 1990? America is a nation born in rebellion. It stands to reason, considering the founding struggle against the British in frontier wars of conquest and against overseas contingencies starting with the Barbary pirates in 1801, that military thinkers developed and tested a wide range of concepts to best insurgent-type forces.

Contrary to the predominant thesis of an American way of war defined by "regular" conflict and a preference for mass, historians W. E. Lee and Andrew Birtle argue that the U.S. Army is "the child of the frontier."[56] Early approaches to what today we would call irregular warfare or counterinsurgency focused on coercing native populations into open battles.[57] As seen in the early American campaigns such as Major General Anthony Wayne's 1794 expedition, the U.S. Army attacked villages, destroying crops and property, to compel native peoples to abandon guerrilla warfare and fight in a more conventional style.[58]

After defeating the British, the American military experimented with different operating concepts and force structure in response to the perceived threat posed by native peoples and the rugged terrain of the frontier. In 1792, President George Washington ordered reorganization of the ground forces for counter-Indian operations under the Legion of the United States.[59] The intellectual underpinnings of the legion lay in the emergence of *petite guerre* during the eighteenth century. Practiced by a variety of actors, *petite guerre* linked small-scale raids and ambushes to confuse and attrite an enemy force to larger campaigns. In calling the force a legion, early American military thinkers sought to "describe the small, mixed corps of light cavalry and light infantry that virtually every contemporary European army employed for the purpose of waging *petite guerre*."[60]

In many ways, this form of warfare triggered a debate about the nature of warfare and American identity. Before the American Civil War there was a tendency "of soldiers to dismiss 'savage' warfare as a form of conflict less worthy of study than 'civilized' wars and the universal reluctance of legislatures, be they located in London, Philadelphia, New York, or Washington, to allocate sufficient funds for the establishment of stable, professional military forces, contributed to this shortcoming."[61] The tendency by military thinkers and politicians to discount the importance of "savage warfare" tended to relegate counterinsurgency-type concepts to informal knowledge transmission networks. Even the name given to the early experimental force design, the Legion of the United States, reflected a larger discourse framing the Americans as destined to expand the edge of civilization into the barbarian frontier, just as elite opinion at the time held that ancient Rome brought order to chaos.[62] There was a tension between being "civilized" but having to fight the "savage."

Outside the legion experiment, this tension related developing concepts and doctrine for irregular warfare to informal knowledge networks. Henry Bouquet's "Reflections on War with the Savages of North-America," William Smith's *An Historical Account of the Expedition Against the Ohio Indians, in the Year 1764*, and James Smith's *A Treatise on the Mode and Manner of Indian War* spread concepts about *petite guerre* among officers and elites interested in the military profession.[63]

Petite guerre was in the West Point curriculum as early as 1835.[64] Between 1835 and 1870, Dennis Hart Mahan incorporated lessons from America's experience in frontier war into his lectures and classes; he instructed "cadets on march, convoy, and signaling procedures suitable for irregular warfare, described how to construct a blockhouse, and gave tips on ways a beleaguered patrol could convert a farmhouse into a fortress."[65] A major theme for Mahan was identifying the principles of Indian warfare and how to use "frontiersmen and friendly Indians as auxiliaries and scouts . . . [gathering] intelligence for the purpose of exploiting intertribal tensions."[66]

In addition to these classroom outlets, military thinkers at West Point and in the War Department kept a small space alive for *petite guerre*. In 1847, Mahan wrote *An Elementary Treatise on Advanced-Guard, Out-Post, and Detachment Service of Troops*, outlining how to employ skirmishers in advance of larger conventional formations.[67] More a technical treatment than doctrinal statement, the textbook outlined how to employ small bands of soldiers to conduct harassing attacks, raids, intelligence gathering, and ambushes in advance of the main army. Similarly, in the 1857 *Regulations of the Army of the United States*, the War Department advocated forming small bands of irregular troops to harass enemy forces and control civilian populations.[68] The manual envisioned future war in which the Army would leverage these informal bands in an economy of force role, using them to control rear areas, gather intelligence, and free up the main force to target the rival military. A form of what we would today call counterinsurgency existed before the American Civil War.

By the mid-nineteenth century, the primary focus of the loose network of military thinkers, West Point faculty and officers in the War Department, was on not *petite guerre* but imagining Napoleonic warfare. In his science of war class, Mahan drew heavily on Antoine-Henri Jomini's *Traité des grandes opérations militaire*. The book used Napoleon's campaigns as a blueprint for developing a geometry of violence, a set of principles about how to fight along interior lines to best concentrate conventional forces.[69]

Napoleon's campaigns deeply influenced the young Mahan. In 1832, the Army sent him to study engineering and tactics in France.[70] In addition to teaching Jomini's interpretation of Napoleon's campaigns, Mahan established the Napoleon Club at West Point as a forum where officers could engage the history of the great general's battles and military thought. Past presidents of the club included Robert E. Lee.[71] For military historian Russell Weigley, Mahan was the chief conduit for bringing Jomini to a generation of cadets who would go on to become the generals of the American Civil War.[72]

The earlier form of savage war collided with a larger understanding of civilized war, limiting its resonance in the emerging military profession and broader American society. While Mahan was lecturing West Point cadets on Indian warfare, they were also reading Swiss diplomat Emmerich Vattel's reflections on ethics and international law.[73] Vattel's works were part of the required instruction of military and internal law. In his book *The Law of Nations*, Vattel argued for a form of Enlightenment warfare that treated the population humanely, to shield them from lawlessness and a descent to cycles of reprisal violence. War was ordering and hence had to follow the principles of rational order for establishing civilization.[74]

After 1796, there were advocacy networks but no incubators or significant elite protection. Between the treatises on frontier wars and Mahan's West Point lectures, an irregular warfare construct emerged advocating harassing adversaries with small units, applying coercion against civilian targets to force open battle, and employing auxiliaries to increase situational understanding and limit force requirements. Yet the emergent theory of victory clashed with the predominant interpretations of the Napoleonic Wars circulating in the halls of West Point. Even in one thinker, Dennis Mahan, this clash of visions of war is apparent. Antebellum-era cadet training embodied diametrically opposed views of how to practice irregular warfare.

The clearest articulation of this balancing act emerged in 1950 in an Army manual, *Operations Against Guerrilla Forces*.[75] After World War II, Sir Henry Clinton's idea of "winning hearts and subduing minds" resurfaced in antiguerrilla operations. Coming out of World War II, officers in the U.S. Army were convinced that the Soviets would wage a protracted global struggle leveraging partisan warfare. This observation emerged from reflections on the success of guerrilla movements in holding down and routing large conventional formations between 1939 and 1945.

According to the 1950 manual,

> Future war may be more global in scope than any war of the past.... [This war] will unavoidably result in guerrilla warfare in its broadest aspects. The era of atomic weapons and other mass destructive means increases the importance of guerrilla warfare from the view of both defense and offense. Scientific developments are constantly producing new means and weapons that readily lend themselves to guerrilla use. Nations benefitting from the use of guerrillas in World War II can be expected to use guerrilla forces as an integral part of their military plans and strategy.... In any campaign of the future, the participant who fails to take proper cognizance of guerrilla warfare, either in the planning or execution stages, may suffer severe setbacks, if not eventual defeat.[76]

In 1949 the Army sent Lieutenant Colonel Russell W. Volckmann to Fort Benning, Georgia, to develop a new doctrinal manual on counterguerrilla warfare.[77] During the Japanese occupation of the Philippines, Volckmann helped organized an insurgency in the mountains in northern Luzon.[78] This experience made him a valuable thinker on counterinsurgency operations. The manual, though written in the Infantry schoolhouse, was the product of one individual synthesizing his personal experiences to produce a new operational concept. It as example of what historian and World War II veteran Irving Holley meant when he referred to doctrine as the distillation of experience.[79]

Volckmann integrated his experience fighting the Japanese, in terms of their operational successes and failures, with observations of Axis counterguerrilla operations in the European theater. German operations provided a significant reference point for Army thinkers. In 1944 the U.S. Army translated the German Army manual *Fighting the Guerrilla Bands* and released it to the force.[80] By 1949, the Army had sponsored publication of over twenty monographs written by German officers on their wartime experience fighting against partisans.[81] These studies and analyses of German antipartisan operations circulated in both close-hold memos and professional journals throughout the 1950s, providing an intellectual forum to think about rear area security operations in Korea and support to anticommunist movements from Greece to China.[82]

German practices emphasized using combined arms maneuver to encircle and destroy guerrilla bands. They focused less on an integrated political-military campaign and more on isolating and interdicting irregular combatants. Since 1871, the German military had approached the question of small wars often in terms of scorched-earth-type tactics designed to compel the population to deny guerrillas sanctuary. The emphasis, much like early American frontier war, was on forcing guerrillas to take the field against superior conventional forces.[83] It was the antithesis of winning hearts and minds.

During World War II, the Germans also used special formations, *Jagdkommando* units, for antipartisan operations. These small units operated independently in dispersed hunter-killer formations and in conjunction with passive security measures that protected critical infrastructure and lines of communication using a mix of police forces and auxiliaries. The central idea of these antipartisan operations was simple: annihilate the threat.

Volckmann's experience led him to view Japanese repressive measures directed at the general population as counterproductive. Coercion without a political strategy to win over the population would only generate future guerrillas. Therefore, Volckmann added aspects of German coercive techniques to a primary political campaign to win popular support. As articulated in *Operations Against Guerrilla Forces*, the first and primary component of any counterguerrilla strategy was a political-military plan based on the unique character of the country and its population.[84] Such a plan should seek to "foster trust and goodwill between the Army and the people by restoring law, order, and socioeconomic stability; [provide] humanitarian relief; and [initiate] programs to alleviate some of the grievances that might fuel resistance movements."[85] In the manual Volckmann argued, "Guerrilla units cannot exist without the support of the population" and that "to be successful, anti-guerrilla operations must be based on a broad, realistic plan that coordinates not only the political, administrative and military phases of the operation but also the activities or adjacent areas and anti-guerrilla commands."[86]

Volckmann drew on the German tradition and *Jagdkommando* to emphasize using guerrilla tactics on the guerrilla by conducting high-tempo operations, including raids and ambushes, to keep the enemy off balance. Guerrillas destabilized the entire political system, targeting a force's political and economic cohesion as well as its ability to maintain freedom of movement.

To attack guerrillas like a guerrilla therefore meant using small bands to disrupt their freedom of movement while denying their ability to influence and leverage the general population. These operations were not strictly military. According to Volckmann,

> The isolation of guerrilla forces from the civilian population may be greatly influenced by the treatment given the civilians. In all areas there are people who want peace and quiet. Friendly and cooperative elements of the populace are carefully cultivated. The news of good treatment spreads rapidly and is an important factor in establishing trust and friendly relations between the civilian population and our military forces. The populace is encouraged to band together to resist extortion and threats from the guerrillas, and the cooperative elements are protected. Law and order is established and strictly enforced. Peacefulness is further stimulated by encouraging the people to resume their normal pursuits.[87]

Volckmann envisioned a mixed campaign in which "a commander, charged with combating hostile guerrillas and extending control over a country, moves his assigned forces into the area, establishes local bases of operations, and takes appropriate security and administrative measures."[88] This campaign called for establishing a governing function over "political, economic, financial, social, and industrial functions."[89] Though written over fifty years before *Field Manual 3-24*, the ideas are remarkably similar, indicating that population-centric counterinsurgency is old wine in a new bottle.

There appears to be a persistent cycle of forgetting counterinsurgency in the U.S. Army. Bureaucracies are supposed to codify and capture knowledge, translating ideas into binding routines. Yet a particular idea, such as how to fight irregular war, can clash with larger civilizational discourses, as seen in earlier *petite guerre* episodes, and deeper debates on the character and nature of organized violence. The military is still embedded within a larger array of social forces. These larger currents can alter the flow of ideas in a defense organization and how concepts emerge into theories of victory and doctrine.

Conclusion

The release of the 2006 counterinsurgency doctrine altered doctrine; it did not usher in a new theory of victory or redefine critical tasks. Incubators and advocacy networks were present, but the degree of doctrinal change was minimal. Furthermore, it is difficult to reject alternative explanations. The roles of exogenous shock and the threat of civilian intervention loom in the shadows, complicating an otherwise heroic story of a general who changed the Army.

With respect to incubators and advocacy networks, the case illustrates military professionals seeking to adapt. Problem-driven search exercises converged in the production of *Field Manual 3-24*. Wallace used observations from exercises and simulations to push the bureaucracy to reconsider counterinsurgency. Yet he did not do so using the form of incubators studied in previous chapters. Rather, Wallace worked within the Combined Arms Center bureaucracy. General Petraeus proved to be a master of generating sites that were removed from the bureaucracy where a broad network of military professionals and civilians could analyze the conflict in Iraq in relation to the larger category of stability operations and counterinsurgency. This case, more than those in previous chapters, illustrates a wider range of actors establishing intellectual forums to reconsider how to fight in Iraq after the fall of Baghdad. Whether out of the conferences in Quantico or from Eliot Cohen's Basin Harbor workshop, incubators appeared as the demand for new approaches to the conflict increased. There appears to have been a responsive practitioner network in Washington.

Like AirLand Battle and Full-Dimensional Operations, the case highlights the crucial role of advocacy networks. Through a mix of briefings and professional journals, a constellation of thinkers around Petraeus diffused the concept of population-centric counterinsurgency. Journals like *Military Review* found their pages exploding with advocacy and reflections on how to apply it in Iraq and Afghanistan. The vibrancy of this dialogue seems to indicate a healthy profession, like the reflective, responsive practitioner network, crafting and disseminating new knowledge.

Senior leaders like Petraeus aggressively worked behind the scenes to protect their concepts. The general engaged in positional legitimation, using his office to protect and propagate the new idea. From writing articles and publishing his counterinsurgency guidance to working behind the scenes to move officers associated with developing the manual into general-officer ranks, Petraeus was on the offensive.

With respect to alternative explanations of change, civilian intervention and the threat of defeat cloud the story. Civilians, even if they were retired officers, in the Defense Department seem to have played an important role in pushing the military to (re)imagine counterinsurgency. The early conferences in Quantico and follow-on workshop held by Eliot Cohen suggest less military autonomy than the previous cases. Although since the 1980s interest had grown in a wide range of military operations short of major war, the setbacks in Iraq provided a significant exogenous shock, motivating civilians to scrutinize the Army.

It is difficult to disentangle where these external pressures stop and the imaginative military professional starts. The later stages of developing *Field Manual 3-24* coincided with a larger strategy review. In September 2006, while Petraeus's team was already working on the new doctrine, General Peter Pace, chairman of the Joint Chiefs of Staff, launched a panel to review the Iraq war policy. This council included individuals who were connected to the broader Petraeus network that was revising counterinsurgency concepts, including Colonels Peter Mansoor and H. R. McMaster.[90] This network was also active through think tanks like the American Enterprise Institute, where retired general Jack Keane campaigned for a new counterinsurgency strategy.[91]

The manual's release in December 2006 coincided with the review panel's release of its findings that current strategy in Iraq was failing. The counterinsurgency concept appears to have preceded the policy window of opportunity.

Alternative explanations linked to technologically induced change and an enduring, attrition-based way of war do not seem to be factors in explaining the emergence of *Field Manual 3-24*. More than any previous theory of victory and associated doctrine, population-centric counterinsurgency does not rely on new capabilities or attrition. If anything, the ghost of irregular warfare has haunted the American military professional since the days of *petite guerre* and frontier wars.

6 Incubators, Advocacy Networks, and Organizational Change

THIS BOOK EXPLORES HOW MILITARY PROFESSIONALS IN THE U.S. Army changed their doctrine. Specifically, it analyzes the unique role played by knowledge networks that allowed new ideas to form and diffuse in an otherwise rigid and complex bureaucracy. The historical cases from the thirty-year period investigated confirm the importance of two institutional mechanisms: incubators and advocacy networks.

Incubators, informal subunits established outside the hierarchy, provided a safe space where officers could escape the iron cage of bureaucracy. These professionals proved adept escape artists. These safe spaces provided critical sites for organizational exploration and speculation. They were the forums in which officers developed new theories of victory articulating how the Army should fight and the form of new future conflicts.

Advocacy networks, the pathways along which new ideas circulated through the broader defense community, provided the connective tissue. These networks connected different constituents in the defense bureaucracy. The networks acted as contagion vectors, infecting other officers and defense officials with new ideas. New doctrine required forums where officers could (re)imagine war and networks along which they could tell their story.

These institutional mechanisms are the focus of this concluding chapter. It reviews the empirical evidence from the cases and considers what they tell us in general about doctrinal change in military organizations. It then uses

TABLE 6.1 Core propositions on doctrinal innovation

Proposition	Doctrine	Observation
Incubators increase the likelihood of emergence of new ideas	Active Defense	Multiple incubators studied the Arab-Israeli War
	AirLand Battle	Multiple incubators analyzed potential battles in the Fulda Gap, including the battle calculus studies and Extended Battlefield network group
	Full-Dimensional Operations	Multiple incubators included the "View of the 1990s" brief, Antaeus, and battle labs
	Counterinsurgency	Multiple incubators were used by military and nonmilitary actors, including the Carr Center for Human Rights and Basin Harbor workshop
Advocacy networks diffuse new ideas across the organization	Active Defense	Advocacy appeared as more limited leadership engagement and political conferences designed to co-opt potential opposition
	AirLand Battle	Senior leaders, in a professional journal blitz, wrote articles in all the major journals to support the new doctrine
	Full-Dimensional Operations	A wider network than in previous cases reached out to not just civilian officials but nongovernment personnel
	Counterinsurgency	As with Full-Dimensional Operations, the mix of civilian and nongovernment personnel diffusing the new theory of victory widened; professional journals became an important forum for disseminating new ideas
Senior leaders help protect new ideas	Active Defense	General DePuy initiated change and acted as a focal point for concept development
	AirLand Battle	General Starry personally participated in studies; General Richardson protected the extended battlefield study
	Full-Dimensional Operations	Multiple senior leaders acted as focal points for change
	Counterinsurgency	General Petraeus became the hub of an intellectual network connecting the Army and broader defense community

the findings, summarized in Table 6.1, to reflect on how military organizations change and the implications for defense policy.

Reflections on Incubators

Protected sites separated from the bureaucracy were a crucial aspect of doctrinal change in each case investigated. These incubators provided the forum where military professionals escaped the iron cage to reimagine warfare. They exhibited three properties of interest for considering how organizations change.

First, officers tend to frame operational problems through careful study and analysis. More often than not, these framing studies reflect an inductive approach to knowledge construction in the military profession. The officer is a pragmatist, who, as Clausewitz outlined in book 2, chapter 5 of *On War*, engages in critical analysis of experience to derive new military theories.[1] In Active Defense, analysis of the Arab-Israeli War provided the foundation for developing a new theory of victory. In the development of AirLand Battle, studies like the Extended Battlefield network proved critical to refining a deep-strike concept. After the last days of the Cold War, the Army relied on concept-driven studies like Antaeus in 1988 and the follow-on joint-exercise Quiet Plan to explore how the organization could respond to a change in strategy.

Second, officers rely on problem-driven simulation to refine new concepts. Creativity is problem driven, linked to a shifting aspect of warfare that bends the logic of an old approach. While at Fort Knox, General Starry helped develop the Active Defense doctrine through the Hunfeld I exercise, testing new defensive concepts. The profession proved able to generate new knowledge, as answers to operational problems, through incubators. Between 1977 and 1979, the Central Battle simulations at V Corps helped invalidate Active Defense and provided the space in which officers could develop new constructs for countering the Soviets. In the 1990s, General Sullivan used a range of initiatives, from the Louisiana Maneuvers to battle laboratories, to usher in an era of experimentation. The profession requires the space to experiment, to test concepts and challenge assumptions about future war.

Third, size matters. Small proved beautiful. Some of the most innovative work and imaginative thinking was done by small cohorts as opposed to sprawling groups. The most successful doctrinal manuals were the product of a small writing team. DePuy relied on his boathouse gang to refine his vision, originally articulated in the "pot of soup" memo. Starry used the faculty of the Army's Command and General Staff College to write AirLand Battle. This practice stands in sharp contrast to the modern practice of writing by committee, in which hundreds of officers make contributions that are cut and pasted by coordinators: knowledge production through satisificing. Long

"To" lines and crowded conference rooms can prove the antithesis of nimble thought and free expression.

Reflections on Advocacy Networks

Looking across the successful episodes of doctrinal change, advocacy networks relied on brokerage to spread ideas and senior leaders to protect them. Brokerage connects previously less connected or distant parties. As a mechanism, this connecting of two sites increases the type of information each previous network had access to. It creates what we might call infection pathways. As military professionals develop new theories of victory they need to reach beyond their immediate peers to infect the larger institution. The more of the institution the networks can connect to, the more likely they are to increase the perceived legitimacy of the advocated idea.

In seeking to create a space to change the Army, General DePuy proved a master of brokering new interorganizational connections. In 1973, he used the "Impetus for Change" paper, summarizing the results of a range of pilot projects and special panels, to justify his proposals for reorganizing the Army. It was an example of outside-in legitimation, using brokerage to spread his idea and then leveraging this wider network to justify change. DePuy similarly used the Octoberfest conferences, analyzing the "new lethality," to entrap potential critics and infect them with his theory of victory. Again in the second Octoberfest, the 1975 Oftcon, DePuy entrapped potential critics through orchestrating a political conference designed to get buy-in from the light infantry community for Active Defense. The general also used references to German tactics to legitimate his operational concept, yoking *Panzergrenadier* tactics and Active Defense in correspondence with members of Congress, the Army staff, and think tanks like RAND. Years later, General Powell showed the same bureaucratic instinct, using the "View of the 1990s" brief to introduce the idea of base force as the framework for transitioning out of the Cold War. The more sites connected, the more likely the idea is to resonate.

The cases illustrate an important role for professional journals. Military journals proved an important arena for socializing ideas to the broader profession. Ideas had to circulate beyond senior leaders. Brokerage in this way can be thought of as occurring at two levels. Senior leaders orchestrate political conferences and briefs as a means of deliberately connecting actors inside and across bureaucracies. Journals—as infection pathways—represent a lower, less orchestrated manner of infection. Their pages are open to not just the talking points of general officers but the retorts of angry majors.

Senior leaders protect new ideas. Without their stamp of approval, in a hierarchical organization change proves elusive. With respect to doctrinal change in the Army, this positional legitimacy proved a key sufficient condition for sparking innovation. In Active Defense, DePuy used a series of Army-wide briefs in 1974 to socialize the lessons learned from the Arab-Israeli War as they related to a new theory of victory for modern combined arms. Similarly, his "pot of soup" memo, sent to all schoolhouse commanders, represented a form of socialization in which commanders were introduced to the new theory of victory and asked to contribute. With respect to AirLand Battle, Starry orchestrated a doctrinal blitz in 1981 targeting middle-tier officers. By writing articles, he sought to protect the emerging AirLand Battle concept and create a space for younger officers to apply it.

Reflections on Military Innovation

How do incubators and advocacy networks, as the types of institutional mechanisms professionals use to escape their iron cage, compare with rival explanations? A second goal of this book is to situate incubators and advocacy networks in relation to existing arguments on the sources of doctrinal innovation.

As shown in Table 6.2, investigation of the episodes of doctrinal change in this book make it impossible to reject the argument that threats to the organization's core mission, whether from rivalry or exogenous shock in the form of potential defeat, incentivize reluctant officers to develop new doctrine. In Active Defense, there were exogenous shocks and no evidence that bureaucratic competition drove doctrinal change. Vietnam loomed in the background, but professional officers shifted their focus to imagining future wars in Europe. The Arab-Israeli War provided a focal point for concept development, departing from ten years of arraying light infantry forces across a Southeast Asian battlefield. Interestingly, the shock seems to have been someone else's war. The Army learned by proxy.

In the development of AirLand Battle, exogenous shocks and bureaucratic competition did not play a role. There was no immediate threat to the Army's core mission or autonomy. Professionals sought to develop new war fighting

TABLE 6.2 Evaluating alternative arguments on doctrinal innovation

Alternative proposition	Doctrine	Observation	Summary
Threats to the organization's core mission, whether from rivalry or exogenous shock in the form of potential defeat, incentivize reluctant officers to develop new doctrine	Active Defense	No significant evidence	*Mixed:* the impetus for doctrinal change is varied and complex
	AirLand Battle	No evidence	
	Full-Dimensional Operations	Mixed	
	COIN, Full-Spectrum Operations	Mixed	
New technology is associated with the emergence of new doctrine	Active Defense	Mixed	*No significant evidence:* the perception of technology and its place in doctrine shifts among the cases
	AirLand Battle	No evidence	
	Full-Dimensional Operations	Mixed	
	COIN, Full-Spectrum Operations	No evidence	
Civilian intervention drives larger magnitude change in doctrine	Active Defense	No evidence	*No significant evidence:* only post–Cold War cases reveal any degree of civilian intervention
	AirLand Battle	No evidence	
	Full-Dimensional Operations	No significant evidence	
	COIN, Full-Spectrum Operations	Mixed	
Doctrinal change is weighted toward an enduring, attritionist American way of war	Active Defense	No significant evidence	*No evidence:* military professionals seem just as likely to manipulate strategic currents and shift their organizational culture as they are to be bound by it
	AirLand Battle	No evidence	
	Full-Dimensional Operations	No evidence	
	COIN, Full-Spectrum Operations	No evidence	

concepts under the framework of a clear mission: provide a conventional deterrent in Europe. That said, the resulting doctrine would likely have narrowed policy options in the event of a military crisis. With its emphasis on deep strike and disruption of enemy staging areas, AirLand Battle was primed for escalation. This dynamic was a function of how the Army (inaccurately) assessed the threat in the late 1970s and early 1980s. It raises the question of how worst-case organizational assessments can impair security and lead to what Barry Posen refers to as inadvertent escalation.[2]

In Full-Dimensional Operations the evidence of exogenous shocks is more mixed. Dramatic budget cuts accompanied the end of the Cold War. Yet military officers seem to have anticipated these cuts as early as 1987 and through projects like Antaeus started to consider how to respond to future threats with a smaller force. There is no significant evidence of civilian intervention. The push and pull of bureaucracy focused more on how cuts would fall across the services. Rather than produce significant service rivalry, this friction led to an onslaught of doctrinal publications as each branch sought to reimagine warfare.

More than budgets, the end of the Cold War itself was a significant shock to the Army's assumptions about the types of conflicts it might fight. To fill this intellectual void, the Army focused on recent conflicts, including Operations Just Cause and Desert Storm. The case suggests, at least anecdotally, that military organizations seek conceptual anchors for thinking about future war. Just as the Arab-Israeli War provided a framework for thinking about the new lethality, the invasions of Panama and Kuwait served as vehicles for thinking about simultaneous attack and precision. This dynamic is also at play in how military organizations tend to use (and abuse) history. Historical cases, in the form of campaigns and famous battles, become a means of synthesizing operating concepts. Doctrine writers use historical cases as a solution to a current problem.[3]

In the development of *Field Manual 3-24: Counterinsurgency Operations*, battlefield setbacks provided the initial impetus for revisiting doctrine. There also were multiple, convergent communities of interest pushing the U.S. Army from inside and outside to reconsider how it approached counterinsurgency. In fact, these communities and the advocacy networks that connected them reached beyond the normal military pathways to civilian academics and nonprofit organizations.

A clear threat in the form of the Soviet Union tended to focus conceptual discussion for the Army. Absent this threat, a greater degree of uncertainty in imagining future wars and preserving organizational autonomy emerged. Yet in each instance incubators and advocacy networks proved important institutional mechanisms for waging a war of ideas in the Army.

With respect to technological shocks as the driver of doctrinal change, there is no significant evidence for that in the cases examined. In Active Defense, concerns about the new lethality contained detailed assessments of the impact of precision-guided weapons. Yet these observations did not exist in isolation. Officers synthesized insights gleaned from battles in the Arab-Israeli War with reflections on the nature of combined arms maneuver to imagine new forms of defense in Western Europe.

In the intellectual development that culminated in the publication of Air-Land Battle in 1982, technological push also does not appear to be a decisive factor. The Army factored in no fundamental changes in weapons systems when studying new concepts. If anything, the causation was reversed. The operational concept in AirLand Battle provided a rationale and a conceptual space to imagine how to employ projected future capabilities. At the strategic level, the relationship was clouded. Beginning with the Soviet SS-20, changing nuclear forces altered threat calculations but in a manner that placed a higher premium on fielding a credible conventional deterrent.

After the Cold War, the lack of an overarching threat focus may have catalyzed a tendency to consider capabilities. The character of war and the entire concept of a postindustrial army abruptly changed owing to the revolution in military affairs (RMA). New technologies, and their demonstration in the Gulf War, affected doctrine development. Alternatively, RMA-infused thinking did not influence counterinsurgency doctrine. Rather, the military professional oscillates between two images of future war: stability operations along with attempts to secure interests in failing states and the continued proliferation of RMA capabilities to state and nonstate actors.

With respect to a cultural thesis and the influence of an enduring American way of war on the development of operational doctrine, the cases provide no significant evidence. In the development of Active Defense, offense and defense, maneuver and attrition blend. While the doctrine emphasized firepower, and suppression correlates with an attrition-based approach, the reality is more complex. From Starry's experiments with a cascading series of tactical counterattacks and DePuy's concept of screening and blocking forces, Active Defense used multiple forms of maneuver to buy time for a second-echelon counterattack. Firepower and attrition were means to an end. Air-Land Battle, with the central idea of a destabilizing attack in depth, is the antithesis of attrition.

There is similarly no evidence for this in Full-Dimensional Operations or *Field Manual 3-24*. The idea of optimizing the Army for a wider range of contingencies (e.g., military operations other than war) runs counter to an attritional orientation. With respect to counterinsurgency, winning hearts and minds reflects a fundamentally different operational problem.

The postindustrial army is the first instance investigated in which the military professional leaned toward an attritional concept. The vision of warfare in the 525-5 pamphlet series and the Force XXI program was on precision firepower and perfect information for identifying and targeting enemy formations en masse. The intent emphasized collapsing the enemy through firepower more than offsetting him through maneuver.

An enduring, attrition-based American way of war did not play an overt role in shaping Army doctrine. The military professional proved to be more pragmatist than ideologue. The officers were Clausewitz's chameleon, assessing the evolving character of war and responding in kind with new concepts.

Implications for Defense Policy: Cultivating the Brain of an Army

In 1878, Emroy Upton, an American Civil War Army veteran and faculty member at West Point, published an account of the world's land forces.[4] Earlier, in 1870, General William T. Sherman, the chief of staff of the Army, had sent Upton to study the world's military forces, hoping to find a new path for the U.S. Army. In 1890 Spenser Wilkinson, a journalist at the Manchester *Guardian*, published *The Brain of an Army: A Popular Account of the German General Staff.* The work was originally an essay that paralleled an ongoing royal commission, led by Lord Hartington, on how Great Britain should organize for national defense.[5] Both treatments focused on how to create thinking organizations. These classics in turn highlight an enduring dilemma at the core of doctrine development in the military profession: How do you create adaptive, learning organizations?

The cases under investigation offer some tentative answers to this question. First, *do not cut off oxygen to the brain.* Training, exercises, and education—the types of ecosystems in which incubators thrive—become easy targets for officials looking for programs to cut. Often these parts of the profession lack external patrons, such as business interests and congressional advocates. Cutting professional military education, field exercises, or small organizations dedicated to research does not make headlines the way a cut to a major weapons program or force strength does. Yet to preserve the capacity for innovation and adaptation, these are exactly the last organizations that should be cut in times of austerity.

Army leaders can increase knowledge production in the profession by protecting funds for framing studies and problem-driven simulation in incubators at multiple levels. These teams should be led by uniformed officers, not contractors. The last twelve years at war have pulled the attention of the officer corps in the United States to near-term tactical fights as opposed to imagining the next war. Because the profession focused on tactics and survival it created an institutional void filled by contractors. Officers were not available for war games or special study groups to develop operational concepts and new stories about future war. Outsourcing imagining war to private contractors risks undermining the profession.

The military needs to own its ideas and ensure they are internally scrutinized by a professional class of officers. It is time to reclaim the profession and incentivize young officers to work on future war studies and conduct experiments instead of contracting these exercises out to hordes of think tanks and for-profit firms staffed by retired officers whose experience is not always relevant to the problem at hand.

Second, senior leaders need to not only protect knowledge construction sites but also *encourage creative destruction* and a constant war of ideas in the profession. More than just connecting multiple networks of key decision makers, this requires leaders to signal a commitment to an intellectually vibrant officer corps. Senior military leaders need to be humble and encourage debate rather than dictate answers. More "pot of soup" memos that circulate for review and commentary are needed than maxims as guidance.

It also requires clever incentives linked to publication and research in the profession. If we are cultivating a "brain of an army," to use Wilkinson's term, the schoolhouse should matter. Professional military education should not be reduced to checking a box for rising warrior bureaucrats. The military should groom reflective professional officers educated in research methods and held to high academic standards that require more than twenty-page theses. Publication in top military journals needs to become a requirement for top performance, beyond seeking awards for writing. Officers must take responsibility for the intellectual vitality of the profession.

The professional military education system should form a key connective hub linking research and concept development with experimentation and service-level war games like the Army's Title 10 exercise, Unified Quest. Just as the classrooms at Fort Leavenworth helped develop AirLand Battle, so too should future generations of officers propose and test new theories of victory while in resident schools. The profession needs a site where knowledge production connects to the core mission and empowers rising leaders to experiment and develop new approaches to land warfare.

This connective hub is unlikely to emerge without significant reform. Modern professional military educational institutions struggle to balance a congressionally mandated curriculum with preserving space to reflect on history and warfare trends. Often staffed by a mix of retired officers and civilian academics, some of whom fail to meet the requirements of tenure at nonmilitary academic institutions, they struggle to look beyond the horizon at future war and often fail to integrate current operating concepts into the curriculum. After the publication of *Field Manual 3-24*, an initial wave of activity at these schools sought to integrate the new doctrine into their curriculum. In 2007 and 2008, the Army, Navy, and Marine Corps held conferences on how to integrate the new doctrine into their professional military education and broader training programs. Yet many of these initiatives failed to materialize as new courses or as a broader change in organizational culture with respect to how the institutions approached teaching counterinsurgency tactics. Between 2006 and 2009, officers in the Army decried their educational institution's failure to respond to the demands of counterinsurgency. Writing in 2009, Major Niel Smith claimed that "the U.S. Army has failed to integrate counterinsurgency (COIN) into Professional Military Education (PME)."[6] A 2009 survey by the National Strategy Information Center found inadequate instruction on irregular warfare across the professional military education system.[7] A 2010 congressional investigation found that institutions like the Army failed to translate the national defense strategy and the vision of the chairman of the Joint Chiefs of Staff, both of which evaluated counterinsurgency as a top priority, into significant curriculum offerings.[8]

Failing to integrate counterinsurgency doctrine in a timely manner is possibly a symptom of a larger disorder. The Army tends to teach the last war. Prior battles become bureaucratic anchors. They produce the illusion of certainty and enduring principles of war. Overly simplified historical anecdotes emerge in place of open speculation and experimentation. The bureaucracy locks in routines and perspectives that simplify the uncertainty and nonlinear dynamics inherent in warfare. Along these lines, Joan Johnson-Freese, an instructor at the Naval War College, questions the extent to which the current education system produces intellectually agile leaders.[9] A 2010 congressional investigation "found that many curricular developments . . . were ineffective in anticipation of emerging opportunities and challenge."[10]

To have a "brain of an army" will require the ability to develop new ideas. A healthy profession is one that produces new knowledge and perfects its art. For the Army, that requires reimagining what professional military education is and how it integrates with the larger concept development and experimentation enterprise. Aligning professional military education with concept development and experimentation helps the Army reach the goal historian

Williamson Murray envisions of building a profession able to "innovate in peacetime and adapt to the unexpected conditions of combat."[11]

In addition to professional journals and the schoolhouse, the war of ideas should take place online in a forum younger officers are comfortable with. This trend toward web-based platforms to enable the lateral sharing of best practices started in 2000 when a group of young officers created a website in their spare time. The idea was to reimagine a professional forum as a series of "peer-to-peer connections and conversations that cut across the Army structure, not limited by geography or the formal organization."[12] The group gifted the site to West Point, where Colonel George B. Forsythe helped them establish the Center for the Advancement of Leader Development and Organizational Learning (CALDOL), and the online sharing network is now at http://cc.army.mil.[13]

The group viewed peer-to-peer networks exchanging ideas about war fighting as deepening the profession. According to the creators of the website, "The Army profession is effective only to the degree that its members take responsibility for it, engage in the collective conversation that shapes it, and see themselves as being connected to their fellow warriors."[14] In agreement with the argument presented in this book about advocacy networks, the website creators viewed themselves as championing a "third-generation leadership" model, in which "connecting leaders in a conversation about their work transforms the individuals who participate as well as the whole profession."[15]

This bottom-up, adaptive approach to professional discourse quickly spread beyond its West Point origins. In 2004, Major General Peter Chiarelli leveraged a series of experimental collaborative command and control systems during his deployment to Iraq as the First Cavalry Division commander, including having his staff develop a web tool, CAVNET, similar to http://cc.army.mil. Starting in March 2005, *Army Magazine*, the flagship publication of the Association of the United States Army, began publishing highlights from http://cc.army.mil. In another shift to peer-to-peer informal exchange networks, in 2005 a group of former marines founded the Small War Foundation and created http://smallwarsjournal.com to exchange best practices associated with irregular warfare and counterinsurgency.

To sustain future innovation, the Army should encourage these peer-to-peer forums and continue, either formally or through organizations like the Association of the United States Army, to reproduce the best content. The key is to ensure that the dialogue is not trapped within the iron cage and the hierarchy of military bureaucracy. The observations need to be spontaneous and random to ensure a vibrant set of ideas in circulation. Of note, http://cc.army.mil and http://smallwarsjournal.com started outside the formal hierarchy. They are, to a large extent, digital incubators albeit in a more disaggregated form than the senior studies reviewed in this book.

Another means of ensuring a wider circulation of ideas within the military is to further develop the idea of officer-broadening assignments. The idea of broadening first appeared in the January 2012 Army chief of staff's "Marching Orders," in which he charged the institution to "develop bold, adaptive, and broadened leaders."[16] Broad opportunities expose Army officers to different institutions and perspectives.[17] The argument is that stepping out of a traditional Army duty position will open future leaders to new ideas. For example, one of the broadening opportunities is for field-grade officers to serve a one-year tour as an Army Fellow at the RAND Arroyo Center in Santa Monica, California. RAND has a long history as a federally funded research center working on doctrinal issues. For example, during the rollout of *Field Manual 3-24* between 2006 and 2008, RAND researchers produced ten monographs on counterinsurgency.[18]

Another example of a successful broadening fellowship is the Chief of Staff of the Army Strategic Studies Group. In 2012, General Ray Odierno founded the group and charged it, a collection of eighteen officers and civilians, with exploring emerging trends to generate new concepts for land forces and recommending to senior Army leaders a road map to develop and integrate these ideas.[19] The group's 2012 report on war fighting in megacities helped shape Unified Quest, the Army Title 10 war game, and concept development in different branches. Senior leaders should continue to encourage these broadening fellowships and use them as special study groups for imagining future warfare and developing future doctrine.

A profession is defined by a shared body of knowledge and expertise. Healthy professions continue to produce new knowledge, forcing critical self-reflection and the destruction of old assumptions as new ideas emerge. For example, no one wants to go to a doctor who routinely prescribes lobotomies. What idea espoused by senior military leaders today not subject to professional criticism will appear just as ridiculous as lobotomies in the future?

Notes

Foreword

1. Quoted in Ministry of Defence, "Strategic Trends Programme: Future Character of Conflict," p. 2, https://www.gov.uk/government/uploads/system/uploads/attachment_data/file/33685/FCOCReadactedFinalWeb.pdf (accessed October 23, 2015).
2. MacGregor Knox and Williamson Murray, *The Dynamics of Military Revolution, 1300–2050* (New York: Cambridge University Press, 2001), 188.
3. I. B. Holley Jr., *Technology and Military Doctrine: Essays on a Challenging Relationship* (Montgomery, AL: Air University Press, 2004), 1.

Chapter 1

1. Thomas Mahnken, *Uncovering Ways of War: U.S. Intelligence and Foreign Military Innovation, 1918–1941* (Ithaca, NY: Cornell University Press, 2002), 169; see also Thomas Mahnken, "Uncovering Foreign Military Innovation," *Journal of Strategy Studies* 24, no. 4 (1999): 26–54.
2. For an analysis of the importance of overcoming routines to enable innovation as a form of learning, see the work of Chris Argyris, including *Reasoning, Learning, and Action* (San Francisco: Jossey-Bass, 1982); *Strategy, Change and Defensive Reform* (Boston: Pitman, 1985); *Overcoming Organizational Defenses* (Needham Heights, MA: Allyn and Bacon, 1990); and *On Organizational Learning* (Cambridge, MA: Blackwell Business, 1993).
3. Mark Edward Lewis, *The Early Chinese Empires: Qin and Han*, vol. 1 (Cambridge, MA: Harvard University Press, 2007).
4. J. van Ooteghem, *Gaius Marius* (Brussels: Académie Royale de Belgique, 1964); Philip Kildahl, *Gaius Marius* (New York: Irvington, 1968).

5. John Jay Johnson, *The Military and Society in Latin America* (Palo Alto, CA: Stanford University Press, 1964), 71–73.

6. Rupert Smith, *The Utility of Force: The Art of War in the Modern World* (London: Penguin), 96; Harald Høiback, "What Is Doctrine?" *Journal of Strategic Studies* 34, no. 6 (2011): 881.

7. The 1875 *Service Regulations* were a response to defeat in the Franco-Prussian War. Joseph Arnold, "French Tactical Doctrine, 1870–1914," *Military Affairs* 42, no. 2 (1978): 61; Jonathan M. House, "The Decisive Attack: A New Look at French Infantry Tactics on the Eve of World War I," *Military Affairs* 40, no. 4 (1976): 164–169.

8. Quoted in Keith B. Bickel, *Mars Learning: The Marine Corps' Development of Small Wars Doctrine, 1915–1940* (Boulder, CO: Westview, 2001), 2. See also Dudley W. Knox, "The Role of Doctrine in Naval Warfare," *U.S. Naval Institute Proceedings* 41, no. 2 (1915): 325–354.

9. This theme is captured in Barry Posen, *The Sources of Military Doctrine: France, Britain, and Germany Between the Wars* (Ithaca, NY: Cornell University, 1986); James Q. Wilson, *Bureaucracy* (New York: Basic Books, 1989), 219–221; Stephen Rosen, *Winning the Next War: Innovation and the Modern Military* (Ithaca, NY: Cornell University Press, 1994), 4; Karl W. Deutsch, "On Theory and Research in Innovation," in *Innovation in the Public Sector*, ed. Richard L. Merritt and Anna J. Merritt (Beverly Hills, CA: Sage, 1985), 17–35; and Marshall W. Meyer, *Change in Public Bureaucracies* (London: Cambridge University Press, 1979).

10. Anthony Downs, *Inside Bureaucracy* (Boston: Little, Brown, 1967), 198–200; Morton Halperin, *Bureaucratic Politics and Foreign Policy* (Washington, DC: Brookings Institution Press, 1974); Jack Snyder, *The Ideology of the Offensive* (Ithaca, NY: Cornell University Press).

11. Rosen, *Winning the Next War*, 8–9.

12. The term "theory of victory" denotes a fundamental idea about how to wage war. Colin Gray first used the term in "A Nuclear Strategy: The Case for a Theory of Victory," *International Security* 4, no. 1 (1979): 54–87. He expands on the idea further in *War, Peace and Victory* (New York: Routledge, 2014), 19. Gray built on Bernard Brodie's *War and Politics* (New York: Macmillan, 1973).

13. Deborah Avant, "The Institutional Sources of Military Doctrine: Hegemons in Peripheral Wars," *International Studies Quarterly* 37, no. 4 (1993): 410; Allan Millett, Williamson Murray, and Kenneth Watman, "The Effectiveness of Military Organizations," *International Security* 11, no. 1 (1986): 37–71.

14. Gordon R. Sullivan, "Army Imperative in Peacetime: Keep the Edge," *Army Times*, January 6, 1992, p. 2.

15. J. F. C. Fuller, *The Conduct of War, 1789–1961* (New Brunswick, NJ: Rutgers University Press, 1961), 254.

16. For a discussion of a grammar of war, see Antulio J. Echevarria II, "Reconsidering War's Logic and Grammar," *Infinity Journal* 1, no. 2 (2011), https://www.infinityjournal.com/article/7/Reconsidering_Wars_Logic_and_Grammar.

17. Høiback, "What Is Doctrine?" 887.

18. Wilson, *Bureaucracy*, 26.

19. Bickel, *Mars Learning*, 5.

20. Andrew Birtle, *U.S. Army Counterinsurgency and Contingency Operations Doctrine, 1860–1941* (Washington, DC: Center for Military History, 2011), 11; Henry Bouquet, "Reflections on War with the Savages of North-America," in *An Historical Account of the Expedition against the Ohio Indians, in the Year 1764*, by William Smith (Philadelphia: W. Bradford, 1765), 37–59; James Smith, *A Treatise on the Mode and Manner of Indian War* (Paris, KY: Joel R. Lyle, 1812).

21. For an overview of Dennis Hart Mahan and his teaching on Indian Wars at West Point, see Bruce Vandervort, *Indian Wars of Canada, Mexico and the United States, 1812–1900* (New York: Routledge, 2003), 55–60. For a general discussion of Mahan as related to the history of West Point, see Thomas Griess, "Dennis Hart Mahan: West Point Professor and Advocate of Military Professionalism, 1830–1871" (PhD diss., Duke University, 1968); Stephen Ambrose, "Dennis Hart Mahan," *Civil War Times* 2 (November 1963): 30–34; and Stephen E. Ambrose, *Duty, Honor, Country: A History of West Point* (Baltimore: Johns Hopkins University Press, 1999).

22. This thought is attributed to Irving Holley Jr.

23. U.S. War Department, *Field Service Regulations, 1905* (Washington DC: Government Printing Office, 1905), 24–40.

24. U.S. War Department, *Field Manual 100-5: Field Service Regulations, Operations* (Washington DC: Government Printing Office, 1941), 22.

25. Department of the Army, *Field Manual 100-5: Field Service Regulations, Operations* (Washington DC: Headquarters, Department of the Army, 1962), 6.

26. Ibid., 3–16, 46–58.

27. U.S. Army TRADOC, *Battlefield Laboratories: The Road to the Post–Cold War Army* (Fort Monroe, VA: Headquarters, U.S. Army TRADOC, 1992), 36.

28. Department of the Army, *Trained and Ready: The United States Army Posture Statement FY 92/93* (Washington, DC: Department of the Army, 1991), 8. For a scholarly treatment along these lines, see Matthew A. Evangelista, *Innovation and the Arms Race: How the United States and the Soviet Union Develop New Military Technologies* (Princeton, NJ: Princeton University Press, 1988).

29. The concept of organizations storing knowledge in codes and procedures is derived from James March, "Exploitation and Exploration in Organizational Learning," *Organization Science* 2, no. 1 (1991): 71–82.

30. Williamson Murray, "Does Military Culture Matter?" *Orbis* 43, no. 1 (1999): 27–42.

31. Letter from Gordon R. Sullivan to general officers, "TRADOC Pamphlet 525-5," September 2, 1994, General Sullivan Gordon Papers, U.S. Army Military History Institute, Carlisle, PA.

32. Sullivan, "Army Imperative in Peacetime," 3.

33. Donn Starry, *Commander's Notes No. 3: Operational Concepts and Doctrine* (Fort Monroe, VA: U.S. Army TRADOC, 1979), 1–2.

34. Department of the Army, *Field Manual 100-5: Operations* (Washington, DC: Center for Military History, 1982), 1-1.

35. Theo Farrell and Terry Terriff, *The Sources of Military Change: Culture, Politics, Technology* (Boulder, CO: Lynne Rienner, 2002), 4; Adam Grissom, "The Future of Military Innovation Studies," *Journal of Strategic Studies* 29, no. 5 (2006): 905–934.

36. Farrell and Terriff, *The Sources of Military Change*, 5.

37. Posen, *The Sources of Military Doctrine*; Rosen, *Winning the Next War*.

38. See Grissom, "The Future of Military Innovation Studies"; and Robert T. Foley, "A Case Study in Horizontal Military Innovation: The German Army, 1916–1918," *Journal of Strategic Studies* 35, no. 6 (2012): 799–827.

39. Farrell and Terriff, *The Sources of Military Change*, 6.

40. Stephen Peter Rosen, *Winning the Next War: Innovation and the Modern Military* (Ithaca, NY: Cornell University Press, 1991), 7–8.

41. Wilson, *Bureaucracy*, 222.

42. Theo Farrell, "Improving in War: Military Adaptation and the British in Helmand Province, Afghanistan, 2006–2009," *Journal of Strategic Studies* 33, no. 4 (2010): 569.

43. Farrell and Terriff, *The Sources of Military Change*, 6.

44. Ibid., 5.

45. James March and Herbert Simon, *Organizations*, 2nd ed. (Cambridge, MA: Blackwell, 1993).

46. Ibid., 199.

47. Ibid., 203.

48. Posen, *The Sources of Military Doctrine*.

49. Williamson Murray and Allan R. Millett, eds., *Military Innovation in the Interwar Period* (Cambridge: Cambridge University Press, 1998), 310.

50. March and Simon, *Organizations*, 208.

51. Downs, *Inside Bureaucracy*, especially 212–222.

52. For a discussion of doctrine as a bridge between tactics and strategy, see Avant, "The Institutional Sources of Military Doctrine," 411.

53. Kimberly M. Zisk, *Engaging the Enemy: Organization Theory and Soviet Military Innovation, 1955–1991* (Princeton, NJ: Princeton University Press, 1993), 4. Similarly, Theo Farrell and Terry Terriff define military innovation as "change in the goals, actual strategies, and/or structure of a military organization." Farrell and Terriff, *The Sources of Military Change*, 5.

54. Organizational sociologists tend to characterize innovation along these lines as a new idea or behavior. See Fariborz Damanpour, "Innovation Type, Radicalness and the Adoption Process," *Communication Research* 15, no. 5 (1998): 45–67; Jerald Hage, *Theories of Organizations: Form, Process, and Transformation* (New York: Wiley, 1980).

55. For discussion on organizations and mission accomplishment as it relates to change, see Morton Halperin, *Bureaucratic Politics and Foreign Policy* (Washington, DC: Brookings Institution Press, 1974), 26–46.

56. Posen, *The Sources of Military Doctrine*. A variation of the civilian intervention thesis concerns how civilian leaders design security institutions and delegate authority as a key determinant of the capacity of military actors to innovate and develop new

doctrine. See Deborah Avant, "The Institutional Sources of Military Doctrine: Hegemons in Peripheral Wars," *International Studies Quarterly* 37, no. 4 (1993): 209–230.

57. This is the core argument Barry Posen uses to explain doctrinal innovation in France, Germany, and the United Kingdom between World War I and World War II in "The Institutional Sources of Military Doctrine."

58. William A. Owens, "Creating a U.S. Military Revolution," in *The Sources of Military Change: Culture, Politics, Technology,* ed. Theo Farrell and Terry Terriff (Boulder, CO: Lynne Rienner, 2002), 205–220; Colin S. Gray, *Strategy for Chaos: Revolutions in Military Affairs and the Evidence of History* (London: Frank Cass, 2002), 1–7; Peter Dombrowski and Eugene Gholz, *Buying Military Transformation: Technological Innovation and the Defense Industry* (New York: Columbia University Press), ix–xiv; Andrew F. Krepnevich, "Cavalry to Computer: The Pattern of Military Revolutions," *National Interest* 37 (Fall 1994): 30–43; Richard O. Hundley, *Past Revolutions, Future Transformation: What Can the History of Revolutions in Military Affairs Tell Us About Transforming the U.S. Military?* (Santa Monica, CA: RAND, 1999); Max Boot, *War Made New: Technology, Warfare, and the Course of History, 1500–Today* (New York: Penguin, 2006); MacGregor Knox and Williamson Murray, *The Dynamics of Military Revolution, 1300–2050,* 2nd ed. (Cambridge: Cambridge University Press, 2001); Michael G. Vickers and Robert C. Martinage, *The Revolution in War* (Washington, DC: Center for Strategic and Budgetary Assessment, 2004); William E. Odem, *America's Military Revolution: Strategy and Structure After the Cold War* (Washington, DC: American University Press, 1993); George Friedman and Meredith Friedman, *The Future of War: Power, Technology, and American Dominance in the 21st Century* (New York: St. Martins, 1996); Michael O'Hanlon, *Technological Change and the Future of Warfare* (Washington, DC: Brookings Institution Press, 2000); Zelmay N. Khalilzad and John P. White, *The Changing Role of Information Warfare* (Santa Monica, CA: RAND, 1999); Hans Binnendijk, *Transforming America's Military* (Washington, DC: National Defense University Press, 2002); James Blacker, "Understanding the Revolution in Military Affairs: A Guide to America's 21st Century Defense," Defense Working Paper 3, Progressive Policy Institute, Washington, DC, 1997; Edward F. Bruner, *Army Transformation and Modernization: Overview and Issues for Congress* (Washington, DC: Congressional Research Services, 2001).

59. Wilson, *Bureaucracy,* 223.

60. Graham Allison and Philip Zelikow, *The Essence of Decision: Exploring the Cuban Missile Crisis* (New York: Longman, 1999).

61. Morton Halperin, *Bureaucratic Politics and Foreign Policy* (Washington, DC: Brookings Institution Press, 1974), 40.

62. Anthony Downs, *Inside Bureaucracy* (Boston: Little, Brown, 1967).

63. Samuel Huntington, "Interservice Competition and the Political Roles of the Armed Services," *American Political Science Review* 55, no. 1 (1961): 40–52.

64. Ibid., 52.

65. Farrell and Terriff, *The Sources of Military Change.*

66. Elizabeth Kier, *Imagining War: French and British Military Doctrine Between the Wars* (Princeton, NJ: Princeton University Press, 1999).

67. Dima Adamsky, *The Culture of Military Innovation: The Impact of Cultural Factors on the Revolution in Military Affairs in Russia, the US, and Israel* (Palo Alto, CA: Stanford University Press, 2010); D. Michael Shafer, *Deadly Paradigms: The Failure of U.S. Counterinsurgency Policy* (Princeton, NJ: Princeton University Press, 1988), 3. See also John Lewis Gaddis, *Strategies of Containment: A Critical Appraisal of Postwar American National Security Policy* (New York: Oxford University Press, 1982).

68. Russell F. Weigley, *The American Way of War: A History of United States Military Strategy and Policy* (Bloomington: Indiana University Press, 1977).

69. For overviews of the emergence of AirLand Battle and its links to broader institutional reform and external conflicts, see Anne W. Chapman, *The Army's Training Revolution, 1973–1990: An Overview* (Fort Monroe, VA: Office of the Command Historian, U.S. Army TRADOC, 1991); U.S. Army TRADOC, *Transforming the Army: TRADOC's First Thirty Years, 1973–2003* (Fort Monroe, VA: Military History Office, U.S. Army TRADOC, 2003); Richard Lock-Pullan, "An Inward Looking Time: The United States Army, 1973–1976" *Journal of Military History* 67, no. 2 (2003): 483–512; Richard Lock-Pullan, "How to Rethink War: Conceptual Innovation and AirLand Battle Doctrine," *Journal of Strategic Studies* 28, no. 4 (2005): 679–702; and Saul Bronfeld, "Fighting Outnumbered: The Impact of the Yom Kippur War on the U.S. Army," *Journal of Military History* 71 (2007): 465–498.

70. On full-spectrum dominance and how it relates to transformation, see U.S. Army, *U.S. Army Transformation Roadmap* (Washington, DC: Headquarters, Department of the Army, 2004).

71. In arguing for endogenous change, this book follows Samuel Huntington, Stephen Peter Rosen, and Kimberly Marten Zisk.

72. For work specifically on the Army profession and its ethic, Don Snider is the authority. See Don Snider and Lloyd J. Matthews, *The Future of the Army Profession*, 2nd ed. (New York: McGraw-Hill, 2005); Don Snider, *Forging the Warrior's Character: Moral Precepts from the Cadet Prayer*, 2nd ed. (New York: McGraw-Hill, 2008); and Suzanne C. Nielson and Don M. Snider, eds., *American Civil-Military Relations: The Soldier and the State in a New Era* (Baltimore: Johns Hopkins University Press, 2009). The intent here is to explore the relationship between doctrinal change and elements of professions.

73. George Ritzer, "Professionalization, Bureaucratization and Rationalization: The Views of Max Weber," *Social Forces* 53, no. 4 (1975): 630–632.

74. Samuel Huntington, *The Soldier and the State: The Theory and Politics of Civil-Military Relations* (Cambridge, MA: Harvard University Press, 1957), 8–10.

75. For more on habitual logics, see Ted Hopf, "The Logic of Habit in International Relations," *European Journal of International Relations* 16, no. 4 (2010): 539–561; and Max Weber, *Economy and Society* (Berkeley: University of California Press, 1978).

76. Morris Janowitz, *The Professional Soldier* (New York: Free Press, 1960); Zisk, *Engaging the Enemy*, 12.

77. On epistemic communities, see Peter M. Haas, ed., "Knowledge, Power, and International Policy Coordination," special issue, *International Organization* 46, no. 1 (Winter 1992). In their work on ideas and foreign policy, Judith Goldstein and

Robert O. Keohane also develop an understanding of the importance of causal and principled beliefs. Judith Goldstein and Robert Keohane, eds., *Ideas and Foreign Policy: Beliefs, Institutions, and Political Change* (Ithaca, NY: Cornell University Press, 1993).

78. Weigley, *The American Way of War*.

79. Edward Rhodes, "Do Bureaucratic Politics Matter? Some Disconfirming Findings from the Case of the U.S. Navy," *World Politics* 47, no. 1 (1994): 1–41.

80. For more on core missions and the redefinition of critical tasks, see Wilson, *Bureaucracy*, 26. For a discussion of the role of environmental pressure, see March and Simon, *Organizations*, 176. For more on problem solving, see work in cybernetics, especially John D. Steinbruner, *The Cybernetic Theory of Decision* (Princeton, NJ: Princeton University Press, 1974).

81. March and Simon, *Organizations*, 176.

82. Stephen Peter Rosen was the first to introduce the term "theory of victory," though the concept is closely related to multiple aspects of classical organizational theory. Rosen, *Winning the Next War*, 19–20. The term is also used in Dima Adamsky, *The Culture of Military Innovation: The Impact of Cultural Factors on the Revolution in Military Affairs in Russia, the US, and Israel* (Palo Alto, CA: Stanford University Press, 2010), 21; and Emily Goldman, "Introduction: Military Diffusion and Transformation," in *The Information Revolution in Military Affairs in Asia*, ed. Emily Goldman and Thomas Mahnken (New York: Palgrave Macmillan, 2004), 1–21.

83. Erving Goffman, *Frame Analysis: An Essay on the Organization of Experience* (Boston: Northeastern University Press, 1974).

84. While this is similar to Alastair Iain Johnston's work on strategic culture, the use of programs here does not share the assumption of a relatively fixed, stable set of cultural understandings. The use of programs implies discourses of war that are always in the making as opposed to constant. See Alastair Iain Johnston, "Thinking About Strategic Culture," *International Security* 19, no. 4 (1995): 32–64.

85. Murray and Millett, *Military Innovation in the Interwar Period*, 310.

86. On action repertoires and standard scenarios, see Allison and Zelikow, *The Essence of Decision*, 163–185.

87. David Johnson, *Fast Tanks and Heavy Bombers: Innovation in the U.S. Army, 1917–1945* (Ithaca, NY: Cornell University Press, 2003).

88. For a discussion on reactive innovation as it relates to organizational theory, see Zisk, *Engaging the Enemy*. For more on the role of career paths in locking in new ways of war, see Rosen, *Winning the Next War*.

89. To institutionalize a higher rate of innovation requires time pressure and deadlines, clarity of goals, and sufficient resources. Time pressure forces bureaucrats otherwise interested in satisficing to deliver outputs to superiors. Clarity of goals relates to mandate and missions. Organizations are also assumed to be more likely to accept a new mission role if they believe it will reinforce or protect their core mission and survival. For more on time pressure and goal clarity, see March and Simon, *Organizations*, 206–207. The concept of sufficient resources is also referred to as

"organizational slack." For more on slack, see Richard Cyert and James A. March, *A Behavioral Theory of the Firm* (Englewood Cliffs, NJ: Prentice-Hall, 1963).

90. J. T. Hage, "Organizational Innovation and Organizational Change," *Annual Review of Sociology* 25 (1999): 597–622; Evangelista, *Innovation and the Arms Race*. Later generations of organizational theorists expand the institutional requirements for innovation to include how information is processed and the division of labor. All things being equal, organizational complexity, or the knowledge capital of individuals within the organization, is directly related to innovation. The greater the degree of complexity, the higher the rate of innovation. Higher complexity is held to be associated with a higher rate of learning. Complex organizations with highly differentiated functions and departments are occupied by specialists who synthesize information and sustain innovation.

91. John B. Wilson, *Maneuver and Firepower: The Evolution of Divisions and Separate Brigades* (Washington, DC: Center for Military History, 1998).

92. Wilson, *Maneuver and Firepower*.

93. "General Craig Outlines National Defense Views," *Army and Navy Journal*, November 16, 1935, p. 205; Robert R. Palmer, *Reorganization of Ground Troops for Combat Study*, vol. 8 (Washington, DC: Historical Section, Army Ground Forces, 1946).

94. The concept is drawn from work on policy change in Europe, specifically the idea of programmatic actors and advocacy coalitions. For a discussion of programmatic actors, see William Genieys, *The New Custodians of the State: Programmatic Elites in French Society* (New Brunswick, NJ: Transaction, 2010); and William Genieys and Marc Smyrl, *Elites, Ideas, and the Evolution of Public Policy* (New York: Palgrave Macmillan, 2008). For a discussion of advocacy coalitions, see Paul Sabatie and Hank Jenkins-Smith, eds., *Policy Change and Learning: An Advocacy Coalition Approach* (Boulder, CO: Westview, 1993). These approaches have not been systematically applied to the question of military reform.

95. Adam Grissom, "The Future of Military Innovation Studies," *Journal of Strategic Studies* 29, no. 5 (2006): 905–934.

96. Susan L. Marquis, *Unconventional Warfare: Rebuilding US Special Operations Forces* (Washington DC: Brookings Institution Press, 1997).

97. Gregory A. Engel, "Cruise Missiles and the Tomahawk," in *The Politics of Naval Innovation*, ed. B. Hayes and D. Smith (Newport, RI: U.S. Naval War College 1994), 18–22.

98. Janowitz, *The Professional Soldier*; Stephen Peter Rosen, "New Ways of War," *International Security* 13, no. 1 (1988): 134–168; Rosen, *Winning the Next War*.

99. Margaret E. Keck and Kathryn Sikkink, *Activists Beyond Borders* (Ithaca, NY: Cornell University Press, 1996); Emanuel Adler, "Seizing the Middle Ground: Constructivism in World Politics," *European Journal of International Relations* 3, no. 3 (1997): 319–363; Peter M. Haas, "Introduction: Epistemic Communities and International Policy Coordination," in "Knowledge, Power, and International Policy Coordination," ed. Peter M. Haas, special issue, *International Organization* 46, no. 1 (1992): 1–35. Dima Adamsky also highlights the importance of senior military leaders as norm entrepreneurs. See Adamsky, *The Culture of Military Innovation*, 135.

100. This premise suggests that resources, as organizational slack, are an insufficient explanation of innovation. What matters is not always budget but the ability of elites to advocate concepts developed in the incubator across the broader organizational communities. For more on organizational slack and its relationship to innovation, see Cyert and March, *A Behavioral Theory of the Firm*; and Scott W. Geiger and Luke H. Cashen, "A Multidimensional Examination of Slack and Its Impact on Innovation," *Journal of Managerial Issues* 14, no. 1 (Spring 2002): 68–84.

101. These protection structures can be viewed as rackets. The price of elite protection is often the distortion of the original construct to fit the senior leader's view of the problem and, by proxy, the optimal solution implied by doctrinal reform.

102. Mark S. Granovetter, "The Strength of Weak Ties," *American Journal of Sociology* 78, no. 6 (1973): 1360–1380.

103. Charles Tilly, *Stories, Identities and Political Change* (Boulder, CO: Rowman and Littlefield, 2003), 21.

104. Andrew Abbott, "Things of Boundaries," *Social Research* 62, no. 1 (1995): 863.

105. Bickel, *Mars Learning*.

106. Terry Terriff, "'Innovate or Die': Organizational Culture and the Origins of Maneuver Warfare in the United States Marine Corps," *Journal of Strategic Studies* 29, no. 3 (2006): 475–503.

107. For more on legitimation strategies in international relations, see Patrick Thaddeus Jackson, *Civilizing the Enemy: German Reconstruction and the Invention of the West* (Ann Arbor: University of Michigan Press, 2006); Patrick Thaddeus Jackson and Martin Hall, eds., *Civilizational Identity: The Production and Reproduction of "Civilizations" in International Relations* (New York: Palgrave Macmillan, 2007); and Patrick Thaddeus Jackson and Ronald R. Krebs, "Twisting Tongues and Twisting Arms: The Power of Political Rhetoric," *European Journal of International Relations* 13, no. 1 (2007): 35–66. Also see the work of Stacy Goddard, including *Uncommon Ground: Indivisible Territory and the Politics of Legitimacy* (Cambridge: Cambridge University Press, 2009); and "When Right Makes Might: How Prussia Overturned the European Balance of Power," *International Security* 33, no. 3 (Winter 2008–2009): 110–142. The concepts build on the work of Charles Tilly and his relational perspective. For more on relational perspectives, see Patrick Thaddeus Jackson and Daniel H. Nexon, "Relations Before States: Substance, Process, and the Study of World Politics," *European Journal of International Relations* 5, no. 3 (1999): 291–332.

108. Alexander L. George and Andrew Bennett, *Case Studies and Theory Development in the Social Sciences* (Cambridge, MA: MIT Press, 2005).

109. Though beyond the scope of this book to investigate, the process should also be evident, albeit with a lag, in professional military education institutions.

110. Posen, *The Sources of Military Doctrine*, 222–244.

Chapter 2

1. In this book I use the term "Arab-Israeli War" because it was the term invoked by the U.S. Army in official documents from the time. This is not meant to promote a

particular view of the war. Rather, the intent is to understand the conflict as decision makers within the Army did, thus using everyday language to reconstruct the operative mode of analysis, synthesis, and dynamic that informed innovation.

2. Henry G. Gole, *General William E. DePuy: Preparing the Army for Modern War* (Lawrence: University of Kansas Press, 2008), 254; see also Saul Bronfeld, "Fighting Outnumbered: The Impact of the Yom Kippur War on the U.S. Army," *Journal of Military History* 71 (2007): 465–498; Paul H. Herbert, *Deciding What Has to Be Done: General William E. DePuy and the 1976 Edition of FM 100-5* (Fort Leavenworth, KS: Combat Studies Institute, U.S. Army Command and General Staff College, 1988), 35.

3. William E. DePuy, personnel note, August 1974, William E. DePuy Papers, box 12, folder 3, U.S. Army Military History Institute, Carlisle, PA.

4. Department of the Army, *Field Manual 100-5: Operations* (Washington, DC: Department of the Army, 1976), 3–5.

5. For more in-depth discussions of the post–Vietnam War Army, see Russell F. Weigley, *History of the United States Army* (Bloomington: Indiana University Press, 1984), 567–192.

6. Richard W. Stewart, *The United States Army in a Global Era, 1917–2003* (Washington, DC: Center for Military History, 2005), 369.

7. For detailed overviews of the shift to the all-volunteer force, see Bernard Rostker, *I Want You! The Evolution of the All-Volunteer Force* (Santa Monica, CA: RAND, 2006); and Robert K. Griffith, *The U.S. Army's Transition to the All-Volunteer Force, 1968–1974* (Washington, DC: Center for Military History, 1997).

8. Stewart, *The United States Army in a Global Era*, 375.

9. Ibid., 376.

10. For an example of these initiatives, see Political Consultative Committee of the Warsaw Pact, "Declaration of the Political Consultative Committee of the Warsaw Pact on the Strengthening of Peace and Security in Europe," July 5, 1966, http://www.cvce.eu/content/publication/2005/12/22/c48a3aab-0873-43f1-a928-981e23063f23/publishable_en.pdf.

11. Central Intelligence Agency, "Current Problems in NATO," 1 OCI No. 0549/69 (January 21, 1969); see also James E. Miller and Laurie Van Hook, eds., *Foreign Relations of the United States, 1969–1976*, vol. 41, *Western Europe; NATO, 1969–1972* (Washington, DC: U.S. Government Printing Office, 2012).

12. North Atlantic Treaty Organization, "The Future Tasks of the Alliance: Report of the Council—'The Harmel Report,'" December 13–14, 1967, http://www.nato.int/cps/en/natolive/official_texts_26700.htm.

13. Joint War Games Agency, "BETA I & II-67: Final Report," April 1967, http://www.dod.gov/pubs/foi/Reading_Room/Joint_Staff/656.pdf.

14. Memorandum from Melvin Laird to Richard Nixon, "NATO Defense Issues," February 20, 1969, in Miller and Van Hook, *Foreign Relations of the United States, 1969–1976*, 41:37, 38.

15. Department of State and National Security Council, "Discussion of United States Policy Toward Europe," in Miller and Van Hook, *Foreign Relations of the United States, 1969–1976*, 41:106.

16. Ibid., 41:106–107.

17. Amos A. Jordan and William J. Taylor, *American National Security: Policy and Process* (Baltimore, MD: Johns Hopkins University Press, 1981), 73–76; Zeb B. Bradford and Frederic J. Brown, *The United States Army in Transition* (Beverly Hills, CA: Sage, 1973), 21–73.

18. Jordan and Taylor, *American National Security*, 73–76.

19. U.S. Department of Defense, *Statement of Secretary of Defense on the FY 1972–1976 Defense Program* (Washington, DC: Government Printing Office, 1971), 25.

20. Terry Terriff, *The Nixon Administration and the Making of U.S. Nuclear Strategy* (Ithaca, NY: Cornell University Press, 1995), 18–20.

21. Harry G. Summers, *The Astarita Report: A Military Strategy for the Multipolar World* (Carlisle, PA: Strategic Studies Institutes, U.S. Army War College, 1982), v.

22. Ibid.

23. Ibid., 20.

24. Ibid., 35–36.

25. Ibid., 37.

26. John Romjue, Susan Canedy, and Anne W. Chapman, *Prepare the Army for War: A Historical Overview of the Army Training and Doctrine Command, 1973–1993* (Fort Monroe, VA: Office of the Command Historian, U.S. Army TRADOC, 2002), 5–8; James Bowden, *Operation Steadfast: The United States Army Reorganizes Itself* (Quantico, VA: U.S. Marine Corps Command and General Staff College, 1985).

27. For a detailed discussion of the history and development of CONARC, see Jean R. Moenk, *A History of Command and Control of Army Forces in the Continental United States, 1919–1972* (Fort Monroe, VA: CONARC Historical Office, 1972).

28. Bowden, *Operation Steadfast*, 10–12.

29. Ibid., 12.

30. Ibid., 45–46.

31. Ibid., 47.

32. Romjue, Canedy, and Chapman, *Prepare the Army for War*, 7.

33. Bowden, *Operation Steadfast*, 18.

34. Romjue, Canedy, and Chapman, *Prepare the Army for War*, 6.

35. Ibid., 9.

36. William E. DePuy, *Implications of the Middle East War on U.S. Army Tactics, Doctrine and Systems* (Fort Monroe, VA: Headquarters, U.S. Army TRADOC, 1974), 3.

37. Ibid., 6.

38. Letter from Creighton Abrams, January 14, 1974, Orwin Talbott Papers, box 2, U.S. Army Heritage and Education Center, Carlisle, PA.

39. DePuy, *Implications of the Middle East War*, 3.

40. John L. Romjue, *From Active Defense to AirLand Battle: The Development of Army Doctrine, 1973–1982* (Fort Monroe, VA: U.S. Army TRADOC, 1984), 20.

41. Letter from William DePuy, January 1, 1974, Orwin Talbott Papers, box 2, U.S. Army Heritage and Education Center, Carlisle, PA.

42. Ibid.

43. DePuy, *Implications of the Middle East War*, 19.
44. Ibid., 18.
45. Letter from William DePuy to Creighton Abrams, January 1974, Orwin Talbott Papers, box 2, U.S. Army Heritage and Education Center, Carlisle, PA.
46. Ibid.
47. William DePuy, concept paper, 1974, William E. DePuy Papers, box 5, folder 2, U.S. Army Heritage and Education Center, Carlisle, PA.
48. DePuy, *Implications of the Middle East War*, 4.
49. Ibid., 5.
50. Ibid., 7.
51. Ibid., 10.
52. Ibid.
53. Ibid., 4.
54. William DePuy, transcript of speech, May 24, 1974, William E. DePuy Papers, box 7, folder 3, U.S. Army Heritage and Education Center, Carlisle, PA.
55. Ibid.
56. DePuy, *Implications of the Middle East War*, 3.
57. Ibid., 20.
58. Ibid.
59. Ibid., 22.
60. Ibid., 24.
61. Letter from William DePuy to Army schoolhouse commanders, July 23, 1974, William E. DePuy Papers, box 2, folder 2, U.S. Army Heritage and Education Center, Carlisle, PA.
62. Ibid.
63. Gole, *General William E. DePuy*, 260.
64. Herbert, *Deciding What Has to Be Done*, 45.
65. Ibid., 81; letter from Donn A. Starry to Paul Gorman, July 1974, Donn Starry Papers, box 3, folder 2, U.S. Army Military History Institute, Carlisle, PA.
66. Donn A. Starry, "Modern Armor Battle II: The Defense," *Armor* 84 (January–February 1975): 39–44.
67. See, for example, David L. Tamminen, "How to Defend Outnumbered and Win," *Armor* 84 (November–December 1975): 39, 44.
68. Herbert, *Deciding What Has to Be Done*, 88.
69. Ibid.
70. Gole, *General William E. DePuy*, 260.
71. Department of the Army, *Field Manual 100-5: Operations*, i.
72. Ibid., 1-1.
73. Ibid.
74. Ibid., 1-2.
75. Ibid.
76. Ibid.

77. Ibid., 2-1–2-32.
78. Ibid., 2-1.
79. Romjue, *From Active Defense to AirLand Battle*, 6.
80. Ibid., 5.
81. Department of the Army, *Field Manual 100-5: Operations*, 3-1.
82. Ibid.
83. Ibid.
84. Ibid., 3-3.
85. Ibid., 3-4–3-6.
86. Ibid., 3-6.
87. Ibid.
88. Ibid., 5-10.
89. Ibid., 5-3.
90. Ibid., 5-2.
91. Ibid., 2-2.
92. Ibid., 5-6.
93. Romjue, *From Active Defense to AirLand Battle*, 8.
94. William DePuy, transcript of speech, May 24, 1977, William E. DePuy Papers, box 7, folder 3, U.S. Army Heritage and Education Center, Carlisle, PA.
95. Herbert, *Deciding What Has to Be Done*, 36.
96. DePuy, transcript of speech, May 24, 1977.
97. Letter from William DePuy to Robert Komer, May 24, 1974, William E. DePuy Papers, box 14, folder 2, U.S. Army Heritage and Education Center, Carlisle, PA.
98. Herbert, *Deciding What Has to Be Done*, 88.
99. Ibid., 9.
100. DePuy also embraced the officers' feedback, adding a chapter on urban combat and coalition warfare at their recommendation. Herbert, *Deciding What Has to Be Done*, 88–90.
101. Letter from DePuy to Komer, May 24, 1974.
102. Letter from William DePuy to Fred Weyland, April 29, 1975, William E. DePuy Papers, box 2, folder 4, U.S. Army Heritage and Education Center, Carlisle, PA.
103. William DePuy, letter in response to Senate testimony, May 12, 1975, William E. DePuy Papers, box 15, folder 2, U.S. Army Heritage and Education Center, Carlisle, PA.
104. Letter from DePuy to Weyland, April 29, 1975.
105. Letter from William DePuy to Gordon Sumner Jr., April 25, 1975, William E. DePuy Papers, box 2, folder 3, U.S. Army Heritage and Education Center, Carlisle, PA.
106. A major form of advocacy was the creation of the National Training Center. Here, General DePuy and his cohort developed a space for tactical adaptation that helped units both learn the new doctrine and experiment with new approaches.

Chapter 3

1. General Glenn K. Otis, transcript of Brazil speech, 1981, Glenn K. Otis Papers, box 1, folder 2, U.S. Army Military History Institute, Carlisle, PA.

2. Department of Defense, *Report of Secretary of Defense James R. Schlesinger to the Congress on the FY 1976 and Transition Budgets FY 1976, FY 1977 Authorization Request and FY 1976–1980 Defense Programs, February 5, 1975* (Washington, DC: Government Printing Office, 1975), I-18.

3. Ibid., I-18.

4. Ibid., I-7.

5. NATO Defence Planning Committee, "Final Communiqué," May 15–16, 1979, http://www.nato.int/docu/comm/49-95/c790515a.htm.

6. Department of Defense, *Report of the Secretary of Defense Harold Brown to the Congress on FY 1980 Budget, FY 1981 Authorization Request and FY 1980–1984 Defense Programs, January 25, 1979* (Washington, DC: Government Printing Office, 1979), 47.

7. Otis, transcript of Brazil speech, 1981.

8. Senate Armed Services Committee, *Procurement of Aircraft, Missiles, Tracked Combat Vehicles*, 95th Cong. (1977), 67 (statement of General Donn A. Starry).

9. Boyd D. Sutton, John R. Landry, Malcolm B. Armstrong, Howell M. Estes III, and Wesley K. Clark, "New Directions in Conventional Defense?" *Survival* 26, no. 2 (1984): 50.

10. John Mearsheimer, "Precision-Guided Munitions and Conventional Deterrence," *Survival* 21, no. 2 (1979): 68–76; John Mearsheimer, "Maneuver, Mobile Defense, and the NATO Central Front," *International Security* 6, no. 3 (1981): 104–122; John Mearsheimer, "Why the Soviets Can't Win Quickly in Central Europe," *International Security* 7, no. 1 (1982): 3–39; John Mearsheimer, *Conventional Deterrence* (Ithaca, NY: Cornell University Press, 1983): 3–39; Richard Betts, "Conventional Deterrence: Predictive Uncertainty and Policy Confidence," *World Politics* 37, no. 2 (1985): 153–179; Sutton et al., "New Directions in Conventional Defense?" 50–70.

11. Mearsheimer, *Conventional Deterrence*, 166.

12. Mearsheimer, "Why the Soviets Can't Win," 6.

13. Robert Lucas Fischer, "Defending the Central Front: The Balance of Forces," Adelphi Paper 127, International Institute for Strategic Studies, 1976; James Blaker and Andrew Hamilton, *Assessing the NATO/Warsaw Pact Military Balance* (Washington, DC: Congressional Budget Office, 1979); Robert Shishko, *The European Conventional Balance: A Primer* (Santa Monica, CA: RAND, 1981).

14. Phillip A. Karber, "Soviet Lessons of Middle East War," in *Final Proceedings of the Fifteenth Annual United States Army Operations Research Symposium* (Bethesda, MD: U.S. Army Concepts Analysis Agency, 1976), 10–15.

15. Mearsheimer, "Precision-Guided Munitions," 71–72.

16. Phillip A. Karber, "The Tactical Revolution in Soviet Military Doctrine," *Military Review* 57, no. 11 (1977): 83–85.

17. John L. Romjue, *From Active Defense to AirLand Battle: The Development of Army Doctrine, 1973–1982* (Fort Monroe, VA: U.S. Army TRADOC, 1984), 16.

18. Sutton et al., "New Directions in Conventional Defense?" 52.

19. C. N. Donnelly, "Tactical Problems Facing the Soviet Army: Recent Debates in the Soviet Military Press," *International Defense Review* 11 (1976): 1405–1412; Graham D. Vernon, *Soviet Operations for War in Europe: Nuclear or Conventional?* National Security Affairs Monograph 77, no. 1 (Washington, DC: National Defense University, 1979).

20. Sutton et al., "New Directions in Conventional Defense?" 51.

21. Ye V. Savkin, *The Basic Principles of Operational Art and Tactics: A Soviet View* (Honolulu: University Press of the Pacific, 2002); A. A. Sidorenko, *The Offensive: A Soviet View*, trans. U.S. Air Force (Washington, DC: Government Printing Office, 1973); David M. Glantz, *Soviet Military Operational Art: In Pursuit of Deep Battle* (London: Frank Cass, 1991); Richard W. Harrison, *The Russian Way of War: Operational Art, 1904–1940* (Lawrence: University of Kansas, 2001); Shimon Naveh, *In Pursuit of Military Excellence: The Evolution of Operational Theory* (New York: Frank Cass, 1997).

22. House Armed Services Committee, *Procurement of Aircraft, Missiles, Tracked Combat Vehicles, Torpedoes and Other Weapons*, 95th Cong. (1977), 67–68.

23. Ibid., 98.

24. Ibid., 72.

25. Mearsheimer, "Why the Soviets Can't Win," 5; Mearsheimer, *Conventional Deterrence*, 166; see also Robert Close, *Europe Without Defense?* (New York: Pergamon, 1979).

26. House Armed Services Committee, *Procurement of Aircraft*, 72.

27. Dennis Ross, "Soviet Threats to the Persian Gulf," *International Security* 6, no. 2 (1981): 159.

28. William B. Quandt, "The Middle East Crises," *Foreign Affairs* 58, no. 3 (1979): 543; Amitav Acharya, *U.S. Military Strategy in the Gulf* (London: Routledge, 1989), 37–49.

29. Dennis Ross, "The Soviet Union and the Persian Gulf," *Political Science Quarterly* 99, no. 4 (1984–1985): 615–636; Rasul B. Rais, "An Appraisal of U.S. Strategy in the Indian Ocean," *Asian Survey* 23, no. 9 (1983): 1043–1051.

30. Ross, "Soviet Threats to the Persian Gulf," 160.

31. Ibid.

32. Ibid.; Scott W. Thompson, "The Persian Gulf and the Correlation of Forces," *International Security* 7, no. 1 (1982): 157–180.

33. Department of Defense, *Fiscal Year 1981 Annual Report* (Washington, DC: Department of Defense, 1980).

34. Thompson, "The Persian Gulf and the Correlation of Forces," 160.

35. Kenneth Waltz, "A Strategy for the Rapid Deployment Force," *International Security* 5, no. 4 (1981): 49–73; Thompson, "The Persian Gulf and the Correlation of Forces."

36. Acharya, *U.S. Military Strategy in the Gulf*, 49–56.

37. Otis, transcript of Brazil speech, 1981.
38. Quoted in Acharya, *U.S. Military Strategy in the Gulf*, 52.
39. Ibid., 53.
40. Congressional Budget Office, *U.S. Projection Forces: Requirements, Scenarios, and Options* (Washington, DC: Government Printing Office, 1978).
41. Edward Luttwak, "The American Style of Warfare, and the Military Balance," *Survival* 21, no. 2 (1979): 57–60; Steven L. Canby, "General Purpose Forces," *International Security Review* 5, no. 3 (1980): 483–506; Steven L. Canby and Edward Luttwak, *U.S. Defense Planning for Non-NATO Contingencies: Analysis of the Operational Forms of Warfare, the Case of Iran* (Potomac, MD: C&L Associates, 1979); Albert Wohlstetter, "Half-Wars and Half-Policies in the Persian Gulf," in *National Security in the 1980s: From Weakness to Strength*, ed. Scott W. Thompson (San Francisco: Institute for Contemporary Studies, 1989), 123–171.
42. Romjue, *From Active Defense to AirLand Battle*, 30.
43. Letter from Edward Meyer to Donn Starry, June 13, 1979, Donn Starry Papers, box 1, folder 3, U.S. Army Military History Institute, Carlisle, PA.
44. Department of the Army, *Historical Survey 1978* (Washington, DC: Center for Military History, 1980), 10.
45. Ibid.
46. Ibid., 11.
47. Ibid.
48. Memorandum from Bob Komer to Edward Meyer, January 20, 1981, Edward Meyer Papers, box 3, folder 1, U.S. Army Heritage and Education Center, Carlisle, PA.
49. Memorandum from Forces Command to Edward Meyer, March 24, 1981, Edward Meyer Papers, box 3, folder 2, U.S. Army Heritage and Education Center, Carlisle, PA.
50. Letter from Richard Cavazos to Donn Starry, July 28, 1982, Donn Starry Papers, box 1, folder 2, U.S. Army Heritage and Education Center, Carlisle, PA.
51. Joshua M. Epstein, "Soviet Vulnerabilities in Iran and the RDF Deterrent," *International Security* 5, no. 4 (1981): 126–158; Thompson, "The Persian Gulf and the Correlation of Forces," 157–180; Kenneth A. Allard, "A Clear and Present Danger: Soviet Airborne Forces in the 1980s," *Parameters* 60, no. 4 (1980): 42–51.
52. Memorandum from Forces Command to Edward Meyer, "Planning Guidance," February 12, 1981, Edward Meyer Papers, box 3, folder 2, U.S. Army Heritage and Education Center, Carlisle, PA.
53. Donn Starry, "Integrated Operations," July 1980, Donn Starry Papers, box 2, folder 3, U.S. Army Heritage and Education Center, Carlisle, PA.
54. Romjue, *From Active Defense to AirLand Battle*, 23.
55. Ibid., 24.
56. Naveh, *In Pursuit of Military Excellence*, 289.
57. Romjue, *From Active Defense to AirLand Battle*, 25.
58. Senate Armed Services Committee, *Procurement of Aircraft*, 74.
59. Ibid., 75.

60. Ibid., 76.

61. Edward A. Dinges and Richard H. Sinnreich, "Battlefield Interdiction: Old Terms, New Problems," *Field Artillery Journal*, January–February 1980, p. 15; Romjue, *From Active Defense to AirLand Battle*, 34.

62. Sutton et al., "New Directions in Conventional Defense?" 53.

63. The original concept also included tactical nuclear weapons. The U.S. Army fielded both tactical nuclear weapons, including the Lance missile system and artillery shells like the W90 neutron bomb shell for four-inch and 155-millimeter systems, and strategic assets like the Pershing II. For operational doctrinal planning purposes, the focus was on fighting only in a nuclear environment because of the inability to control nuclear escalation or targeting. Division commanders and their subordinates, the primary audience of operational doctrine, did not have targeting or release authority. That is, they required presidential approval to use even tactical nuclear weapons. Though fielded by the Army, strategic systems like the Pershing II were programmed in advance at higher echelons and not easily retasked. Thus, in conceptualizing how to strike a mobile second echelon, these systems were impractical and focus was on conventional capabilities. Romjue, *From Active Defense to AirLand Battle*, 40.

64. Department of the Army, *Tactical Command and Control*, TRADOC Pamphlet 525-2 (Fort Monroe, VA: Headquarters, U.S. Army TRADOC, 1980).

65. Romjue, *From Active Defense to AirLand Battle*, 41.

66. Letter from James Richardson to Donn Starry, "Extended Battlefield Concept," May 4, 1981, Donn Starry Papers, box 1, folder 2, U.S. Army Heritage and Education Center, Carlisle, PA.

67. Ibid.

68. Romjue, *From Active Defense to AirLand Battle*, 37.

69. Department of the Army, *Historical Survey 1978*, 14.

70. Donald Hicks, *DARPA/DNA Long Range Research and Development Planning Program* (Washington, DC: Department of Defense, 1975), 1–2.

71. Richard H. Van Atta, Michael J. Lippitz, Jasper C. Lupo, Rob Mahoney, and Jack H. Nunn, *Transformation and Transition: DARPA's Role in Fostering an Emerging Revolution in Military Affairs*, vol. 1, *Overall Assessment* (Alexandria, VA: Institute for Defense Analysis, 2003), 7.

72. Ibid., S-4.

73. Ibid.

74. General Accounting Office, "Decisions to Be Made in Charting Future of DOD's Assault Breaker," February 28, 1981, p. 2.

75. Senate Armed Services Committee, *Department of Defense Appropriations for FY77, Part 8: Research and Development; Testimony of William Perry Before the United States Senate*, 95th Cong. (1978), 5598.

76. Department of Defense, "Remarks as Given by Secretary of Defense William J. Perry to the National Academy of Engineering," October 3, 1996, http://www.defense.gov/releases/release.aspx?releaseid=1057.

77. Van Atta et al., *Transformation and Transition*, 10.

78. Cable from Donn Starry to TRADOC, "The AirLand Battle," January 29, 1981, Donn Starry Papers, box 2, folder 5, U.S. Army Heritage and Education Center, Carlisle, PA.

79. Romjue, *From Active Defense to AirLand Battle*, 44; Department of the Army, *Military Operations: Operational Concepts for the AirLand Battle and Corps Operations, 1986*, TRADOC Pamphlet 525-2 (Fort Monroe, VA: Headquarters, U.S. Army TRADOC, 1981).

80. Romjue, *From Active Defense to AirLand Battle*, 6.

81. Donn A. Starry, "Extending the Battlefield," *Military Review* 61, no. 3 (1981): 31–50; Donn A. Starry, "Extending the Battlefield," *Field Artillery Journal*, September–October 1981, pp. 6–19.

82. William R. Richardson, "Winning on the Extended Battlefield," *Army*, June 1981, pp. 35–42; Clyde J. Tate and L. D. Holder, "New Doctrine for the Defense," *Military Review* 62, no. 7 (1981): 2–9; Huba Wass de Czege and L. D. Holder, "The New FM 100-5," *Military Review* 62, no. 7 (1982): 54–69.

83. David E. Grange, "Infantry and Air Defense in the AirLand Battle," *Air Defense Magazine*, October–December 1981, pp. 24–25; Michael S. Lancaster, "The Armor Force in the AirLand Battle," *Armor*, January–February 1982, pp. 26–32; Jerry M. Sollinger, "AirLand Battle: Implications for the Infantry," *Infantry*, March–April 1982, pp. 22–25; Carl H. McNair and Josef Reinsprecht, "Army Aviation Forces in the AirLand Battle," *US Army Aviation Digest*, July 1981, pp. 6–13.

84. Romjue, *From Active Defense to AirLand Battle*, 51–55.

85. Ibid., 56.

86. Ibid., 61.

87. Ibid., 63.

88. Ibid., 66.

89. Department of the Army, *Field Manual 100-5: Operations* (Washington, DC: Center for Military History, 1982), i.

90. Ibid., 1-1.

91. Ibid.

92. Ibid., 2-2.

93. Ibid.

94. Ibid.

95. Ibid.

96. Ibid.

97. Ibid.

98. Ibid.

99. Ibid., 2-3.

100. Ibid.

101. Ibid., 7-13.

102. Ibid.

103. Ibid., 7-14.

104. Ibid., 7-13.

105. Ibid.
106. Romjue, *From Active Defense to AirLand Battle*," 59.
107. Department of the Army, *Field Manual 100-5: Operations*, 7-22–7-25.
108. Romjue, *From Active Defense to AirLand Battle*, 27.
109. Ibid., 29.
110. Ibid.
111. Donn Starry, "Concepts," Donn Starry Papers, box 2, folder 5, U.S. Army Heritage and Education Center, Carlisle, PA.
112. Romjue, *From Active Defense to AirLand Battle*, 77.
113. Donn A. Starry, "Armor Conference Keynote Address," *Armor*, July–August 1978, p. 33.
114. Romjue, *From Active Defense to AirLand Battle*, 24.
115. Because large portions of the document were still classified at the time of this writing, my analysis relies on the unclassified portions analyzed by Romjue, *From Active Defense to AirLand Battle*, 25.
116. U.S. Army TRADOC, *Annual Historical Review, FY 1978* (Fort Monroe, VA: Headquarters, U.S. Army TRADOC, 1978), 1–3.
117. Romjue, *From Active Defense to AirLand Battle*, 26.
118. Ibid.
119. Yoav Ben-Horin and Benjamin Schwarz, *Army 21 as the U.S. Army's Future Warfighting Concept* (Santa Monica, CA: RAND, 1988), 4–5.
120. Ibid.
121. Ibid., iv.
122. Ibid.; U.S. Army TRADOC, *AirLand Battle 2000 Concept* (Fort Monroe, VA: Headquarters, U.S. Army TRADOC, 1982), 25–27.
123. Cable from Donn Starry to TRADOC commanders, "Concept Based Requirement Strategy," January 5, 1981, Donn Starry Papers, box 1, folder 5, U.S. Army Heritage and Education Center, Carlisle, PA.
124. U.S. Army TRADOC, *Annual Historical Review, FY 1981* (Fort Monroe, VA: Headquarters, U.S. Army TRADOC, 1982), 4–5.
125. U.S. Army TRADOC, *Army 21 Interim Operational Concept* (Fort Monroe, VA: Headquarters, U.S. Army TRADOC, 1985).
126. Ibid., 4–5.
127. Ibid.
128. Ben-Horin and Schwarz, *Army 21*, 11–15.
129. Ibid., 10; TRADOC *Annual Historical Review, FY 1983* (Fort Monroe, VA: Headquarters, U.S. Army TRADOC, 1984).
130. Donn A. Starry, "Reflections," in *Camp Colt to Desert Storm: The History of U.S. Armored Forces*, ed. George F. Hofmann and Donn A. Starry (Lexington: University Press of Kentucky, 1999), 551–552.
131. At TRADOC, Starry did receive briefs on using tactical nuclear weapons and enhanced radiation weapons but was skeptical regarding the early use of nuclear weapons. Van Atta et al., *Transformation and Transition*.

Chapter 4

1. Colin L. Powell, "National Military Strategy of the United States," January 1992, http://history.defense.gov/Portals/70/Documents/nms/nms1992.pdf; John M. Shalikashvili, "National Military Strategy of the United States of America," 1995, http://history.defense.gov/Portals/70/Documents/nms/nms1995.pdf.

2. Department of the Army, *Field Manual 100-5: Operations* (Washington, DC: Headquarters, Department of the Army, 1993); Department of the Army, *Force XXI Operations: A Concept for the Evolution of Full-Dimension Operations for the Strategic Army of the Early Twenty-First Century*, TRADOC Pamphlet 525-5 (Fort Monroe, VA: Headquarters, U.S. Army TRADOC, 1994).

3. Department of the Army, *Fiscal Year 1992 Army Posture Statement* (Washington, DC: Department of the Army, 1991), 1.

4. Department of the Army, *Fiscal Year 1995 Army Posture Statement* (Washington, DC: Department of the Army, 1994), 34–37.

5. Gordon R. Sullivan, *Collected Works of the Thirty-Second Chief of Staff, United States Army: Gordon R. Sullivan, General, United States Army, Chief of Staff, June 1991–June 1995* (New York: Diane, 1996), 456.

6. Ibid., 451. The figures are in 1994 dollars.

7. Department of the Army, *Fiscal Year 1992 Army Posture Statement*, 1.

8. Senior officer associated with writing concepts and doctrine in the early 1990s, interview by the author, September 5, 2009.

9. Department of the Army, *Fiscal Year 1992 Army Posture Statement*, 1.

10. Ibid., 4–5.

11. Department of the Army, *Fiscal Year 1993 Army Posture Statement* (Washington, DC: Department of the Army, 1992), 18.

12. Department of the Army, *Fiscal Year 1992 Army Posture Statement*, 3.

13. Ibid.

14. Ibid., 4.

15. Ibid., 5.

16. Ibid., 6.

17. Field-grade officer associated with writing concepts and doctrine in the early 1990s, interview by the author, September 5, 2009.

18. House Subcommittee on Defense, Committee on Appropriations, *FY92 Defense Posture: Statement by General Colin L. Powell, U.S. Army, Chairman of the Joint Chiefs of Staff Before the United States House of Representatives*, 102nd Cong. (1991), 6.

19. Senate Committee on Appropriations, *Department of Defense Global Overview: Statement by General Colin L. Powell, U.S. Army, Chairman of the Joint Chiefs of Staff Before the United States Senate*, 102nd Cong. (1991), 130.

20. House Subcommittee on Defense, Committee on Appropriations, *FY92 Army Postures: Statement by General Carl E. Vuono Chief of Staff United States Army Before the United States House of Representatives*, 102nd Cong. (1991), 5.

21. Senate Committee on Appropriations, *Department of Defense Appropriations for Fiscal Year 1992: Statement by General Colin L. Powell, U.S. Army, Chairman, Joint Chiefs of Staff Before the United States Senate*, 102nd Cong. (1991), 136.

22. Lorna Jaffe, "The Development of the Base Force, 1989–1992," July 1993, p. 2, http://www.dtic.mil/doctrine/doctrine/history/baseforc.pdf.

23. Ibid., 12.

24. Ibid., 6. Interestingly, Paul Wolfowitz is a key part of this story. Wolfowitz worked on developing integrated planning scenarios while serving in the Department of Defense between 1977 and 1980 and later led the defense committees tasked with responding to "National Security Review 12."

25. The statement was prefaced with "I do not expect this review to invent a new defense strategy for a new world. On the contrary, I believe that our fundamental purposes are enduring and that the broad elements of our current strategy—our Alliances, our military capabilities—remain sound." George Bush, "National Security Review 12," March 3, 1989, http://bush41library.tamu.edu/files/nsr/nsr12.pdf.

26. Jaffe, "The Development of the Base Force," 9.

27. Ibid., 3–4, 10; Joint Chiefs of Staff, "1990 Joint Military Net Assessment," January 20, 1990, p. ES-4, http://www.dtic.mil/dtic/tr/fulltext/u2/a344529.pdf.

28. Jaffe, "The Development of the Base Force," 12.

29. Don Snider, *Strategy, Forces and Budgets: Dominant Influences in Executive Decision Making, Post–Cold War, 1989–91* (Carlisle, PA: Strategic Studies Institute, 1993), 11. The concept was not without controversy and debate. Yet those debates decreased after the fall of the Berlin Wall in November 1989. For an account of the types of debates between the services and the Joint Chiefs of Staff over what became known as Base Force, see Snider, *Strategy, Forces and Budgets*, and Jaffe, "The Development of the Base Force."

30. Jaffe, "The Development of the Base Force," 21.

31. Thomas K. Adams, *The Army After Next: The First Postindustrial Army* (Palo Alto, CA: Stanford University Press, 2008), 26; U.S. Joint Chiefs of Staff, *National Military Strategy of the United States* (Washington, DC: Government Printing Office, 1992).

32. House Subcommittee on Defense, Committee on Appropriations, *Fiscal Year 1993 Army Posture: Statement by Michael P. W. Stone, Secretary of the Army, Before the United States House of Representatives*, 102nd Cong. (1992).

33. House Subcommittee on Defense, Committee on Appropriations, *FY92 Defense Posture*, 47.

34. Senate Committee on Appropriations, *Department of Defense Global Overview*, 55.

35. Ibid., 55–56.

36. Ibid., 57.

37. Donald H. Rumsfeld, *Prepared Testimony to the Senate Armed Services Committee*, 107th Cong. (2001), http://www.defense.gov/Speeches/Speech.aspx?SpeechID=374.

38. Snider, *Strategy, Forces and Budgets*, 9.

39. Mark D. Sherry, *The Army Command Post and Defense Reshaping, 1987–1997* (Washington, DC: Center for Military History, 2008), 24.

40. Ibid., 25.

41. Ibid., 29.

42. Powell, "National Military Strategy."

43. Department of the Army, *Fiscal Year 1992 Army Posture Statement*, 24.

44. Sullivan, *Collected Works*, 88.

45. Ibid., 23.

46. Department of the Army, *Fiscal Year 1992 Army Posture Statement*, 11.

47. Ibid., 9.

48. Ibid., 12.

49. Ibid., 13.

50. Department of the Army, *Fiscal Year 1993 Army Posture Statement*, 36.

51. Anthony Lake, "From Containment to Enlargement," speech given at Johns Hopkins University School of Advanced and International Studies, Washington, DC, September 21, 1993, http://fas.org/news/usa/1993/usa-930921.htm.

52. Anthony Lake, *A Strategy of Enlargement and the Developing World* (Washington, DC: U.S. Department of State, 1993).

53. Senate Subcommittee on Defense Appropriations, *Department of Defense: Statement by the Honorable Les Aspin Secretary of Defense Before the United States Senate*, 103rd Cong. (1993), 10.

54. Department of the Army, *Fiscal Year 1994 Army Posture Statement* (Washington, DC: Department of the Army, 1993), 17.

55. Adams, *The Army After Next*, 3; Frederick W. Kagan, *Finding the Target: The Transformation of American Military Policy* (New York: Encounter, 2006), 154.

56. House Subcommittee on Defense, Committee on Appropriations, *Fiscal Year 1995 Defense Posture: Statement by the Honorable William J. Perry, Secretary of Defense Before the United States House of Representatives*, 103rd Cong. (1994), 3.

57. House Subcommittee on Defense, Committee on Appropriations, *Fiscal Year 1995 Defense Posture: Statement by General John M. Shalikashvili, Army, Chairman of the Joint Chiefs of Staff Before the United States House of Representatives*, 103rd Cong. (1994), 51.

58. House Subcommittee on Defense, Committee on Appropriations, *FY92 Defense Posture: Statement by the Honorable Richard B. Cheney Secretary of Defense Before the United States House of Representatives*, 102nd Cong. (1991), 1.

59. Frank N. Schubert and Theresa L. Kraus, *The Whirlwind War: The United States Army in Operations* DESERT SHIELD *and* DESERT STORM (Washington, DC: Department of the Army, 1995), 174–205.

60. Barry Posen, "Command of the Commons: The Military Foundation of U.S. Hegemony," *International Security* 28, no. 1 (2003): 5–46.

61. Department of the Army, *Fiscal Year 1993 Army Posture Statement*, 6.

62. Department of the Army, *Fiscal Year 1994 Army Posture Statement*, 62.

63. Ibid., 63.

64. This perspective was echoed by a senior retired officer associated with the Future Battles Directorate at TRADOC during the early 1990s. Retired flag officer, interview by the author, September 8, 2009.

65. Department of the Army, *Fiscal Year 1994 Army Posture Statement*, 67.

66. Ibid.

67. House Subcommittee on Defense, Committee on Appropriations, *FY92 Defense Posture*, 137.

68. Retired officer associated with the chief of staff of the Army's office, interview by the author, September 11, 2009.

69. Department of the Army, *Fiscal Year 1995 Army Posture Statement*, 5.

70. John L. Romjue, *American Army Doctrine for the Post–Cold War* (Honolulu: University of Hawaii Press, 1997), 35.

71. Sullivan, *Collected Works*, 18.

72. Ibid., 19.

73. Alvin Toffler, *Future Shock* (New York: Bantam, 1984); Alvin Toffler, *The Third Wave* (New York: Bantam, 1984); Alvin Toffler, *Powershift: Knowledge, Wealth, and Violence at the Edge of the 21st Century* (New York: Bantam, 1991); Alvin Toffler and Heidi Toffler, *War and Anti-War: Making Sense of Today's Global Chaos* (New York: Bantam, 1995).

74. For an overview of RMA, see Colin S. Gray, *Strategy for Chaos: Revolutions in Military Affairs and the Evidence of History* (London: Frank Cass, 2002); MacGregor Knox and Williamson Murray, *The Dynamics of Military Revolution, 1300–2050*, 2nd ed. (Cambridge: Cambridge University Press, 2001); and Adams, *The Army After Next*.

75. Gordon R. Sullivan and James M. Dubik, *War in the Information Age* (Carlisle, PA: Strategic Studies Institute, U.S. Army War College, 1994), xxv.

76. Senior officer, interview by the author, September 5, 2009.

77. House Subcommittee on Defense, Committee on Appropriations, *Fiscal Year 1993 Army Posture: Statement by General Gordon Sullivan, Chief of Staff, United States Army Before the United States House of Representatives*, 102nd Cong. (1992), 17.

78. Senate Committee on Appropriations, *Department of Defense Global Overview: Statement by General Gordon Sullivan, Chief of Staff, United States Army Before the United States Senate*, 102nd Cong. (1992), 6.

79. Gordon R. Sullivan, "Doctrine: A Guide to the Future," *Military Review* 78, no. 2 (1992): 4.

80. Sullivan and Dubik, *War in the Information Age*, xv.

81. Gordon R. Sullivan, "Power Projection and the Challenges of Regionalism," *Parameters* 23 (1993): 9.

82. Romjue, *American Army Doctrine for the Post–Cold War*, 25; see also Carl E. Vuono, *The U.S. Army: A Strategic Force* (Washington, DC: Department of the Army, 1990).

83. House Subcommittee on Defense, Committee on Appropriations, *FY92 Army Postures: Statement by the Honorable Michael P. W. Stone, Secretary of the Army, Before the United States House of Representatives*, 102nd Cong. (1991), 2.

84. Romjue, *American Army Doctrine for the Post–Cold War*, 28.

85. Retired flag officer, interview by the author, September 8, 2009. In particular, he said that the key obstacles to reform at the Pentagon were the deputy chief of staff for Operations and Plans, who felt threatened by some of the more extreme digitization plans, and personnel at the Combined Arms Center at TRADOC, who viewed themselves as the keepers of conceptual innovation and imagination but were reluctant to test the boundaries of advances in information technology.

86. Romjue, *American Army Doctrine for the Post–Cold War*, 3.

87. Ibid., 38.

88. Ibid., 70.

89. Senior officer, interview by the author, September 5, 2009.

90. Romjue, *American Army Doctrine for the Post–Cold War*, 75.

91. Ibid.

92. Department of the Army, *Fiscal Year 1994 Army Posture Statement*, 70.

93. Ibid., 53.

94. Ibid.

95. U.S. Army TRADOC, *Battlefield Laboratories: The Road to the Post–Cold War Army* (Fort Monroe, VA: Headquarters, U.S. Army TRADOC, 1992), 2.

96. Ibid., 76.

97. Department of the Army, *Fiscal Year 1994 Army Posture Statement*, 58.

98. Ibid.

99. Ibid.

100. Sullivan, *Collected Works*, 103.

101. Senior retired officer associated with the LAM initiative and the TRADOC Future Battles Directorate in the early 1990s, interview by the author, September 11, 2009.

102. Ibid.

103. House Subcommittee on Defense, Committee on Appropriations, *Fiscal Year 1995 Army Posture: Statement by the Honorable Togo D. West, Secretary of the Army, Before the United States House of Representatives*, 103rd Cong. (1994), 159.

104. Senior officer, interview by the author, September 5, 2009.

105. Sullivan, *Collected Works*, 100.

106. U.S. Air Force, *Air Force Manual 1-1: Basic Aerospace Doctrine for the United States Air Force* (Washington, DC: U.S. Air Force, 1992).

107. Romjue, *American Army Doctrine for the Post–Cold War*, 113.

108. Department of the Army, *Field Manual 100-5: Operations*, 1-1.

109. Department of the Army, *Fiscal Year 1995 Army Posture Statement*, 60.

110. Ibid., 61.

111. Sullivan, *Collected Works*, 277.

112. Retired flag officer, interview by the author, September 8, 2009.

113. Department of the Army, *Field Manual 100-5: Operations*, 1-1.
114. Ibid., 1-2.
115. The principles are objective, offensive, mass, economy of force, maneuver, unity of command, security, surprise, and simplicity. See Department of the Army, *Field Manual 100-5: Operations*, 2-4–2-6.
116. Ibid., 2-8.
117. Ibid., 2-9.
118. Ibid., 3-5.
119. Ibid., 4-1–5-5.
120. Ibid., 6-3.
121. Ibid., 7-12.
122. Ibid., 13-0.
123. Ibid., 13-4.
124. Romjue, *American Army Doctrine for the Post–Cold War*, 41.
125. See White House, "National Security Strategy of the United States," August 1991, http://nssarchive.us/NSSR/1991.pdf.
126. Romjue, *American Army Doctrine for the Post–Cold War*, 44–45.
127. Ibid., 45. Some examples of these articles include John W. Reitz, "Managing Intellectual Change: Army's Revision of FM 100-5," *Army*, September 1992, pp. 45–47; Frederick M. Franks Jr., "Full-Dimensional Operations: A Doctrine for an Era of Change," *Military Review* 72, no. 12 (1993): 5–10; James R. McDonough, "Versatility: The Fifth Tenet," *Military Review* 73, no. 12 (1993): 11–14; H. Hugh Shelton and Kevin Benson, "Depth and Simultaneity: Half the Battle," *Military Review* 73, no. 12 (1993): 57–63.
128. Frederick Franks, "Briefing of FM 100-5, Operations (Preliminary Draft) to CSA and ARSTAF," November 5–6, 1992, Frederick M. Franks Papers, box 1, U.S. Army Heritage and Education Center, Carlisle, PA.
129. Frederick Franks, "Notes, FM 100-5 Off Site Conference, Fort Story VA, 5–6 Nov," November 10, 1992, Frederick M. Franks Papers, box 1, U.S. Army Heritage and Education Center, Carlisle, PA.
130. Romjue, *American Army Doctrine for the Post–Cold War*, 138–139.
131. House Subcommittee on Defense, Committee on Appropriations, *Fiscal Year 1995 Army Posture: Statement by General Gordon Sullivan, Chief of Staff, United States Army Before the United States House of Representatives*, 103rd Cong. (1994), 4.
132. Ibid., 169.
133. Sullivan, *Collected Works*, 437.
134. Ibid.
135. Department of the Army, *Force XXI Operations*, i.
136. Ibid., iv.
137. Ibid.
138. Senior retired officer, interview by the author, September 11, 2009.
139. Department of the Army, *Force XXI Operations*, 1-1.
140. Ibid., 2-2.

141. Ibid.
142. Ibid., 2-4.
143. Ibid.
144. Ibid., 1-2.
145. Ibid., 1-1.
146. Ibid., 1-5.
147. Ibid., 2-7.
148. Ibid., 2-8.
149. Ibid., 2-9.
150. Ibid., 3-4.
151. Ibid., 3-10.
152. Ibid., 2-10.
153. Ibid.

Chapter 5

1. Andrew Jackson O'Shaughnessy, *The Men Who Lost America: British Leadership, the American Revolution, and the Fate of the Empire* (New Haven, CT: Yale University Press, 2014), 11. For more on British military thought related to counterinsurgency in the eighteenth century, see ibid.

2. Richard Stubbs, *Hearts and Minds in Guerrilla Warfare: The Malayan Emergency, 1948–1960* (Singapore: Eastern Universities Press, 2004), 263. For further analysis of British counterinsurgency operations during the Malayan Emergency, see ibid.

3. David Petraeus, "Multi-national Forces–Iraq Commander's Counterinsurgency Guidance," *Military Review*, September–October 2008, p. 211.

4. Fred Kaplan, *The Insurgents: David Petraeus and the Plot to Change the American Way of War* (New York: Simon and Schuster, 2013), 82.

5. William S. Cohen, *Report of the Quadrennial Defense Review* (Washington, DC: Department of Defense, 1997).

6. For an overview of some of the conferences sponsored by U.S. Marine Corps Combat Development Command, see Barak A. Salmoni, ed., *Pedagogy for the Long War: Teaching Irregular Warfare; Conference Proceedings* (Quantico, VA: Marine Corps Training and Education Command and U.S. Naval Academy, 2008).

7. Kaplan, *The Insurgents*, 88.

8. Ibid., 108–116.

9. Department of Defense, *Quadrennial Defense Review Report* (Washington, DC: Department of Defense, 2006), 2–11.

10. John Nagl, foreword to *The New Counterinsurgency Era: Transforming the U.S. Military for Modern Wars*, by David Ucko (Washington, DC: Georgetown University Press, 2009), viii.

11. Defense Science Board, *Transition to and from Hostilities* (Washington, DC: Office of the Under Secretary of Defense for Acquisition, Technology, and Logistics, 2004).

12. Ibid., 5.

13. Kaplan, *The Insurgents*, 119.

14. Ibid., 120–121.

15. For an overview of the Army and its resistance to, but eventual acceptance of, the stability operations mission, see Jennifer Taw, *Mission Revolution: The U.S. Military and Stability Operations* (New York: Columbia University Press, 2012); and Thomas S. Szayna, Derek Eaton, and Amy Richardson, *Preparing the Army for Stability Operations: Doctrinal and Interagency Issues* (Santa Monica, CA: RAND, 2007).

16. Department of Defense, "Directive 3000.05: Military Support for Stability, Security, Transition, and Reconstruction (SSTR) Operations," November 28, 2005, http://fas.org/irp/doddir/dod/d3000_05.pdf.

17. Kaplan, *The Insurgents*, 133.

18. Robert Kerr, "Meet the Press: New Combined Arms Center Commander Discusses Iraq, Training, Leaders, Lessons-Learned," *Fort Leavenworth Lamp*, August 23, 2003, p. 1.

19. Tom Clancy and Frederick Franks, *Into the Storm: A Study in Command* (New York: Berkley, 2004), 125.

20. Donald P. Wright and Timothy R. Reese, *On Point II: Transition to the New Campaign; The United States Army in Operation Iraqi Freedom, May 2003–January 2005* (Fort Leavenworth, KS: Combat Studies Institute Press, 2008), 78–80.

21. Kaplan, *The Insurgents*, 133.

22. Department of the Army, *Field Manual Interim 3-07.22: Counterinsurgency Operations* (Washington, DC: Department of the Army, 2004).

23. Kaplan, *The Insurgents*, 136.

24. Ibid., 104–105.

25. Kalev Sepp, "Best Practices in Counterinsurgency," *Military Review*, May–June 2005, pp. 8–12.

26. James Russell, *Innovation, Transformation, and War: Counterinsurgency Operations in Anbar and Ninewa Provinces, 2005–2007* (Palo Alto, CA: Stanford University Press, 2011).

27. For a detailed overview of the establishment of the COIN Academy, see Ucko, *The New Counterinsurgency Era*, 75–80.

28. For a tactical-level perspective on operations in Tal Afar, see Jay Baker, "Tal Afar 2005: Laying the Counterinsurgency Groundwork," *Army*, June 2009, pp. 61–68; and Christopher Hickey, "Principles and Priorities in Training for Iraq," *Military Review*, March–April 2007, pp. 22–32.

29. Multi-national Force–Iraq, *Counterinsurgency Handbook* (Camp Taji, Iraq: Counterinsurgency Center for Excellence, 2006).

30. Ibid., 2.

31. Ibid., 6; David Kilcullen, "Twenty-Eight Articles: Fundamentals of Company-Level Counterinsurgency," *Small Wars Journal* 1 (March 2006), http://www.au.af.mil/info-ops/iosphere/iosphere_summer06_kilcullen.pdf.

32. Multi-national Force–Iraq, *Counterinsurgency Handbook*, 3.

33. Ibid., 2.
34. Kaplan, *The Insurgents*, 137.
35. Octavian Manea, "Reflections on the 'Counterinsurgency Decade': *Small Wars Journal* Interview with General David H. Petraeus," *Small Wars Journal*, September 1, 2013, smallwarsjournal.com/printpdf/14544.
36. Kaplan, *The Insurgents*, 137.
37. The workshops included "Measuring the Humanitarian Impact of War," held November 8–9, 2004, at the Carr Center in Washington, D.C., and "Working with Civilian Actors," held April 5–6, 2004, at the Carr Center in Arlington, Virginia.
38. Kaplan, *The Insurgents*, 140; Adam Joyce, "A Revolution from the Middle: How the U.S. Army Transformed Its Way of War," paper presented at the International Studies Association panel "Concepts at War," April 3, 2013, San Francisco, CA.
39. Kaplan, *The Insurgents*, 143–144.
40. David H. Petraeus, "Learning Counterinsurgency: Observations from Soldiering in Iraq," *Military Review*, January–February 2006, pp. 2–12.
41. Eliot Cohen, Jan Horvath, Conrad Crane, and John Nagl, "Principles, Imperatives, and Paradoxes of Counterinsurgency," *Military Review*, March–April 2006, pp. 49–53.
42. For an overview of the conference, see Thomas Ricks, "How to Fight This War," in *The Gamble: General David Petraeus and the American Military Adventure in Iraq, 2006–2008* (New York: Penguin, 2009), chap. 2.
43. John Nagl, "Constructing the Legacy of FM 3-24," *Joint Forces Quarterly* 58, no. 3 (2010): 118.
44. Ibid.
45. Kaplan, *The Insurgents*, 23.
46. David H. Petraeus, interview by Alexander Alderson, June 14, 2007, cited in Alexander Alderson, "US COIN Doctrine and Practice: An Ally's Perspective," *Parameters*, Winter 2007–2008, p. 38.
47. David H. Petraeus, "Preface," in "Counterinsurgency Reader," special issue, *Military Review*, October 2006.
48. Department of the Army, *Field Manual 3-24: Counterinsurgency* (Washington, DC: Department of the Army, 2006).
49. Ibid., 1-1.
50. Ibid., 1-23.
51. Kaplan, *The Insurgents*, 215.
52. Ralph Peters, "Politically Correct War: U.S. Military Leaders Deny Reality," *New York Post*, October 18, 2006, http://www.unc.edu/depts/diplomat/item/2006/1012/pete/peters_pcwar.html.
53. U.S. Army and Marine Corps, *The U.S. Army/Marine Corps Counterinsurgency Field Manual* (Chicago: University of Chicago Press, 2007).
54. Gian Gentile, *Wrong Turn: America's Deadly Embrace of Counterinsurgency* (New York: Free Press, 2013).

55. Elisabeth Bumiller, "West Point Is Divided on a War Doctrine's Fate," *New York Times*, May 27, 2012, http://www.nytimes.com/2012/05/28/world/at-west-point-asking-if-a-war-doctrine-was-worth-it.html.

56. Andrew Birtle, *U.S. Army Counterinsurgency and Contingency Operations Doctrine, 1860–1941* (Washington, DC: Center of Military History, 1998), 7; W. E. Lee, "Early American Ways of War: A New Reconnaissance, 1600–1815," *Historical Journal* 44 (2001): 269–289. For an in-depth analysis, see John Grenier, *The First Way of War: American War Making on the Frontier, 1607–1814* (Cambridge: Cambridge University Press, 2005). These arguments can be contrasted with Russell Weigley's treatment of American military history in *The American Way of War: A History of United States Military Strategy and Policy* (Bloomington: Indiana University Press, 1960).

57. There are ethical and definitional concerns with viewing wars against Native Americans as counterinsurgency given that indigenous populations were polities in their own right engaged in a complex, contentious relationship with early European settlements and, later, the American government.

58. For an overview of Wayne's campaign, see Alan D. Graff, *Bayonets in the Wilderness* (Norman: University of Oklahoma Press, 2008); and Wiley Sword, *President Washington's Indian War* (Norman: University of Oklahoma Press, 1993).

59. For an overview of the legion, see Andrew Birtle, "Origins of the Legion of the United States," *Journal of Military History* 67, no. 4 (2003): 1249–1261; and Francis Paul Prucha, *The Sword of the Republic: The United States Army of the Frontier, 1783–1846* (Bloomington: Indiana University Press, 1977).

60. Birtle, "Origins of the Legion of the United States," 1251; see also Christopher Duffy, *The Military Experience in the Age of Reason* (New York: Atheneum, 1988), 268–279; David Gates, *The British Light Infantry Arm, 1790–1815* (London: B. T. Batsford, 1987), 10–35; Johann Ewald, *Treatise on Partisan Warfare*, translated and annotated by Robert Selig and David Skaggs (New York: Greenwood, 1991), 1–38.

61. Birtle, *U.S. Army Counterinsurgency*," 10.

62. Russell Weigley, *History of the United States Army* (Bloomington: Indiana University Press, 1984), 91–94. For a discussion of Enlightenment discourse and war, see Armstrong Starkey, *War in the Age of Enlightenment, 1700–1789* (Westport, CT: Praeger, 2003); and Bruce Buchan, "Pandours, Partisans, and Petite Guerre: The Two Dimensions of Enlightenment Discourse on War," *Intellectual History Review* 23, no. 3 (2013): 329–347.

63. Birtle, *U.S. Army Counterinsurgency*, 11; Henry Bouquet, "Reflections on War with the Savages of North-America," in *An Historical Account of the Expedition Against the Ohio Indians, in the Year 1764*, by William Smith (Philadelphia: W. Bradford, 1765), 37–59; James Smith, *A Treatise on the Mode and Manner of Indian War* (Paris, KY: Joel R. Lyle, 1812).

64. See Chapter 1.

65. Birtle, *U.S. Army Counterinsurgency*, 12.

66. Ibid.

67. Dennis Hart Mahan, *An Elementary Treatise on Advanced-Guard, Out-Post, and Detachment Service of Troops with the Essential Principles of Strategy and Grand Tactics* (New York: Wiley and Putnam, 1847).

68. War Department, *Regulations for the Army of the United States, 1857* (New York: Harper, 1857).

69. Antoine-Henri Jomini, *Traité des grandes opérations militaire* (Paris: Magimel, 1816). For a summary of the ideas of Napoleon and how they influence American military thought, see Joseph Harsh, "Battlesword and Rapier: Clausewitz, Jomini, and the American Civil War," *Military Affairs* 38, no. 4 (1974): 133.

70. John Waugh, *The Class of 1846: From West Point to Appomattox: Stonewall Jackson, George McClellan, and Their Brothers* (New York: Random House, 2010), 14. Lafayette took Mahan under his wing while the young officer studied in France.

71. James J. Schneider, "The Loose Marble—and the Origins of Operational Art," *Parameters*, March 1989, p. 27.

72. Russell Weigley, *Toward an American Army: Military Thought from Washington to Marshall* (Westport: Greenwood, 1962), 38–78. For an alternative view that sees Mahan as not just a disciple of Jomini but advocating a more refined reading of Napoleon's operational art, see James L. Morrison Jr., "Military Education and Strategic Thought, 1846–1861," in *Against All Enemies: Interpretations of American Military History from Colonial Times to the Present*, ed. Kenneth J. Hagan and William R. Roberts (New York: Greenwood, 1986), 122.

73. For an overview of Emmerich Vattel's work and impact, see Charles Fenwick, "The Authority of Vattel," *American Political Science Review* 8, no. 3 (1914): 375–392; Richard Devetak, "Law of Nations as Reason of State: Diplomacy and the Balance of Power in Vattel's 'Law of Nations,'" *Parergon* 28, no. 2 (2011), 105–128; and Patrick Finnegan, "Study of Law as a Foundation of Leadership and Command: The History of Law Instruction at the United States Military Academy at West Point," *Military Law Review* 112 (2004): 181.

74. Buchan, "Pandours, Partisans, and Petite Guerre."

75. Department of the Army, *Special Text 31-20-1: Operations Against Guerrilla Forces* (Fort Benning, GA: Infantry School, 1950).

76. Ibid., 11.

77. The best historical treatment of Russell W. Volckmann's contribution to American counterinsurgency doctrine is Andrew J. Birtle, *U.S. Army Counterinsurgency and Contingency Operations, 1942–1976* (Washington, DC: Center of Military History, 2007).

78. For his account, see Russell W. Volckmann, *We Remained: Three Years Behind Enemy Lines in the Philippines* (New York: W. W. Norton, 1954).

79. See Irving B. Holley Jr., *Ideas and Weapons* (Washington, DC: Air Force History and Museums Program, 1997), vii.

80. Analysis of the manual and associated campaigns was rereleased in 1954 as part of an effort to counter future communist guerrilla movements. See Department

of the Army, *German Antiguerrilla Operations in the Balkans (1941–1944)*, Pamphlet 20-243 (Washington, DC: Department of the Army, 1954).

81. Birtle, *U.S. Army Counterinsurgency and Contingency Operations, 1942–1976*, 133.

82. Examples include Lloyd Marr, "Rear Area Security," *Military Review* 31 (1951): 57–62; and Hellmuth Kreidel, "Agents and Propaganda in Partisan Warfare," *Military Review* 39 (1959): 102–105.

83. Charles D. Melson, "German Counterinsurgency Revisited," *Journal of Military and Strategic Studies* 4, no. 1 (2011): 1–33.

84. Department of the Army, *Special Text 31-20-1*.

85. Birtle, *U.S. Army Counterinsurgency and Contingency Operations, 1942–1976*, 135.

86. Department of the Army, *Special Text 31-20-1*, 35.

87. Ibid., 40–41.

88. Ibid., 41.

89. Ibid.

90. Thomas E. Ricks, *The Gamble: General Petraeus and the American Military Adventure in Iraq* (New York: Penguin, 2010), 90.

91. Ibid., 95–96.

Chapter 6

1. Carl von Clausewitz, *On War*, ed. and trans. Michael Howard and Peter Paret (Princeton, NJ: Princeton University Press, 1989).

2. Barry Posen, *Inadvertent Escalation: Conventional War and Nuclear Risks* (Ithaca, NY: Cornell University, 1992).

3. An example of using a historical case is the battle of Tannenberg in World War I.

4. Emroy Upton, *The Armies of Asia and Europe: Embracing Official Reports on the Armies of Japan, China, India, Persia, Italy, Russia, Austria, Germany, France, and England; Accompanied by Letters Descriptive of a Journey from Japan to the Caucasus* (New York: D. Appleton, 1878).

5. The relationship between the essay and the commission is detailed in the preface to the second edition. Spenser Wilkinson, *The Brain of an Army: A Popular Account of the German General Staff* (London: Constable, 1913).

6. Niel Smith, "Overdue Bill: Integrating Counterinsurgency into Army Professional Education," *Small Wars Journal*, December 3, 2009, http://smallwarsjournal.com/jrnl/art/integrating-coin-into-army-professional-education.

7. Richard Shultz, Roy Godson, and Querine Hanlon, *Armed Groups and Irregular Warfare: Adapting Professional Military Education* (Washington, DC: National Strategy Information Center, 2009).

8. House Subcommittee on Oversight and Investigations, Committee on Armed Services, *Another Crossroads? Professional Military Education Two Decades After the Goldwater-Nichols Act and the Skelton Panel*, H.R. 111-4 (2010), 74.

9. Joan Johnson-Freese, *Educating America's Military* (New York: Routledge, 2013); Kevin P. Kelley and Joan Johnson-Freese, "Getting to Good in Professional Military Education," *Orbis*, Winter 2014, pp. 119–131.

10. House Subcommittee on Oversight and Investigations, Committee on Armed Services, *Another Crossroads?* xiii.

11. Williamson Murray, "Is Professional Military Education Necessary?" *Naval War College Review*, January 2014, p. 147.

12. Scott Snook, Nitin Nohria, Rakesh Khurana, eds., *The Handbook for Teaching Leadership: Knowing, Doing, and Being* (Thousand Oaks, CA: Sage, 2012), 388.

13. Nancy M. Dixon, Nate Allen, Tony Burgess, Pete Kilner, and Steve Schweitzer, *Company Command: Unleashing the Power of the Army Profession* (West Point, NY: Center for the Advancement of Leader Development and Organizational Learning, 2005), 3.

14. Ibid., 6.

15. Ibid., 177.

16. "Marching Orders: America's Force of Decisive Action," January 2012, http://www.chapnet.army.mil/pdf/38th%20CSA%20Marching%20Orders%20(January%202012).pdf.

17. See United States Army Human Resources Command, "Broadening Opportunity Programs," https://www.hrc.army.mil/Officer/Broadening%20Opportunity%20Programs_Building%20a%20cohort%20of%20leaders%20that%20allow%20the%20Army%20to%20succeed%20at%20all%20levels%20in%20all%20environments (accessed July 23, 2015).

18. These publications include Austin Long, *On "Other War": Lessons from Five Decades of RAND Counterinsurgency Research* (Santa Monica, CA: RAND, 2006); David Gombert, *Heads We Win: The Cognitive Side of Counterinsurgency (COIN)* (Santa Monica, CA: RAND, 2007); William Rosenau, *Subversion and Insurgency* (Santa Monica, CA: RAND, 2007); Daniel Byman, *Understanding Proto-insurgencies* (Santa Monica, CA: RAND, 2007); Angel Rabasa, Lesley Anne Warner, Peter Chalk, Ivan Khilko, and Paraag Shukla, *Money in the Bank: Lessons Learned from Past Counterinsurgency (COIN) Operations* (Santa Monica, CA: RAND, 2007); Martin C. Libicki, David C. Gombert, David R. Frelinger, and Raymond Smith, *Byting Back: Regaining Information Superiority Against 21st-Century Insurgents* (Santa Monica, CA: RAND, 2007); Bruce R. Pirnie and Edward O'Connell, *Counterinsurgency in Iraq (2003–2006)* (Santa Monica, CA: RAND, 2008); David C. Gombert, John Gordon IV, Adam Grissom, David R. Frelinger, Seth G. Jones, Martin C. Libicki, Edward O'Connell, Brooke Stearns Lawson, and Robert E. Hunter, *War by Other Means: Building Complete and Balanced Capabilities for Counterinsurgency* (Santa Monica, CA: RAND, 2008); John Mackinlay and Alison Al-Baddawy, *Rethinking Counterinsurgency* (Santa Monica, CA: RAND, 2008); Seth Jones, *Counterinsurgency in Afghanistan* (Santa Monica, CA:

RAND, 2008); Peter Chalk, *The Malay-Muslim Insurgency in Southern Thailand: Understanding the Conflict's Evolving Dynamic* (Santa Monica, CA: RAND, 2008); and Austin Long, *Doctrine of Eternal Recurrence: The U.S. Military and Counterinsurgency Doctrine, 1960–1970 and 2003–2006* (Santa Monica, CA: RAND, 2008).

19. For more on the Strategic Studies Group, see its website at http://csa-strategic-studies-group.hqda.pentagon.mil/SSG_Index.html.

Index

Page numbers in italics indicate material in figures or tables.

Abrams, Creighton, 29, 31, 33, 36–37
Active Defense doctrine, 21; advocacy networks for, 47–52, 54, *143*; blending offense/defense, 149; DePuy and, 25–26, *143*; fundamental tasks of, 46; as fusion of ideas, 42–43; German acceptance of, 50–51; incubators for, 47, 53, *143*; intraservice cooperation and, 36–39, 55; invalidated by V Corps, 68–70, *144*; memory and experience in, 55; versus power projection doctrine, 113; shaped by conflict analysis, 35–36. *See also* Arab-Israeli/Yom Kippur War
Adamsky, Dima, 13
adaptation, defined, 8–9
advocacy networks, 145–146; across services, 106; for Active Defense, 47–52, 54, *143*; for AirLand Battle doctrine, 59, 84–86; for Base Force concept, 123; benefit of small size, 144; and classified briefings, 30; and communities of interest, 148; as contagion vectors, 142; cross-cutting connections through, 2; defined, 19; DePuy's/TRADOC's use of, 47–52, 54; diffusion of ideas through, 22, 23, 59, 84, *143*; enabling brokerage, 20; for Extended Battlefield, 72; for Full-Dimensional Operations, 118, 121, 124; as institutional mechanisms of change, 4, 15; legitimating incubators, 21; lobbying Army chief of staff, 52; Mahan's use of, 136–137; online forums as, 153; personal correspondence as, 51, 54; as positive feedback loops, 19; rallying the base, 123; for rewriting COIN, 125–126, 132–133, 140–141; seeking broad organizational consensus through, 85–86, 117–118; as sources of doctrinal innovation, 146–148; testimony before Congress, 51–52. *See also* letters, communication and lobbying via; professional journals
Afghanistan, 63–68, 133–134

189

Africa, 64, 91
Air Defense Artillery School, 108
Air Force Manual 1-1: Basic Aerospace Doctrine, 112
AirLand Battle doctrine: versus Active Defense, 79; advocacy networks for, 59, 84–86, *143*; articles supporting, 75, 86; coordinating with Air Force, 76, 106; expanded focus of (1993), 113; formal publication of, 75; incorporating into *FM 100-5*, 7, 75–77, 116; incubators for, *143*; little civilian involvement in, 14; not a response to shocks and competition, 86, 146–147; origins of, 14, 59–60, 104, 122; post–Cold War, 116; primed for escalation, 147; refining of, 76; renamed Concept-Based Requirements System, 82, 85; as response to problem-driven search, 86; technological push not a factor, 148–149; tenets of, 77–78; 2000 version of, 82–84; as umbrella concept, 83–84
AirLand Operations (Pamphlet 525-5), 105
air suppression, 36–38, 41, 47, 67
all-volunteer force, 26–27
American way of war, 1, 125–126, 134, 137, *147*; Active Defense as, 55; AirLand Battle as, 86; as attritionist, 13, 39–40, 149–150; Extended Battlefield as, 75; Force XXI as, 124; need for new, 40; *petite guerre* as, 134–135, 141; RMA and, 103–104
Ancker, Clinton, III, 129
Anderson, Gary, 126–127
Antaeus Studies, 96, 113, 122–123, *143*, 144, 147
antipartisan operations, 138–139
antitank weapons, 38, 41, 50, *58*, 61–62, 123
Arab-Israeli/Yom Kippur War: DePuy's comments on, 25; *FM 100-5* on, 26, 43–53; as framework for new lethality concept, 25, 37–39, 148; implications of, for European theater, 33–35, 37–42; lessons-learned cycle following, 33–34, 51–52; oil embargos following, 64; studies of, as incubators, *143*; tank and artillery losses in, 33, 37–38, 40. *See also* Active Defense doctrine
"armed nation building," 134
Armor School, 108
armor versus light community, 48
Army Combat Development Command, 32
Army Green Book (Sullivan), 113
"The Army in the Post-industrial World" (Sullivan), 97
Army journal, 117
Army Magazine, 153
artillery, 33, 35–36, 42, 46–47, 50–52
Aspin, Les, 98–99
Assault Breaker program, 74, 85
Association of the United States Army, 153
Astarita, Edward F., 29–30, 53
"Astarita Report," 29–30, 32, 54, 55
asymmetric threats, 90, 99–100, 103, 126–127
attritionist strategy, 13, 39–40, 86, 124, *147*, 149–150

balance of power, 56–60, 68, 77
Base Force concept, 94–96, 99, 123
Basin Harbor workshop, 133, *143*
"battle calculus," 68–69
Battle Command Training Program, 128
"Battlefield Development Plan," 81–83
battlefield dynamics, 107–109, 114–115, 120–121
battle labs, 108–109, *143*, 144
Battle of Tannenberg, 79
battle space, 107–108, 112
bias, 9, 16, 73, 99, 107, 123
Biden, Joe, 134

Birtle, Andrew, 134
blocking forces, 43, 55, 79, 149
"boathouse gang," 43, 110, 144
bottom-up innovation, 8, 153
Bouquet, Henry, 5, 135
Brain of an Army (Wilkinson), 150–152
brigades, emphasis on, 14
British forces, 13, 125, 134, 150
brokerage, 20, 54, 86, 123, 145
Brown, Harold, 74
budgetary constraints, 87–88; during Cold War, 88, 93–97; driving reform, 116, 121; as exogenous shocks, 147; and Force XXI, 121–122; and Full-Dimensional Operations, 121–122, 147; protecting training from, 150; and size of ground forces, 90; and technological overmatch, 101–103; and third wave of warfare, 111
bureaucracy: Active Defense and, 47–53; COIN and, 129; competitive pressure within, 11; concepts as blueprint for cooperation, 84; iron cage versus anomalous change, 3–4; isolating battle labs from, 108; locking in perspectives, 152; new ideas as threat to, 20; overcoming interservice rivalries, 36–39; Pamphlet 525-5 and, 105; positional legitimation within, 21, 54; post-Vietnam debates and, 30; separating development agencies from schools, 32
Bush, George H. W., 76, 94, 99, 175n25
buy-in, 23, 47–50, 108, 116, 145

CALDOL, 153–154
"capabilities and threat based army," 101, 109
capabilities following concepts, 123
Carnegie Corporation, 130
Carr Center for Human Rights, 130, 133, *143*
Carter, Jimmy, 64–65, 97

Casey, George, 129–130
Cavazos, Richard, 67
CAVNET web tool, 153
Central America, 64
Central Battle: as doctrinal statement, 80; and Extended Battlefield concept, 70–74, *71*; and Fulda Gap, 60–63; shaping the, 70; and three days of war, 63–68; as V Corps challenge, 68–70, 144
Cheney, Richard B., 100
Chiarelli, Peter, 153
"child of the frontier," U.S. Army as, 134
civilian influence on doctrinal change, 147, 147–148; advocacy networks, 19–20; and COIN, 140–141; disagreement on force ratios, 60; expected pathways of, 11–12, *12*; intervention thesis, 8, 158–159n56; mobilizing community to prevent, 50; no compelling evidence for, 14, 86, 104, 124
Clark, Wesley, 107
Clausewitz, Carl von, 4, 79, 144, 150
Clinton, Bill, 98–99
Clinton, Henry, 125, 137
close air support, 35–37
Cohen, Eliot, 127, 131, 133, 141
COIN doctrine: advocacy networks for, 125–126, 131–133, 140–141; Basin Harbor workshop, 133, *143*; Carr Center for Human Rights, 130, 133, *143*; COIN Academy, Camp Taji, 129; as MOOTW, 116; as "new old" idea, 134–140; Petraeus and "coinistas," 126, 130, 140–141; previous initiatives in Afghanistan, Iraq, 126
Cold War: budgetary constraints, 88, 93–97; from containment to dominance, 92; doctrine as engine of change, 106; end of, 87, 148; Eurocentric focus during, 11; force reductions following, 90; reform after, 14, 116, 124; use of incubators, 100

combat development agencies, 32
combat service support lab, 108
Combined Arms Center: briefing civilian leadership, 76; Concept Development Directorate within, 83; Foss and, 105–106; Petraeus as commander, 130; study groups on Extended Battlefield, 70, 72; TRADOC and, 43, 47; Wallace as commander of, 128, 140
combined arms team, 45, 47, 52
command and control concept, 45, 107–108
Command General Staff College, 75–76
"command of the commons," 100
committees, use of, 31, 144
competition and doctrinal change, 11, 12, 55, 86, 146
complexity, organizational, 18, 162n90
CONARC, 31–32, 81
concealment to enable movement, 45
Concept-Based Requirements System. See AirLand Battle doctrine
Concept Development Directorate, 83, 85
concepts: as blueprint for bureaucratic cooperation, 84; concept-driven simulation, 53; "concepts team," 43; "concept-to-production" cycle, 111; conceptual and bureaucratic anchors, 148, 152; conceptual innovation sequence, 34, 35; driving acquisitions, 82; formation process at TRADOC, 104–109; as foundation of doctrine, 80–81; general-officer panel reviews of, 83; military definition of, 6; as narratives, 83; socializing of, from top down, 86; translated into doctrine, 78
Concepts, Doctrine, and Development, 107
conferences. See workshops/conferences
conscription, reforms after, 14

contingency corps/operations, 65, 67, 79–80, 89, 95–97
continuum of military operations, 97–98
controversy, generating, 22, 54, 128, 132
corporateness, 16
Counterinsurgency Handbook, 130
"Counterinsurgency in Iraq" workshop, 131. *See also* COIN doctrine
cover to enable movement, 45
Craig, Malin, 18
Crane, Conrad, 131
creative destruction, 151
creativity as problem driven, 144
cross-reinforcement, 47. *See also* suppression
culture and doctrine, 13, 13–14, 149
Culver, John, 51
Czechoslovakia, 27

"daring thrust" attack, 62
Darley, Bill, 133
DARPA, 73–74, 85
Davidson, Janine, 128
"D-Day force," 66
"deadly embrace" of COIN, 133
decision-making rate, 69
deep-strike concepts, 70–73, 78–79, 115, 121, 123
defeats, reactions to, 2–3, 11–14, 12, 26
Defense News journal, 117
Defense Planning and Resources Board, 93
defensive operations. *See* Active Defense doctrine
democratic engagement, 98–99
DePuy, William: on air defense suppression, 37; analysis of SAM envelope by, 35–36; on blocking forces, 43, 55, 79, 149; developing Active Defense doctrine, 25–26, 75, 143; development of concepts into doctrine, 80–81; on evolution of weapons, 38; focus on

near-term fight, 81; Fort Benning speech, 39–41; and horizontal advocacy networks, 22–23; "Impetus for Change" paper, 31–32, 145; as lead advocate of change, 42; and National Training Center, 167n106; navigating bureaucracy, 36–37, 54, 81; Octoberfest conferences, 48–49, 54, 145; perspective on doctrine formation, 41–42; "pot of soup" memo, 41–42, 54, 144, 146; providing safe space for new concepts, 106, 146; unfinished manuscript on battle tactics, 25; use of tables and charts by, 38

Desert Shield, 91, 96–97, 106

Desert Storm, 95, 97, 110, 120, 148

destabilization, 99

Dickman, Joseph T., 18

diffusional legitimation, 21

digitized battlefield, 88, 99–100, 103

"Directive 3000.05" (Defense Department), 128–129

division, shift to brigades from, 14

doctrinal change, 8–10; exogenous shocks and, 147–148; inter-unit rivalry over, 11–12; and intervening institutional mechanisms, 21; from service coordination or rivalry, 73; sources of, 11–14; technological shocks and, 148–149; threshold of, *10*

doctrine, 3–5, 80; built around concepts, 6–7, 81, 104–108; as intellectual foundation, 81; joined with force development, 32–33; as means of organizational change, 121; permeating Army, 112; personalized reflections as, 5, 137–138; writing of, 43

"Doctrine: A Guide to the Future" (Sullivan), 104

Downs, Anthony, 9

drill, 1, 2, 5

early entry concept, 107–108, 121

economic dimensions of power, 63. *See also* budgetary constraints

economy of force missions, 98

education, 32, 150–152

An Elementary Treatise on Advanced-Guard, Out-Post, and Detachment Service of Troops (Mahan), 135

Eleventh Air Assault tests (1963–1965), 108

emulation versus adaptation, 9

engagement cycle, 105

Enlightenment warfare, 136

epistemic community, military as, 16

equipment: linking new doctrine to, 51; losses of, in Arab-Israeli War, 33, 37–38; shortages of, 67

Europe: and AirLand Battle concept, 75; conventional deterrence in, 60; estimated Soviet strength in East, 58; as expected next battleground (1976), 44–45; implication of Arab-Israeli War for, 37–42; post-Vietnam reorientation to, 26, 28–30

exogenous shock(s): creating imperative for change, 11; end of Cold War as, 111, 124; role of, in doctrinal change, 12, 15, 55, 140, 146–148, *147*; setbacks in Iraq as, 141

expertise as professional feature, 15

Extended Battlefield concept: as American way of war, 75; Combined Arms Center study groups on, 70, 72; Franks on Gulf War, 120–121; incubators and advocacy networks for, 72; responding to Soviet threat, 70–74, *71*

failed states, 92, 99

Farrell, Theo, 8, 9

Field Artillery School, 108

field commanders, soliciting reviews from, 72, 83

Field Manual 3-0: Operations (2001, 2008), 7
Field Manual 3-07.22: Counterinsurgency Operations, 129, 133
Field Manual 3-24: Counterinsurgency Operations: balancing of political-military campaigns, 126; as doctrinal innovation, 125; "hearts and minds" variant, 132; historical antecedents to, 139; promoted by incubators and advocacy networks, 133; RAND monographs on COIN, 154; reactions to, 132; setbacks as impetus for, 148; weakness in education on, 152
Field Manual 90-8: Counterguerrilla Operations (1986), 134
Field Manual 100-5, 5, 7, 49, 117; "Battle Planning and Coordination" section, 78–79; as capstone document, 105; "Combat Fundamentals" chapter, 77; "How to Fight" chapter, 45, 81; "Identifying the Challengers" section, 77; moved to TRADOC, 43; as near-term guide, 111–112; seeking institutional buy-in with, 116–117; *Field Service Regulations, Operations* (1941), 5; *Field Service Regulations* (1962), 5, 7; *Operations* (overview), 7, 43–53; *Operations* (1968), 5, 7; *Operations* (1976), 7, 26, 38, 43, 45, 47, 49–50; *Operations* (1982), 6, 7, 75–76; *Operations* (1993), 7, 89, 105–106, 111–112, 115–117
Field Manual 100-20: Military Operations in Low Intensity Conflict (1990), 134
Fields, Craig, 127
Fields Study, 127–128
Field Service Regulation (1905), 5
fighting forward as NATO doctrine, 46
Fighting the Guerrilla Bands (German Army), 138
fire coordination, 115

firepower, massing, 45–46
First Armored Division, 40–41, 100
first battle, winning the, 44, 53
First Expeditionary Division, 18
Fiscal Year 1992 Army Posture Statement, 90–91
flexible response, 28, 60–61
FLOT (forward line of troops), 70, 71
Foch, Ferdinand, 3
Focus 21, 84. *See also* AirLand Battle doctrine
fog of war, dissolving, 88
Foley, John V., 31
follow-on forces attack, 70, 76
force design and development, 31–34
force generation, 69, 81, 110
force packages, 94–95, 99
force posture, 61, 90, 96, 100–101, 110
force projection Army, 112
force ratios, 40, 45, 60, 69, 78
force reductions, 26–27, 90, 99
Forces Command, 32
Force Structure, Resources, and Assessment (J8), 93–94
Force XXI: budgetary constraints and, 121–122; enemy as "new warrior class" in, 120; experiments, 128; *FM 3-0* (2001), 7; Full-Dimensional Operations under, 88–89, 118; goals and fundamental hypothesis of, 118–119; incubators and advocacy networks for, 122–123; inducing shock to break enemy, 121; Pamphlet 525-5, 6, 89, 112, 119; precision fire power and perfect information, 149; resembling attrition-based warfare, 124, 149; threat perspective of, 119–120
"Force XXI Campaign Plan" (Sullivan), 118–119
Forsythe, George B., 153
forward defense: and AirLand Battle, 59; balancing of forces in, 66; battle simulations testing, 68–69;

conventional deterrence, 54; within extended battlefield, 70; versus forward presence, 93; NATO strategy of, 28–29, 54; post–Cold War shift from, 98; reinforcing, 66; shifting to power projection, 87, 118
forward line of troops (FLOT), 70, 71
Foss, John W., 96, 105–106
framing studies, 53, 84, 144, 150
Franks, Frederick M., Jr.: enabling radical statements, 119; establishing battle labs, 108; five battlefield dynamics of future war, 107; and LAM, 111; and origin of AirLand Battle 2010 project, 82–83; using *Field Manual* to seek buy-in, 116–117; using TRADOC as engine of change, 106–108
Frederickean Army, 111
Fulda Gap, 143; under Active Defense, 68; battle calculus of, 68–69; under Extended Battlefield concept, 72; and NATO forward defense, 66; Soviet attack scenario in, 62, 63
Full-Dimensional Operations doctrine: "battlefield dynamics" of, 121; budgetary constraints and, 121–122, 147; deterrence to offense to OOTW, 113–114; as first post–Cold War doctrine, 88; and *FM 100-5* (1993), 119; incubators and advocacy networks for, 118, 122, 143; no significant civilian intervention, 121; not an attritional orientation, 149; as power-projection doctrine, 121; senior leadership as focal points for, 143
Fuller, J. F. C., 4
Full-Spectrum Operations doctrine, 113–114, 147
functional versus systems management, 31
Future Battles Directorate, 88, 119–120
future wars: assessments/analysis of, 13, 84, 107, 119; and contingency planning, 67; and doctrine, 111–112; imagination and, 15–16, 26, 55, 82, 118; innovation as preparation for, 10, 14; study of being outsourced, 150–151; two images of, 149

Galvin, John, 132
generational lead, 100, 103
Germany, 29–30, 46, 52, 82, 138
GLCMs, 59
goal clarity, 161–162n89
Goldwater-Nichols Act (1986), 96
Gorman, Paul, 43
"graduate level" of war, 132
Grant, Ulysses S., 79, 102
Greenway, John R., 70
ground troops, 29–30, 44
guerrilla tactics against guerrillas, 139
Gulf War (1990–1991), 96, 100, 107, 149

Halperin, Morton, 11
Hamiltonians versus Jeffersonians, 16
Harmel, Pierre, 27
"Harmel Report," 27, 54
Hartington (Lord), 150
Hartzog, William W., 119
Harvard University, 130
"hearts and minds," 125, 132
Henriques, Richmond B., 75
Herbert, Paul H., 49
heuristics, micro and macro, 13
An Historical Account of the Expedition Against the Ohio Indians (Smith), 5, 135
historical cases in doctrine formulation, 79, 148, 152
Hix, William, 129
Hoffman, Martin, 128
Holder, L. D., 75
Holley, Irving, 137
horizontal innovation, 8
Horvath, Jan, 129–131
hostilities short of war, 97–98
Huffman, Burnside E., Jr., 34

Hunfeld I war game, 43, 144
Huntington, Samuel, 11, 15–16

IBM, 31
"immature theaters," 97, 106–107
"Impetus for Change" (DePuy), 31–32, 145
inadvertent escalation, 147
incubator(s): acceptance of, 20–21; for Active Defense doctrine, 47, 53; ad hoc nature of, 85; and advocacy networks, 21; for AirLand Battle doctrine, 59, 84–85, 122, *143*; Army War College as, 18; battle labs as, 108, 111; defined, 1–2; defining character of land warfare, 122; for envisioning future war, 119; as escape from bureaucracy, 142; for Extended Battlefield doctrine, 72; for Force XII, 122; framing studies as, 150; for Fulda Gap "battle calculus," 68–69, *143*; for Full-Dimensional Operations, 118, 122; importance of, 19, 133; as institutional mechanisms of change, 4, 15; LAM as, 111; problem-driven simulation as, 150; protected sites as important, 143–144; for rewriting COIN doctrine, 131, 132; searching for relevance and missions, 123; seen as threat by bureaucrats, 20; use of to overcome inertia, 17–18
independence of action, 78
inductive approach, 144
Infantry School, 108
information technology, 88, 103, 110–111, 119–120
innovation, doctrinal, *35*, *143*; alternative causal pathways of, 55, 146–147, *147*; civilian intervention not required for, 104; complexity and, 18; concepts as basis of, 83; defined, 8–9, 10; horizontal and bottom-up, 8; importance of incubators for, 123;
institutional requirements for, 9, 161–162n89; internal and external catalysts for, 16; during peacetime, 153; in response to challenges, 9; in response to strategic assessment, 14; role of resources in, 163n100
institutionalized knowledge: adaptation versus innovation in, 8–9; formal doctrine as, 4, 105; of individual memories, 9; problem-driven search as, 16–17, 53, 84, 86, 140, 144; satisficing in, 161–162n89; of weaknesses, 110
Instructions for Large Unit Commander (von Moltke), 3
insurgency, 66, 90, 116
"Integrated Operations" memo, 68
Intelligence School, 108
interservice rivalries, 36–39, 73, 76
Iran, 58, 63, 67, 99
Iraq, 64, 90, 92, 99, 126–127, 130–131
iron cage of bureaucracy, 3, 15, 17
irregular warfare, 126–127, 134
"islands of conflict," 84
Israel. *See* Arab-Israeli/Yom Kippur War
ITASS, 73–74, 85

J5 (Strategic Plans and Policy), 93–94
J8 (Force Structure, Resources, and Assessment), 93–94
Jagdkommando units, 138–139
Janowitz, Morris, 16
Jay, John, 1
Jeffersonians versus Hamiltonians, 16
Johnson, Lyndon B., 29
Johnson-Freese, Joan, 152
Johnston, Alastair Iain, 161n84
Joint Military Net Assessment (1990), 93
Joint Warfighting Center, 128
Jomini, Antoine-Henri, 136
journals. *See* professional journals
JSCP, 92
Just Cause, 96–97, 120, 148

Keane, Jack, 141
Kennedy, John F., 29
Kier, Elizabeth, 13
Kilcullen, David, 127, 130
knowledge: formal institutions of, 15; networks of, 1, 133, 135, 142; protecting production of, 150; synthetic approach to constructing, 42. *See also* institutionalized knowledge
Knox, Dudley W., 3
Komer, R. W., 50–51, 66
Korea, 59, 75, 98–99, 138
Kuwait, 90, 148

Laird, Melvin R., 26–27, 28
Lake, Anthony, 98
LAM (Louisiana Maneuvers), 19, 108–111, 144
land combat: post-Vietnam, 29–30; SAM envelope for, 35; tanks in Arab-Israeli War, 25, 33–38, 47; tanks in Cold War Europe, 39–43, 50–52, 55, 58, 61–62, 68, 74, 91; tanks in Persian Gulf, 91, 100, 102; use of terrain, 38, 47. *See also* Active Defense doctrine
Latin America, 91–92
The Law of Nations (Vattel), 136
leadership. *See* senior leadership
"Learning Counterinsurgency" (Petraeus), 131
Lee, Robert E., 136
Lee, W. E., 134
legitimacy, 54, 132, 145
lethality on the battlefield, 25, 37–39, 43–44, 55, 145, 148
letters, communication and lobbying via, 51; Abrams's orders to TRADOC (1974), 33–34; Cavazos's use of, 67; DePuy's use of, 35–37, 41–42, 50–52, 54; "Integrated Operations" memo, 68; Meyer's use of, 65–66; Petraeus's use of, 130–131; Richardson's use of,

72; Sullivan's use of, 112, 118–119; "TRADOC Pamphlet 525-5" (Sullivan), 6. *See also* white papers
levels of war, 77
light versus armor community, 48
Loh, John M., 106
Louisiana Maneuvers, 19, 108–111, 144

Mahan, Dennis Hart, 5, 135–137
Mahanian decisive battle concept, 16
Mahnken, Thomas, 2
Malayan Emergency (1952), 125
Mansoor, Peter, 141
"Marching Orders" (2012), 154
Marine Corps Combat Development Command, 108
Marine Corps Warfighting Laboratory, 108
Marine Gazette, 20
Marius Reforms, 2
marketing campaign for doctrine, 117–118
Marshall, Andrew, 74
Marshall, George C., 109–110
"massive systemic shock," 121
Mattis, James, 131
Maurice of Nassau, 2
McCaffrey, Barry R., 100
McMaster, H. R., 141
McNair, Leslie J., 109
Mearsheimer, John, 60–62
mechanized warfare, 58; AirLand Battle addressing, 75, 79; and "Astarita Report," 29–30; British Army and, 13; component parts of, 50; in *FM 100-5* (1976), 47, 50; German concepts of, 50–52; historical case studies of, 68–69; infantry fighting vehicles, 51–52, 58, 61; versus light infantry, 98, 106–107, 115; Oftcon II on, 48; versus "other wars," 60, 66; in postindustrial world, 77–79, 97, 106–107; U.S.

mechanized warfare (*continued*)
  Army's shift to, 48; Warsaw Pact plans for, 61–62, 63. *See also* Arab-Israeli/Yom Kippur War
media, early briefings of, 117
megacities, war fighting in, 154
memory and experience, 54–55
Meyer, Edward C., 65–66, 72, 73, 80, 90
micro and macro heuristics, 13
Middle East, 59, 63–64, 67, 75, 92. *See also* Arab-Israeli/Yom Kippur War; Iraq; Kuwait; Syria
Military Review, 117, 129, 131, 132–133, 140
"Modern Armor Battle II: The Defense" (Starry), 43
modern battlefield: four principles of fighting on, 45; increased lethality of weapons, 38, 44–45; mechanized warfare as defining feature, 47; military-technical revolution, 104; need for early air suppression, 36–37; proliferation of weapons, 45; versus World War II, 38–40
MOOTW (military operations other than war): versus attritional orientation, 124, 149; conceptual experimentation for, 123–124; in *FM 100-5: Operations* (1993), 7; post–Cold War, 14, 115–116; rules of war and, 121. *See also* OOTW (operations other than war)
Morelli, Donald R., 80, 82
Mosul, Iraq, 129
"move" doctrines, 22, 38, 40–42, 47, 78
"Multi-national Forces–Iraq Commander's Counterinsurgency Guidance," 125
multipolar world concerns, 56, 59
Murray, Williamson, 153

Nadaner, Jeffrey, 128
Nagl, John, 127, 131
Napoleon Bonaparte, 136
nationalism, 90–91, 119

"National Military Strategy" in 1990s, 87, 92–93, 112–113
"National Security Review 12," 93
"National Security Strategy," 113, 117
National Training Center, 167n106
NATO: CIA memo on (1969), 27; concerns about SS-20 and Backfire, 58–59, 149; conventional forces (1969), 28; Flexible Response strategy, 60; and non-NATO resource shortfalls, 67; planning for nuclear battlefields, 73; Special Group on Arms Control, 59. *See also* Active Defense doctrine; Fulda Gap
Naval Postgraduate School, 129
Naval Warfare (1994), 112
near-term fight, 81
nesting, 54, 85
new warrior class, 87
new world order, 87, 90, 96, 99
Nixon, Richard, 26, 28–29, 63
Nonaligned Nations, 64
nongovernment personnel, 143
non-NATO contingencies, 65–67
nonprofit organizations, 148
nonstate actors, 87, 90–91, 120
nuclear forces, 28, 58, 72–73, 95, 149, 171n63

Octoberfest/Oftcon II, 48–49, 54, 145
Odierno, Ray, 154
"offensive spirit," 77–78
oil embargos, 63–64
101st Airborne Division, 66–67, 129
one-and-a-half-war contingency model, 29
online forums, 153
On War (Clausewitz), 144
OOTW (operations other than war), 23, 113–114. *See also* MOOTW (military operations other than war)
operational concepts, 6–8, 34, 77, 83, 88, 113

operational level of war, 8, 30, 68, 77–78, 81, 85–86
Operations Against Guerrilla Forces (1950), 137–138
Operations manual. *See Field Manual 100-5*
Operation Steadfast, 31–32
ordering, war as, 136
organizational: complexity, 18, 162n90; flexibility, 78; slack, 163n100
other-war scenarios, 60, 63, 66, 96
Otis, Glenn K., 56, 59, 64, 68
outside-in legitimation, 86

Pace, Peter, 141
pace of warfare, 113
Pakistan, 63
Pamphlet 525-5: *AirLand Operations*, 105; *Force XXI Operations*, 89, 112, 119; origin of, 105; on precision firepower and perfect information, 149; scope of, 112
Panama, 96–97, 148
Panzer and *Panzergrenadier* tactics, 50–52
parallel ideas, 85
Parameters journal, 117, 133
Parker Panel, 31
peacekeeping and enforcement, 97–98
peer-to-peer connections online, 153
Pentagon, 178n85
Perry, William J., 74, 99
Pershing, John J., 18
Persian Gulf, 63–67
Peters, Ralph, 132
petite guerre (small war), 113, 126, 131, 134, 140
Petraeus, David, 133; "coinistas" group, 130; going outside bureaucracy, 140; incubators and advocacy networks preceding, 125–126; refining theory of victory, 130; use of positional legitimation, 141

"Pilot Study on the Department of Army Organization" (Whipple and Foley), 31
"Planning Guidance" Joint Chiefs memo, 67
planning horizon, 81–82, 107
Pokorny, Anthony G., 81
policeman of the world concept, 87
"politically correct war," 132
Posen, Barry, 8, 9, 22, 100, 147, 159n57
positional legitimation, 21, 54, 123, 141, 146
postindustrial battlefield: as attritional concept, 149; "battlefield dynamics" and, 121; battle labs and LAM, 111; and capability-based concept development, 124; digitization and asymmetric threats, 99–100; *FM 100-5: Operations* (1993) and, 112; Force XXI response to, 118, 122; and RMA, 149
"pot of soup" memo, 41–42, 54, 144, 151
Powell, Colin L., 87, 93–95, 122–123
power-projection doctrine, 87, 92, 96–97, 99, 110, 118
pragmatism, 144, 150
precision-strike capabilities, 96–97, 101, 148
"preemptive maneuver" attack, 62
primacy of U.S. military, 88, 98, 107
"Principles, Imperatives, and Paradoxes of Counterinsurgency" (Cohen, Horvath, Crane, and Nagl) 131
Principles of War (Foch), 3
private industry decision making, 31
problem-directed search, 16–17, 53, 84, 86, 140, 144
problem solving in organizational theory, 9
professional journals: bridging informal networks with, 133; failures to use, 133; German monographs in U.S., 138; *Marine Gazette*, 20; *Military Review*, 117, 129, 131, 132–133, 140;

professional journals (*continued*)
  officer debates and advocacy in, 20, 22; *Parameters*, 117, 133; proposed requirement for officers, 151, 153; senior leaders' use of, 59, 86, 133, 140, *143*, 145–146
professional soldiers, 14–15, 31–32, 150
propositions of this book, *21*, 21–24, 23
Prussian Army, 1–3
publications, 132. *See also* professional journals

Quadrennial Defense Review Report (2006), 127–128
Quantico conferences, 127, 140–141
"Quiet Study," 93, 144

RAND Arroyo Center, 154
rapid deployment capacity: intra-Army discussions on, 67; Joint Task Force, 65; no specific objective threat requiring, 101; post–Cold War, 92, 98, 101; post–Gulf War, 115; post-Vietnam, 31
"Reflections on War with the Savages of North America" (Bouquet), 5, 135
Regulations for the Order and Discipline of the Troops of the United States (von Steuben), 1
Regulations of the Army of the United States (1857), 136
"Reorganization of the 101st Airborne Division (Air Assault)" memo, 66–67
reserves, 27, 41, 46, 67–68
Rhodes, Edward, 16
Richardson, James, 72, 75–76
RMA (revolution in military affairs), 11, 14, 103, 120, 149
Rogers, Bernard, 70, 76
Romjue, John, 34, 71, 117
Root, Eliu, 18

Root Reforms, 5
Rosen, Stephen Peter, 8
Rumsfeld, Donald, 95, 127–128

SAM envelope, 35
satisficing, 144, 161–162n89
Saudi Arabia, 63
"savage" warfare, 135–137
"scan, swarm, strike, scatter" sequence, 84
scenario-based planning, 29, 44, 53, 82–83, 93. *See also* worst-case scenarios
Schlesinger, James R., 27
Schmidle, Robert "Rooster," 127
scholarly models, 15
schoolhouses (Army): as advocacy networks, 20; and currently deployed troops, 128; DePuy's use of, 41–43, 146; developing deep-strike concept, 70; need for emphasis on, 151; planning use of tactical nuclear weapons, 72; TRADOC's use of, 47, 83; under unified command, 32; Volckmann's use of, 137; Wallace's use of, 128; and war of ideas, 151, 153
science fiction, 110–111
Scribner, Edwin G., 80
second-echelon forces: alternatives to deep strike, 115; divisions and regiments, 69; post-Soviet, 106–107; and Soviet advantage, 14; and Warsaw Pact, 60–63, 68–73, 82
Secretaries of Defense, 50; Donald Rumsfeld, 95, 127; Harold Brown, 65, 74; James Schlesinger, 52; Les Aspin, 98; Melvin Laird, 28; Richard Cheney, 100; William Perry, 99
seeing deep, 69
senior leadership: and alliances with midlevel officers and bureaucrats, 19; championing ideas, 133; as focal points, *143*; as institutional node,

25–26; lobbying Congress, 97; as norm entrepreneurs, 19; orchestrating connections between actors, 145–146; protecting new ideas, 20, 146; targeting of, 54; use of Antaeus Studies by, 123; use of professional journals by, 59, 86, 133, 140, 143, 145–146. *See also* advocacy networks; incubators

Sepp, Kalev, 129
Sewall, Sarah, 130–131
Shafer, D. Michael, 13
Shalikashvili, John M., 99
Shang Yang, 2
shared situation awareness, 103
Sherman, William T., 150
Short, Edward, 130
Signal School, 108
simulation: during Iraq invasion, 128, 140; problem-driven, 53, 84, 122, 140, 144, 150; testing forward defense, 68–69; value of, 128; V Corps Central Battle, 43, 68–69, 78, 84, 144. *See also* battle labs; war games
simultaneous attack and operations, 115, 121, 148
small teams innovate best, 144
small war (*petite guerre*), 113, 126, 131, 134, 140
Small War Foundation, 153–154
Smith, James, 5, 135
Smith, Niel, 152
Smith, William, 5, 135
solving the wrong problem, 17
Southwest Asia, 63
Soviet threat, response to: AirLand Battle concept, 74–80; Central Battle Active Defense doctrine, 68–70, 80–81; and Concept-Based Revolution, 80–84; as conceptual focus, 148; doctrinal shift in mid-1970s, 61; and Extended Battlefield concept, 70–74;

Fulda Gap, 60–63; numerical advantage, 14; U.S. projected gap (1980s), 56–58, *57*, *58*

Soviet Union: arms production rates, *58*; breakthrough tactics of, 46, 62; "Brezhnev doctrine," 27; client/proxy states, 63–64, 68; collapse of, 88; concerns about retrenchment of, 92; increasing short-warning attack capabilities, 61; invasion of Afghanistan, 63–68; mass, momentum, continuity principles, 62; "rescuing Blitzkrieg" following Arab-Israeli War, 61; tanks in Arab-Israeli War, 37

Special Operations Command, 19
spectrum of operations, *114*
"spectrum supremacy," 121
speculation, defined, 2
stability operations, 127–128, 132, 149
standard operating procedures, 11
"standing start" posture, 62
Starry, Donn: advocating eight-year planning horizon, 81–82; and AirLand Battle doctrine, 74–76, 84, *143*; assuming command of TRADOC, 81; "Battlefield Development Plan," 81–83; "Concept Based Requirement Strategy," 82–83; contributing chapters to *FM 100-5*, 43; and DARPA studies, 85; definition of "concept" by, 6; emphasizing operational level of war, 81; engaging middle-tier officers, 146; establishing Central Battle as doctrine, 80–82; experiments on role of tank, 42–43, 68–69, 84; experiments on small counterattacks, 42–43, 55; on Fulda Gap, 62; Hunfeld I war game, 43, 144; "Integrated Operations" memo, 68; on mechanized and "other" wars, 60; Meyer letter to, 65; "Modern

Starry, Donn (*continued*)
Armor Battle II: The Defense," 43; testifying before Senate, 60; use of advocacy networks, 59; use of incubators, 23, 53, 59, 69–70; on visualizing targets, 69
Stone, Michael P. W., 91, 105
Strategic Assessment Group, 29
Strategic Plans and Policy (J5), 93–94
Strategic Studies Institute, 104. *See also* U.S. Army
streamlining, 32
strength of weak ties, 133
subversion of legitimate regimes, 90
"Successful and Unsuccessful Counterinsurgency Practices" (Sepp), 129
Sullivan, Gordon R.: announcing Force XXI, 118–119; and battle labs, 108–109, 144; on doctrine, 6, 106, 112; on *FM 100-5* (1993) as intellectual bridge, 112–113; importance of focus on future, 6; on information age warfare, 103; interest in Toffler's work, 102–103; and LAM, 111, 144; on multipolarity, 96; on postindustrial battlefield, 97, 102–104; promoting experimentation, 144; role of in initiating reform, 106; on Third Wave Warfare, 102; use of positional legitimation, 123; use of TRADOC, 106
Sumner, Gordon, Jr., 52
suppression, 36–38, 41–43, 47, 67
surge planning for Afghanistan, 133–134
synchronization, 78, 114
Syria, 25, 64
systems versus functional management, 31

Tactical Air Command, Air Force, 76, 106, 108
tactical versus operational levels of war, 8, 30, 68, 77, 81
tactics versus strategy, 5–6
Tal Afar, Iraq, 129–130
tanks, 33, 37–38, 40, 42, 47
Tannenberg, Battle of, 79
target servicing, 69, 70, 81
Tate, Clyde J., 75
technology, 88, 101–103. *See also* information technology
Templar, Gerald, 125
Terriff, Terry, 8
terrorism, 66, 90, 92, 120
theories of victory, 8, 156n12, 161n82; advocacy networks diffusing, 22, 143; AirLand Battle, 59; Arab-Israeli War and Active Defense, 38, 144; bundles of assumptions in, 16–17; Central Europe, 46–47; defined, 16–17; DePuy and shoot-to-move, move-to-concentrate, 22–23, 26, 38, 42, 47, 53–55, 145–146; emergent, 8, 10; emerging through incubators, 20, 22, 69, 94; formalizing into doctrine, 4, 75, 77; leaders' championing of, 22; multiple coexisting, 97; nesting and, 54; Petraeus and COIN, 130, 134, 137, 140–141; rate of change in, 122–123; redefining of critical tasks, 81; role of advocacy networks in, 22; role of senior leadership in, 22; tank as central decisive weapon, 42
Third Armored Cavalry Division, 129
third wave of warfare, 102, 111
"Thirteen Observations from Soldiering in Iraq" (Petraeus), 130–131
Thomas, Jim, 126–127
"three days of war," 65, 80, 86, 90, 113
Toffler, Alvin, 102–103, 110, 120
Toffler, Heidi, 102, 110
Total Force, 27
TRADOC: Analysis Center, 83; battle labs, 108–109, 143, 144; Commanders Conferences, 82; concept formation process at, 104–109; consensus-

building campaign for *FM 100-5* (1993), 117–118; creation of, 31–33; DePuy's use of, 22–23; developing Active Defense doctrine, 25–26; establishment as critical node of, 47; incorporating both OOTW and high-intensity combat, 113; linking new doctrine to equipment requirements, 51; lobbying for Active Defense doctrine, 47–53; Octoberfest conferences, 48, 54; post–Cold War adjustments, 89, 116; presentations to Congress, 51–52; testing and refinement of Active Defense, 49–50; weapons performance tables and charts, 38. *See also* Arab-Israeli/Yom Kippur War; Pamphlet 525-5

Traité des grandes opérations militaire (Jomini), 136

Transition to and from Hostilities, 127

A Treatise on the Mode and Manner of Indian War (Smith), 5, 135

"triad of nuclear forces," 95

trusted networks, 125

Twenty-Fourth Infantry Division, 100

"twin pillar" approach, 63

two-and-a-half-war doctrine, 29

two-war doctrine, 14, 87, 95

Tyler, Patrick, 95

Unified Quest war game, 151, 154

"United States Counterinsurgency: An Australian View" (Kilcullen) 127

unit readiness, 31

University of Chicago Press, 132

Upton, Emroy, 150

U.S. Army: Army 21 concept, 84; attritionist way of war, 13; battles against native population, 134–136, 183n57; forgetting previous knowledge, 139–140; Fort Benning, 39, 108, 137; Fort Bliss, 108; Fort Hood, 48; Fort Huachuca, 108; Fort Knox, 42, 48–49, 53, 108, 144; Fort Leavenworth, 43, 70, 105–108, 110, 131–132, 151; Fort Lee, 108; Fort Monroe, 43, 108–109, 111; Fort Sill, 108; Intelligence Center, 132; Material Command, 33–34; Material Systems Analysis Agency, 34; reorganization under Operation Steadfast, 31; Strategic Studies Group, 154; study of Germany, 138; as tactical organization, 32; War College, 18, 104, 133

U.S. House of Representatives, testimony before: by Sullivan, 103, 118; by West, 103

U.S. Marine Corps, 20, 108

U.S. Senate, testimony before: by Aspin, 98; by Powell, 87, 95; by Starry, 60; by Sullivan, 103; by Vuono, 92, 101

"U.S. Strategy Plans for Insuring No Rivals Develop" (Tyler), 95

Vattel, Emmerich, 136

V Corps, 43, 68–69, 78, 84, 128, 144

versatility as tenet of war, 113–114

Vicksburg, siege of, 79

victory. *See* theories of victory

Vietnam War, 14, 26, 28–30, 48–49, 132

"View of the 1990s," 94, 123, *143*

Volckmann, Russell W., 137–139

von Moltke, Helmuth, 3

von Steuben, Baron Friedrich Wilhelm, 1

Vuono, Carl, 92, 101–102, 105–106

Wallace, William Scott, 128–130, 133, 140

War Colleges, 18, 104, 130, 133, 152

war everywhere, 87, 114

war games, 20; as additional layer of review, 83; Berlin in, 28; Extended Battlefield, 72; Hunfeld I, 43; informed by Arab-Israeli War, 34

war of ideas, 151

war of information, 132

Warsaw Pact, 27, 60

Washington, George, 134

Wass de Czege, Huba, 75
Wayne, Anthony, 134
weak ties, strength of, 133
web-based officer interaction, 153
Weber, Max, 15
Weigley, Russell, 13, 136
West, Togo D., 111
Westmoreland, William C., 31
West Point, 136
Weyland, Fred, 51–52
Whipple, Winthrop, 31
white papers, 65–66, 73, 81, 105. *See also* letters, communication and lobbying via
Wilkinson, Spenser, 150
will to resist, breaking enemy's, 121
Wilson, James Q., 4, 8, 11
win-win to win-hold, 99
Wolfowitz, Paul, 126, 175n24
workshops/conferences, 133, 140, *143*; Basin Harbor workshop (Eliot Cohen), 127, 131, 133, 141, *143*; Carr Center workshops, 130–131; "coinistas" recruited from, 130; "Counterinsurgency in Iraq," 131; Fort Leavenworth COIN conference, 131–132; Octoberfest conferences, 48–49, 54; Quantico irregular warfare conferences, 127, 140–141; within Warsaw Pact, 61
"world in transition" concept, 120
World War II, 19, 38, 108, 138
"worldwide mobility," 97
worst-case scenarios: Arab-Israeli War, 39; Cold War Europe, 53, 60, 62, 82; digitization and asymmetric threats, 99–100; Fulda Gap, 62; and inadvertent escalation, 147; military professionals' bias toward, 16, 26, 73, 99–100, 105, 123; Soviets outside Europe, 64; tactical use of nuclear weapons, 72–73; TRADOC assumptions, 107

Xerox, 31

Yemen, 63, 64
yoking, 20
Yom Kippur War. *See* Arab-Israeli/Yom Kippur War

Zisk, Kimberly Marten, 10

The authorized representative in the EU for product safety and compliance is:
Mare Nostrum Group
B.V Doelen 72
4831 GR Breda
The Netherlands

www.ingramcontent.com/pod-product-compliance
Lightning Source LLC
Chambersburg PA
CBHW031817220426
43662CB00007B/686